The Lady of the Hare

THE LADY OF THE HARE

A Study in the Healing Power of Dreams

JOHN LAYARD

FOREWORD BY ROBERT JOHNSON

SHAMBHALA
Boston & Shaftesbury
1988

Shambhala Publications, Inc.
Horticultural Hall
300 Massachusetts Avenue
Boston, Massachusetts 02115
www.shambhala.com

Printed in the United States of America

Distributed in the United States by Random House, Inc.,
and in Canada by Random House of Canada Ltd

LIBRARY OF CONGRESS CATALOGING-IN-PUBLICATION DATA

Layard, J. (John)
The lady of the hare: a study in the healing power of dreams/John Layard.
p. cm.
Reprint. Originally published: London: Faber and Faber, [1944].
Includes index.
ISBN 0-87773-456-9 (pbk.)
1. Dreams—Religious aspects—Christianity—Case studies. 2. Hares—Miscellanea. 3. Psychoanalysis. 4. Jung, C. G. (Carl Gustav), 1875–1961 I. Title.
BF1078.L38 1988 88-15866
154.6'3—dc19 CIP

BVG 01

CONTENTS

PART ONE

THE DREAM ANALYSIS

CONTENTS

PART TWO

THE MYTHOLOGY OF THE HARE

CONTENTS

THE HARE IN CHINA

THE HARE IN NORTH AMERICA

CONTENTS

CONTENTS

CONTENTS

CONTENTS

PART THREE

MORE DREAMS ABOUT HARES AND RABBITS

ILLUSTRATIONS

PART I

PART II

ILLUSTRATIONS

PART III

FOREWORD

John Layard is memorialized in my mind by a tenderly warm incident. He and I and a few others were in the first class in the newly formed C. G. Jung Institute in Zurich, Switzerland, in 1948. We were all new to each other and very self-conscious, I the most since I was the youngest of the group.

There was a vivid discussion of schizophrenia, a subject dear to Jung since it was he who first took this dreadful illness from the uncurable category. The main point of the lecturer was that schizophrenia can best be cured by the close relationship of the patient with a very feminine element in the therapist. This is rarely found in any therapist of any school—and, strangely, more likely to be found in a man than a woman! There was a long and dramatic silence after this statement as we tried to absorb the implications of this bit of information. Then the lecturer went on to say that John Layard was such a person and was the carrier of that particular gentle feminine quality.

I was thrilled to hear that so warm and gentle a feminine quality persists into our hard-bitten twentieth century and honored to be in the presence of a person of this character.

It was true of John Layard; he was a gentle soul, soft when allowed, strong when necessary. I am reminded of a comment on gentleness coming from an American Indian legend. It observed that when a man is firm inside and gentle without, he is a healer. When he is hard outside and soft inside, he is useless.

John Layard was a man of the right proportions, soft and gentle outwardly, strong within. I can give no greater compliment.

ROBERT JOHNSON

ACKNOWLEDGEMENTS

The author's gratitude is due in the first place to the Lady of the Hare, appearing in this work under the pseudonym of 'Mrs. Wright', who has kindly allowed it to be published and from whom the author learnt quite as much as she learnt from him; and in the second place to the members of the Psychological Study Group in Oxford to whom Part I, dealing with the Dream Analysis, was first communicated, and who by their encouragement, criticism, and support have materially assisted him. In accordance with his view that Psychology should not restrict itself to the narrow field of curative medicine, but should illuminate and be illuminated by all the Humanities, this study group has as its foundation members a Professor of Logic, a Professor of the Philosophy of the Christian Religion, a College Tutor, a College Chaplain, a Priest, an Anthropologist, a Psychologist, and a Psychiatrist, whose initials with their consent appear here as a mark of his grateful esteem.

H.H.P.	H.P.K.	G.A.
L.W.G.	V.W.	R.G.M.
N.H.K.A.C.	M.F.	

The author is further indebted to the following friends who kindly read and criticized all or parts of the manuscript during its preparation for the press: Canon L. W. Grensted, Nevill Coghill, Esq., Dr. H. G. Baynes, Dr. Gerhard Adler, the Rev. Father Victor White, O.P., Dr. William Cohn, Dr. H. Meinhard, and Mrs. E. Martin-Clarke.

He also wishes to tender thanks to the firm that has undertaken to break new ground by the publication of this narrative, and in particular to the two partners most directly concerned: T. S. Eliot and Richard de la Mare.

JOHN LAYARD

1 *Northmoor Road,*
Oxford

INTRODUCTION

Many books have been written setting out the theory and practice of psychology, but few give full accounts of case histories. This is partly because the subject-matter is often too intimate to publish, and in any case is apt to be very lengthy, and partly also because of the difficulty experienced by the analyst in giving what is equally essential to a critical understanding of the analytical process, namely, an accurate account of his own role in the human drama.

So far as I know this is the first document relating to the practice of Analytical Psychology (which is the branch of psychological practice founded by Jung) in which any serious attempt has been made to record in any detail the analyst's own part in the process as well as the patient's.

In mentioning Jung in this context I do not mean to throw any of the blame for whatever mistakes may be detected in the handling of this case on to his method. Indeed, no method is more than a guide or framework within which each individual practitioner deals with a problem to the best of his personal ability, adding a little bit here and taking away there. Rather do I deliberately risk censure for the sake of giving the public some insight into a minute corner of that vast field of psychic experience concerned with the integration of personality through the activation of the redemptive process imminent but so often unrecognized within us all, both inside and outside religious communities, which it is the task of psychology as well as of religion to further.

Psychology is at once a new science and a very old one. It is old in that it seeks to unite the two opposing forces in human nature by means of a third factor, which is that of acceptance by the conscious mind of those primitive contents that form part of our psychic heritage, which, if not admitted, operate as negative autonomous complexes, but, when accepted, prove to be the keystone supporting the bridge. It is new in so far as it provides a new technique by means of which this unity may be approached and that which has hitherto been most feared or despised may be thereby transformed into spiritual strength.

This process is by no means antagonistic to religion, and is based on the rediscovery of what I believe to be the universal redemptive process underlying all religions, embracing body as well as spirit in its healing power. We all have in us the constituent elements of salvation. The trouble is that many of us don't know it. The aim of Analytical Psychology is to make conscious this salvation process, latent within us all but inoperative till we become receptive enough to perceive it and give it that honour which alone will release it from its prison in the deep caverns of the soul.

One of the channels through which this process expresses itself is that of dreams. All primitive peoples recognize this, and accordingly pay great attention to them, and it is thought by some that all mythology and all knowledge of the other side of life came to mankind through this channel, later canalized into dogma which is its static representation, true but lacking in redemptive efficacy so long as it is divorced from its organic source.

Though God spoke to the prophets in dreams and visions the Church is now apt to frown on them, considering them either to be vain fancies, a view that has now percolated to the common man, or else, if they are clearly important, to be, except in rare instances, of the Devil. The truth is that they may be taken as being of God in the sense that they still, as of old, contain messages that, if we know how to read them, point the way to spiritual growth, but equally as being of the Devil if we fail to see below their manifest content which so often darkens and distorts the spiritual meaning that lies beneath. For among the many levels on which any given dream may be interpreted there are always two diametrically opposite methods of approach. One of these sees in every image a purely personal content and thus often produces very negative results. The other is concerned with the impersonal forces behind the personal content, and seeks to activate the latent power which they possess to heal the ills which the former method does little more than disclose. A case in point is that of a dreamer who dreamt that he was raging at his mother, saying, 'You never listen to what I say!' This was, he said, quite literally true. Taken in this concrete sense the dream only intensified the opposition and provided no solution at all. Taken more deeply, however, the mother, who in her personal aspect appeared such a negative figure, nevertheless represented in the inner recesses of his psyche the pregnant qualities in his own nature which he, owing to his inability to understand, was thus opposing and helping to destroy. The positive message of the dream was that, in wasting his substance complaining that his actual mother would not listen to him, he was thereby violating his own soul in the form of the Eternal Mother lying hidden under the imperfections of his own mother-image, and would do better to ask her what she wanted of him. If he would only listen to her instead of trying to force her to listen to him, his own pregnant nature would respond and come to his help, and he would be one step on the way to becoming redeemed, and incidentally towards improving his relations with the actual mother.[1]

It is on this point as to which of these two methods of approach it is most expedient to stress, namely, that in which personal issues predominate or that in which the impersonal forces within are activated to perform their healing function in their own way, that Jung differs from other psychological teachers. Freud and his psychoanalytical followers, who think that religion with its insistence on supra-personal forces is an escape, tend to see the personal aspect only. The Analytical Psychologist, on the other hand, tries to see both, and of the two lays the main emphasis on the creative interpretation that treats personal issues as being only surface phenomena, knowing that the deeper forces have only to be made relatively conscious for them to purge the dross of personal conflicts with their healing power.

For this reason the barrier to publication of case histories by psychologists who place the main emphasis of their analysis

[1] The eternal mother here referred to is an aspect of the *anima* to which reference is made on p. 87.

on personal issues, and rightly hesitate to make public all the intimate details which it reveals, is by no means insuperable in the case of a Jungian analysis which does not concentrate on such details to any comparable extent but tends to resolve them in the crucible of more fundamental factors that express themselves less in terms of logical formulations than through symbols, which, as will be seen in the following account, have a dynamic power of their own.

Analysis conducted on these lines tends the deeper it goes to recognize symbols of an ever less personal nature, reaching down layer by layer through the stages of cultural evolution to early Christian times and beyond to the primitive beliefs out of which Christianity developed, and then returning upward again to make a synthesis of the varied experiences it has evoked. Some persons draw the bulk of their unconscious symbolism from one source, some from others out of the inexhaustible well, and, contrary to the general supposition, the deeper the analysis the quicker the cure. The case history here given has been selected for an initial publication on account of its direct use of Christian symbolism of a type known to all, though the forcefulness of it may surprise some who have regarded such symbols as mere fanciful imagery and not, as they are, the actual mirror of nature in the pregnant unconscious.

I deliberately refrain in this introduction from giving any psychological theory, because I wish to present the case as nearly as possible from the point of view of the patient happily ignorant of all such theories. Being a hard-working country woman helping her husband to earn his living from the soil, she was not overburdened with the secondhand substitutes for life doled out by modern city conditions, and lived in a small cottage devoid of any modern convenience in as direct contact with nature as is possible in these islands to-day. For this reason, the simplest approach had to be made, and was richly rewarded. Nor were any technical terms used throughout the analysis, though certain concepts were of course at the back of the analyst's mind, a brief note about some of these being inserted in the Theoretical Discussion beginning on p. 86.

This already disposes of the idea that education with a capital E is a necessary prerequisite to being analysed. Education in its commonly used sense of book-education may help, but is more usually a hindrance, and is of use only if it has been so conducted as not to be opposed to, but as fulfilling the natural law.

One brief word is needed to explain the relation between analyst and patient. This explanation is necessary only on account of the confusion introduced by psychologists themselves with regard to the phenomenon called transference. Transference is the shifting of emotions primarily directed towards the parents on to the analyst. Such emotions are always ambivalent. The parents are the life-givers and also the prime agents by whom instinct is inhibited in order to transform it into social behaviour. In the latter role they frequently figure as oppressors, and it is this, together with the possessive aspect of the parental relationship, that is the main object of inquiry among psychoanalysts of the school founded by Freud. Emphasis on personal reactions of this kind leads inevitably to the projection of love or hate on to the analyst, and, to protect themselves against this, Freudian analysts have evolved a complicated technique by means of which they believe themselves to be acting with complete impersonality. The frequent result is, however, an intense personal dependence of the patient upon the analyst, a dependence never satisfied on account of the artificiality of the technical barriers that are erected and which then have to be resolved by a yet more complicated technique which sometimes works but sometimes does not, and which in any case is apt to take a very long time.

The Analytical Psychologist of the Jungian school does not have to defend himself in anything like the same measure, because he does not seek to represent the personal parents but on the contrary concentrates as much as possible on the impersonal factors that lie beneath personal relationships. He has in mind the redemptive process which, once activated in the patient, tends to resolve personal complexes as farmyard manure is resolved and rendered innocuous in running water.

For this reason the personal loves and hates, because unhesitatingly accepted, become absorbed into the healing process. Therefore he does not need the paraphernalia of defence put up by the Freudian, but faces his patient as one human being faces another in ordinary human converse. The result is a deep mutual respect flowing between the two in their joint endeavour.

The process is quicker and surer than any purely reductive analysis conducted on personal lines, and is more fundamental. In other words, to put it briefly, 'Freud employs a reductive method, Jung a *prospective* one. Freud treats the material analytically, resolving the present into the past, Jung *synthetically*, building up out of the actual situation towards the future.'[1]

The analysis described in this book was unusually quick because the patient had never lost contact with the power of faith, either in persons or in essential religious truths. It took place in twelve interviews at intervals of a week or occasionally a fortnight. It did not pretend to have solved all the patient's problems, but it did revolutionize the dreamer's attitude to life, and laid the foundation for further progress which will be described in a later volume. Even before these later developments, however, the patient herself was so impressed with the new light it shed on so many aspects of the redemptive process, which she recognized as being applicable not only to herself but to mankind in general, that she readily gave permission for it to be published under the sole necessary disguise of altering all names.

NOTE ON THE MYTHOLOGY OF THE HARE

The above remarks refer exclusively to the first part of this book dealing with the actual analytical situation. This left, however, one large question-mark with regard to the interpretation of what was perhaps her most crucial dream in which she sacrificed a hare, from which the book takes its name. This dream (No. 9 in the series), which led to an intense experience

[1] *The Psychology of C. G. Jung*, by Jolan Jacobi (London, 1942), pp. 66, 67.

that largely altered the dreamer's life, was during the analysis interpreted along lines applicable to any form of animal sacrifice as symbolizing the transformation of instinct into spiritual power, but the reason why the hare should have been selected by the dreamer's unconscious in preference to any other animal remained obscure till chance brought to my notice the widespread mythological beliefs regarding the hare in many parts of the world, both ancient and modern. These proved so remarkably consistent throughout the world, and in addition corresponded to and illuminated so many details of this dream and of those immediately following it, that it became evident that the hare was to be numbered among what Jung calls the 'Archetypes', by which is meant symbolic images pregnant with power that have had great influence in the past and which live on in the deeper levels of the unconscious of Modern Man, unknown to and therefore inoperative in most, but ready to spring forth into effective action once the internal redemptive process is activated and begins to work. To complete this analytical account I have therefore included a Second Part dealing with *The Mythology of the Hare* which will be found to explain more fully than appeared in the analysis itself why this dream had such a notable effect.

NOTE ON THE ILLUSTRATIONS TO PART I

One criticism that may be levelled against this book is that, with the exception of the patient's own drawing of the angel on p. 33, the illustrations to Part I dealing with the actual dream material are only approximate reproductions of her own sketchy indications. This is due to the fact that such indications as she did make were all made on odd scraps of paper and so faintly and tentatively drawn that; even if they could have been reproduced, which is doubtful, they would have necessitated a great deal of explanation and consequent unnecessary waste of wartime paper. As they were all, however, in the nature of diagrams and not pictures, I therefore submitted them, together with the necessary explanations, to my friend Mr. Rupert Shephard, who has kindly traced some and redrawn others in pen and ink, introducing just enough perspective to indicate the relative positions of the various characters appearing in the dreams. They have all been submitted to the patient, and several were subsequently altered in accordance with her suggestions. She now passes them all as being good approximations to the visual impressions she wished to convey.

PERSONS APPEARING IN THE DREAMS

(all names are fictitious)

MRS. WRIGHT

MR. WRIGHT, her husband, a skilled cowman

MARGARET, their daughter

BERTHA, Mrs. Wright's unmarried sister

KATE, Mr. Wright's sister, a nurse

EILEEN, one of Mr. Wright's other sisters

THE VICAR

THE REV. MAC X, Presbyterian Minister

MISS HARDACRE

ABRAHAMS, the butcher

MRS. SMART, a neighbour

MRS. R., a neighbour

Part One
THE DREAM ANALYSIS

INTRODUCTORY

During the summer of 1940 the Vicar of a small village with whom I was acquainted told me of an extremely backward girl of 16,[1] and asked whether anything could be done to help her. She was the only daughter of a superior labourer named Wright who had migrated from Northern Ireland to England in order to take up a situation as cowman for a neighbouring farmer. They were, he said, god-fearing people and he would point them out to me in church. At first sight, apart from a habit of holding her head down as if slightly shrunk into her shoulders, the girl appeared outwardly normal, on the plump side and with ruddy cheeks. If there was anything specially noticeable about her it was perhaps a rather extreme quietness and circumspection, though this was in itself not necessarily out of keeping with the till recently feudal character of the village. The Vicar said, however, that it was indeed but the outward and visible symptom of a nature so retiring that she would speak to no-one but her mother and consequently had no real friends in the village, spending her time doing nothing but odd jobs in and about her parents' cottage and everlastingly reading any books she could lay hands on.

I said I had no idea whether I could do anything for her, but would, if the Vicar liked, see her mother.

After some time Mrs. Wright came to see me,[2] and we had a short talk during which I formed a very good opinion of the simplicity and sincerity of the mother but could gather little

[1] When subsequently exempted from wartime National Service she was classed as a High Grade Mental Defective.

[2] Mrs. Wright was 54 at the time of this interview.

information about her daughter Margaret apart from the fact that, when about three years old, she had suffered from convulsions, the origin of which was obscure, that she had left school before her time as she was considered too stupid to learn, and that the only folk she had any interest in outside the immediate family circle were old people, for whom she liked doing small services. Otherwise the only additions I could get to the Vicar's account were that she was a 'good girl' though utterly lacking in initiative, combined with his yet further emphasis on her voracious reading. I told Mrs. Wright, as I had told the Vicar, that I had no idea whether anything could be done, but that if the girl liked, and only if she did so, I would see her. Mrs. Wright said that, owing to some obscure physical ailment she had recently taken her daughter as an outpatient to a hospital in the neighbouring big town, but that the doctor had been so rude to her because she would not speak that it had upset her very much and she had retired to bed with a high temperature. I said that, as making contact would in any case be a delicate matter and depended very much on the girl acting from her own free will, I would not arrange to see her till she had recovered from this shock and from the resistance it must have caused to anything she could conceivably regard as 'treatment', and that it would be better to wait till she was up and about again before any suggestion was made that she should see me.

Next day I happened to see both parents at a village gathering, but as they said nothing about the girl, I did not either. I then had to go away on business for a week, and when I came back the Vicar told me that the parents had on the morning before the village meeting taken her to another hospital where she had been detained 'for observation' and kept in bed while her temperature continued to rise and fall. There she stayed for some time not greatly affected one way or another, apart from not liking the strange food—so different from what her mother cooked—while the doctors failed to make any diagnosis whatever.

INTRODUCTORY

INTERVIEW WITH THE DAUGHTER, 31ST JULY 1940

Meanwhile I had myself moved into the neighbouring city, whither Mrs. Wright one day brought her daughter, who had now left the hospital, to see me. I had provided tea and coffee and chocolate biscuits so as to produce as homely an atmosphere as possible and, with these as my assistants, asked the mother to leave the daughter alone with me. For an hour I tried every device to amuse or interest the daughter, but failed to produce anything more than a monosyllabic 'Yes' or 'No', except on a single occasion when, asked what kinds of book she liked reading, she managed to whisper the words 'Edgar Wallace'. When I inquired what any of the stories were about, dumbness once more enveloped her. She would look back with expressionless eyes, obviously harbouring terror behind an appearance of calm serenity which was the defence she had built up against any approach. Even attempts to make her more comfortable were fruitless. As an example of this, when I suggested that it might be more convenient for her if she put the half-filled cup she had been balancing for the past ten minutes on her immaculately clean dress down on to the small table by her side, she indeed put it down, though not to please herself but rather as a gesture of obedience to an imagined authority. Naturally, all this time, all her muscles were tense, but a whole hour failed to relax them. Worst of all, she was not even, on the face of it, confused, so that there was no possibility of putting her at her ease. Nor yet did she once smile, but throughout the whole interview sat like a statue, and even a wide range of pictures of various kinds failed to arouse so much as a twitter of response, either of approval or the reverse. At the end of an hour it was I who was beaten. Nothing seemed to have touched her, and in despair I went out to confess my utter failure to her mother.

FIRST INTERVIEW WITH THE MOTHER

31*st July* 1940 (*continued*)

As it was a beautiful summer's day, warm and radiant, I had asked the mother to wait outside in the garden. I told her what had happened, saying that I had failed to get anything out of her daughter, and she said, 'No, Margaret hardly ever speaks to anyone but me'. I was, however, struck by Mrs. Wright's calmness and lack of any of those dominating qualities that one would normally have presumed in the mother of such a girl. I told her I was sorry I had not been able to achieve anything, saying that if I had a children's clinic I might set her daughter down in it and try to observe her in that way, but that, not having one, I failed to see what I could do. I did mention, however, that her daughter was evidently in a state of constant terror, and that her automatic and senseless obedience to any suggestion must cover a resentment that might very well lie at the root of her trouble. Seeking to find out the cause of her terror, I then asked Mrs. Wright whether she knew of anything that had happened during her daughter's childhood that might have given rise to such a deep and all-pervading inhibition.

This did not at first lead to any response, nor yet did my inquiries as to whether her daughter had ever had any sexual difficulties. Mrs. Wright said her daughter's periods were quite regular, and that, except for a little constipation she knew of no physical trouble of that kind.

This did, however, finally stir memories, for, after a long pause, she said, 'I have never told you about my sister.' The mother then told me that she was herself formerly a nurse specializing in midwifery, necessitating frequent absences from home, for which reason her elder sister Bertha had had a large share in the baby's upbringing, and for a considerable period had had the child in her sole charge. Mrs. Wright did not think that Bertha had been cruel to Margaret in any way, but said it was true that her sister was a very disappointed woman, never having married and having thrown over the only suitor she ever had owing to what Mrs. Wright described as 'false pride' over some peccadillo he had committed or was said to have committed. This had soured her sister for life, so much so that now, in her old age, none of her relatives would put up with her except Mrs. Wright herself, with whom she was now living, and had lived for many years. Mrs. Wright then described how very difficult she was, ending up by saying, 'Margaret cannot abide her. She never speaks when she is there, and always goes out of any room her aunt comes into.' I pointed out that this could not be very good for Margaret, and she then said, 'No, perhaps it's not', and went on to describe the loathing and contempt her sister Bertha had for her daughter, and how she never ceased criticizing her, saying her mother spoilt her and trying to make her do this and that, which made the family atmosphere far from pleasant. Asked how her husband liked it, Mrs. Wright said, 'He doesn't, but Bertha has no other home, and he agrees with me in saying we cannot possibly turn her out.' When I again pointed out that her sister's influence on Margaret might be very much worse than Mrs. Wright realized, she said, 'Perhaps that is so, but nothing will make me turn her out. I am the only sister who can put up with her, and if I turned her out her death would be on my hands and I could not bear it. Besides, she is my sister, and I couldn't do that, whatever happened.' I saw that, however bad the presence of the aunt might be for Margaret, there was a quality of loyalty and positive staunchness about Mrs. Wright that would be so damaged if she could ever have been persuaded to violate it—which was in itself very doubtful—that it would also injure her attitude towards her own daughter and so defeat its object. Moreover, anyone failing to perceive this would lose her confidence and forfeit the expression of a similar loyalty towards himself. So, in the interest of the very daughter to whose well-being the presence of the aunt was most harmful, it was quite clear that the aunt must stay. For this reason, after making quite clear to Mrs. Wright the probable effect on her daughter and after assuring myself that she was rather more fully aware than before of this aspect of the problem, I wholeheartedly acquiesced, contenting myself only with suggesting that, even allowing for her feelings of staunch loyalty towards her sister, there must be something that we did not at the moment quite understand about Mrs. Wright's own psychology that caused her to allow her good nature to be trespassed on so much to the detriment of her daughter.

Mrs. Wright, whose intelligence had become more and more apparent during this conversation, quite readily agreed, saying she could not herself make out why, having a husband she loved and having all her days striven to do her best, life should have proved so difficult for her. I said that, if we could find out why this was, we might be able to get at Margaret's problem through hers, and that, so far as I could see, this was the only way we could. She said, 'I'd do anything for Margaret. But what can I do?" I told her there was one way, and that was by somehow getting at the unconscious factors that seemed to nullify her own attempts at success. I said that dreams often showed us things about ourselves we did not consciously know, and asked whether she ever dreamt. She said, 'No, I never dream. Except, of course, when I was pregnant, as all women do.' I asked her whether she remembered any of the dreams she had had then, and she said, 'Yes, I once dreamt that my husband had died. It was a terrible dream. How can a woman have a dream like that about a man she loves?' I asked her whether she would like to have a talk about that some time. She said she would, and it was arranged that she should come next time without Margaret.

SECOND INTERVIEW

3rd August

There had been an unfortunate misunderstanding about the date of the interview, with the result that when Mrs. Wright arrived, I had only half an hour to spare. I was afraid that a first interview under such inauspicious circumstances might be abortive and spoil the whole analysis. As it turned out, however, that half-hour laid the foundation for very rapid progress.

Mrs. Wright lost no time beating about the bush, and opened the conversation directly by telling me that she had once had a vision of an angel. She had told it to her sisters at the time, but they laughed at it so much that she had never mentioned it to anyone again until now. This incident occurred while on a visit to America to look after her brother, during or after which she had first learned the elements of professional nursing. I understood her to say at the time that the incident occurred when she was 14 years old, though in a later interview[1] she said she must have been 19.

1. Vision (*The Warning Angel*)

'The vision occurred when I was wide awake one evening at dusk, when there appeared to me an angel. The angel looked lovely, the most beautiful thing I had ever seen, and stood with right arm raised above her head, with her forefinger pointing upwards. Her raiment was of dazzling white linen. Her face seemed to be made of light. Her eyes were dark. Behind her head there was a shining golden light.'

Mrs. Wright knew somehow that the vision was a portent of evil. She thought it meant that some loved one had died, and for some time expected to receive letters from home to that effect. No such letters, however, arrived, but shortly after-

[1] Fourth interview, on 14th August.

wards she herself was almost killed by being run over by a tram, though by God's grace she escaped unhurt.

I made no comment on this narrow escape, because the meaning of the warning was at that time by no means clear, though it became so later. When she had assured herself that I was taking her vision seriously and was not laughing at it as everyone else had done, she said:

2. VISION (*Warning Yellow Lights*)

'I quite often have Lights.' Asked what she meant, she said that a yellowish light sometimes appeared to her, also usually at dusk, and always at some spot where no material light could possibly be, and was always a warning of somebody's death. It was a dull yellow light, such as might be given out by an old stable lamp (though no lamp, of course, was visible) and quite different from the shining golden light she had seen behind the angel's head. The warnings indicated by these lights had often come true, and usually, if not always, referred to the death of one of her patients. The indication was so precise that the lights always appeared in the direction in which her patients lived.

I made no comment on this either, other than the silent comment of my extreme interest, remarking only to myself that yellow is the colour of intuition,[1] and dullness as opposed to brilliance indicates the quality of death.

She then told me the first of what she had previously described as her two 'pregnancy dreams'.

3. DREAM (*Death of husband while ploughing*)

She said: 'I dreamt that my husband was killed. He had gone out ploughing, and had been cut in half by the plough. I saw the horses careering about. When I woke up, I touched my husband in bed to make sure that he was alive.'

Quite naturally the Freudian explanation that this was a wish fulfilment dream leapt to my mind, but it was difficult to

[1] I later found that there are two intuition colours, yellow and blue, yellow being the extraverted and blue the introverted. (See footnotes on pp. 44 and 82.)

SECOND INTERVIEW

Fig. 1. VISION OF THE WARNING ANGEL

An exact reproduction of Mrs. Wright's own drawing, which she pleads as being quite inadequate to express the radiant beauty of the face looking down upon her, of the perfect symmetry of the right arm and hand, and of the golden light shining behind the angel's head.

reconcile this with the fact that I knew the husband to be a very decent and unusually balanced man, whom she truly loved. Instinctively this simple and cynical interpretation, though it might have some element of truth, revolted the sense of reverence I had already conceived towards the dreamer's problem. I also found it difficult to visualize just how a man *could* be cut in half by a plough, so I asked her if she could describe the dream to me in greater detail, pointing out that a man usually walked *behind* and not in front of his plough. How was it then that he seems to have been in front of it? And also at what part of his body had he been cut in half? In answer to the first question she said that that was just the puzzle. She had no idea why he had got in front. In answer to the second she said that he had not actually been cut in half, but that the coulter of the plough had pierced his abdomen, and that she had been horrified to see the red blood gushing out.

Though there was here an obvious reference to the wound in Christ's side from which flowed the redeeming blood, I made no further comment about this dream, as she was keen to go on to tell me the other.

4. Dream (*Deep Water*)

She started straight off by saying, 'I was by deep water'. I could not refrain from remarking on the beauty of the English language and its foundation in dream imagery, and said: 'You really were in deep water, weren't you?' She smiled, and said, 'I had never thought of it in that way, but it's true.' Then she went on, 'In the dream it seemed that I was by the side of a lake. The lake was very deep and the water was muddy. Dreams of deep muddy water always mean trouble for me. On the far side of the lake was a beautiful green pasture. On my side there was a steep mountain. I wanted to get to the green pasture, but for some reason I cannot understand, I thought I had to climb the mountain to get there. I started climbing, but the surface of the mountain was made of loose stones and earth, and I kept on slipping down.'

There was no need for me to say anything further about the

meaning of muddy water. Had Mrs. Wright been a so-called 'educated' woman, it might have taken a whole hour to explain what this meant, but her simple Irish intuition knew all about it already. Nor was there any need to point out the biblical allusion to the green pastures as her rightful goal. The question I put to her was why, instead of swimming or taking a boat across the lake or going round it, to get to the green pasture, she had to take the 'stony path' up the mountain, which in fact would never have led there at all. She said, 'Life has always been difficult for me. I don't know why it should be, as I have always tried to do my best.' I said, 'Perhaps what you have thought the best was not. If you had managed to get up the mountain, you would have found yourself in a very much worse situation than the one in which you actually were. But God was kind to you, and put the stones and loose earth there so as to make you fall down. Now we know what the angel was warning you about. Her finger was pointing upwards.' She said, 'Yes, and the finger was the central point of the vision.' I pointed out that the angel was, in fact, warning her not to go up the hill. I then asked her what she actually thought the angel in her vision had been pointing towards. She said, 'It was pointing to heaven.' Mrs. Wright was a very religious woman, so this was a delicate point. I said, 'But the green pasture was heaven, and the dream says that going uphill is the wrong way.' She said, 'I was always taught that heaven was up above.' I said that perhaps God's angel was telling her that it was not. This part of the conversation ended on the query: Where then is heaven? Is it up the mountain to the right, or is it on the other side of the lake, where the green pasture is, to the left?

I asked her whether she saw any connection between this dream and the dream about her husband's death. She said, 'There seems to be something wrong about them both.' But she did not know what. I pointed out that in each case things were the wrong way round. Just as in the second dream she was going the wrong way to go to the green pasture, so in the first dream her husband was at the wrong end of the plough. If he had not been in front he would not have been killed, nor would the horses have shied. Her wrong assumption that she must climb the mountain in order to get to heaven was a répetition of the same motive of putting the husband in front of the plough. It was like 'putting the cart before the horse'.

This was as much as I thought necessary to say at this early stage. The words 'animus' or 'shadow'[1] did not cross my lips during the whole analysis, though the concepts of them were vital to it. The husband was not mentioned again, till at a later stage it became clear that the fatal wound in his side represented an incident in the crucifixion of her own well-meant but mistaken ideals.[2]

The whole interview had lasted just half an hour, but it had been enough.

[1] See page 87.

[2] Mrs. Wright's true willing sacrifice took place later in Dream 9, in which she sacrificed the Hare, thus reliving the experience of Dream 3 on a deeper level. This, when explained, proved to be the central point in her analysis (see p. 51).

THIRD INTERVIEW

8th August

Mrs. Wright opened the interview by telling me a dream.

5. Dream

'I was in an unknown place. It was the evening, and I was trying to get home. It was in a big unknown city, with lots of people around. I went to find out what time the bus left to go home. The bus driver said it left at 10.99.

'As I had some time to wait, I went to see my sister-in-law.[1] This woman is in real life a nurse, like myself, but she was always jealous of me because I got all the jobs and she didn't. The reason for this was that, while I did not mind doing small jobs about the house as well as nursing, she stood on her dignity and would not do anything beside what she was paid for, and insisted on being waited on and having meals in a room by herself.

'In the dream I knocked at her door, but all she would answer was "*m*", as if to say, "Oh drat, this woman coming to bother me again". However, she opened the door, but instead of letting me in, pulled up a chair and sat on it in the doorway.

'While she was sitting there, with me standing outside, I heard a man's voice inside mumbling something, but I could not hear what. I had the impression she was hiding him (and her relationship with him) from me.

'I saw her sister Eileen[2] there too.

'After that I lost them in the throng. I finally found myself in the bus, thankful I had not missed it and should get home all right.'

[1] Her husband's unmarried sister Kate, whose character is described later in the comment on this dream.

[2] Her husband's youngest sister, not discussed at the time, but who, as I learnt later, was inclined to be hysterical like Bertha. She also is unmarried.

The dreamer's intuition was such as to make it unnecessary for me to labour the point that catching the bus was a very positive sign, and that going 'home' meant finding her real self, as a child returning to the security of its parents or, in adult phraseology, to God. The evening also represented the time of casting off daytime attitudes, and of communing with God as he revealed himself in dreams.

She said that in the dream '10.99' seemed quite a natural time, which seemed peculiar only when she woke up. She had tried to translate it into actual time, but realizing that it came only to the meaningless hour of 11.39, had come to the conclusion that what it really meant was 'nearly 11', referring to the 'eleventh hour', implying that the situation, though urgent, was not yet too out of hand to mend.

The scene was neither in Ireland nor any other place that she knew, and therefore represented a purely psychological situation of which she was as yet unaware. It was, of course, clear to the analyst that the husband's sister was her *Shadow*, and the unknown man whom the *Shadow* was preventing her from seeing was her *animus*.[1] I did not, however, use any such technical terms to her, but pointed out quite simply that the door at which she was knocking was the door into her soul. I then went on to point out that, though in actual life she was herself the better nurse, who got the jobs precisely because she was human and humble enough not to stand on her dignity, nevertheless the sister-in-law in the dream represented an unconscious, rigidly obstructive element in herself, preventing full contact with her soul (and also probably with her husband), and that this part of herself was withholding some essential knowledge, represented by the 'lover' whose voice she could hear but could not understand.

Using her own religious experience as a basis on which to build, I compared the door through which her sister-in-law prevented her from going with the screen separating the nave of the church from the chancel, and suggested the 'lover' inside might well represent the priest who himself represented our Lord, the 'lover' of mankind. Alternatively his voice might

[1] See page 87.

represent the 'still small voice' of conscience. I reminded her that God 'moves in a mysterious way', and suggested that perhaps the reason why she could not understand what he said was because it might disagree with a ready-made conception of God, that might possibly not tally with the truth. She said she must try to find out what this nasty thing in her was. I told her that it was not so much a matter of finding out the nasty thing as of *seeing through* the nasty thing, to find out the healing truth which it masked.

So much for the collective symbolism of the dream. Hoping to find out possibly some more particular implication, and knowing the importance of doors as symbols, I asked her whether she could describe her sister-in-law's door more fully. She looked round the room in which we were sitting, which happened to be a College room with inner door leading to the bedroom, and said, 'It was a cream painted door, rather like that'. This could, of course, have been interpreted as an unconscious sexual projection on to the analyst, identifying the analyst with the unknown lover inside. Had this been pointed out, it would have produced either a positive sexual transference, which is the last thing an Analytical Psychologist wants, or else (which would have been more probable in this case) a justified revulsion leading to hopeless resistance, or even more probably to a breaking off of the analysis. No such suggestion was, of course, made, with the desired result that no such transference occurred throughout the whole analysis, which was on the other hand characterized by a deep respect of the analyst towards the patient, as well as of her to him.

All that I did point out, was the confirmation which this afforded of the symbolism of the inner and outer chamber, repeating on the one hand the motive of the nave and chancel of a church, and on the other hand that of her own conscious and unconscious processes. I closed the interview by suggesting that she might try to draw or paint her vision of the angel. She modestly protested her inability to draw, but I showed her published drawings of other patients, which convinced her that skill in draughtsmanship was by no means necessary in the analytical process.

FOURTH INTERVIEW

14th August

Mrs. Wright to-day brought her drawing of the angel reproduced in Fig. 1.

She said she was feeling much better since the last interview. She had, before reaching the end of the road outside my house come to the conclusion that she had made a great mistake in thinking that she could ever alter her sister's attitude. She heartily agreed with the comment 'Am I my brother's keeper?' She then said that, after coming to the end of the road, she had turned down into the main street of the town, where she had seen in a shop window some verses called 'Wit's End Corner', which went right home to her as they described the position she had been in for years. She had written them down on the back of her drawing of the angel. They were:

WIT'S END CORNER

Are you standing at 'Wit's End Corner'?
Yearning for those you love,
Longing and praying and watching
Pleading their cause above?
Trying to lead them to Jesus
Wondering if you had been true,
He whispers at 'Wit's End Corner'
'I'll win them as I won you'.

Are you standing at 'Wit's End Corner'?
Then you are just at the spot
To learn of the wondrous resources
Of Him who faileth not.
No doubt to a brighter pathway
Your footsteps will soon be led,
But only at 'Wit's End Corner'
Is the God who is able proved.

Though to the sophisticated mind these verses may sound somewhat banal, the psychological situation they portray often turns out to be the corner-stone of salvation. They imply, not only that a person will not as a rule think of submitting to analysis unless he is indeed at his wit's end, but also that it is in the inferior function that salvation is invariably found.

She then said that she had a dream which justified the interpretation put on the one which she had brought last week.

6. DREAM

'I was going to a wedding, but before I got there I met my niece, who is now actually 19 years old but who in the dream appeared to be still only 14. This girl, though too young to be married, was dressed as a bride, and with her was an unknown boy of about 13, with beautiful face and flaxen hair. I kissed my niece. Then I bent down to kiss the boy. [When she said this she covered her face with her hands and silently wept. When she had recovered she went on]: But he turned his face away and would not kiss me.'

I asked why she wept. She said because he would not kiss her. While I was wondering what this meant, she added gently as if comforting herself, 'But he had a smile on his face, it was not a bad smile but a shy one. He was really too shy to let me kiss him.'

I then asked, 'Was he the bridegroom?' and she said, 'I do not know, he was dressed more like a page, and had a velvet suit on. I had expected to find the real bride and bridegroom in the church. But I never got there, but met these two on the way instead. I do not know whether he was the bridegroom or not. He *may* have been.'

I pointed out that the niece's real age, 19, was the same as her own when she had had the vision of the angel, so that in this respect the niece resembled herself (now beautified through her acceptance of the 'nasty' side of herself, represented by her sister-in-law in the previous dream) but that the scene really referred to the time when Mrs. Wright was herself 14, which was the niece's age in the dream. This age of puberty represented the parting of the ways, and I reminded her that she had first told me that she was 14 when she had the vision. I called attention to the fact that, though she had thought she was going to witness a marriage of fully sexed adults, what she had actually witnessed, was the union of a non-nubile girl with a non-nubile boy. That is to say that the marriage in question represented not a sexual union but a spiritual one, in the same way that the birth of Christ from an untouched virgin represented the spiritual rebirth of mankind. Thus, the marriage was more in the nature of the marriage of Christ with his Church, and also of the union of the conscious self with the soul. The boy represented her soul, beautiful but as yet shy. Being young, he represented growth, embracing all the potentialities of the adult. I pointed out also that just as the niece was an improved and beautified version of that side of herself which had been represented by her sister-in-law in the last dream, improved and beautified owing to the dreamer's acceptance of her own inferior function, so also the boy represented the unseen 'lover' in the previous dream, then hidden because unconscious, but now, for the same reason, come out into the open for her to view. As she was not very well acquainted with her soul, however, he was represented as being shy and not yet quite ready to embrace her. The improved relations between herself and this important component of her psyche were, however, very marked, and she would doubtless have further opportunities of getting on better terms with it. I told her that the problem was not only her own individual problem, but one which the whole modern world shared. For Christianity had got 'old' and was now having to be reborn out of our dreams, as it had previously been revealed in the Revelation of Saint John, in which dream processes were recognized as containing the highest spiritual values.

She said, 'Everything seems topsy-turvy now.' I said, 'Yes, things are quite literally topsy-turvy, so that it may well be that the heaven you are seeking is not overhead any longer, but by the inscrutable wisdom and bounty of God has changed its position, and is now to be found within instead of above.'

FIFTH INTERVIEW

20th August

Mrs. Wright opened the interview by saying in her quiet inward way that things had during the past week immensely improved at home. She no longer minded little things that used to worry her. The relationship with her sister was much better, and for the first time for years things were 'just as they used to be' before her mother died and they were all a happy family at home.

She then told me a dream.

7. Dream

Scene I

'I was walking up a gently rising path, when a man looked over my left shoulder. He was tall and lean, and had a pointed beard which was reddish brown with light glistening from it. As he looked over my left shoulder I was afraid, and recoiled with a shiver of fear, saying: "Please, don't touch me." He did not touch me, but passed by, and as he did so the words of Our Lord came into my head, "*Fear not*". And I ceased fearing. He passed by, and I noticed he was wearing a blue suit. It came into my mind that his face was like Christ's. He went straight on, and then disappeared.

Scene II

'Then I found myself approaching a place where there was a kind of circus going on. But I felt "This is not the place for me". It did not seem to be wholesome, and also one had to pay to get in.

Scene III

'So I retraced my steps, and then found myself going into a room in which there were a gentleman and two ladies. Also Margaret was there, in a brown dress she often wears. This is the first time Margaret has come into my dreams for a long time. She didn't look up at me at all as she usually does, as if to say, "Help me; tell me what to do", but just sat there calmly happy.

'The two ladies were sitting at a table, each studying an open book with patterns of embroidery on it. The patterns were like patchwork, made up of two colours: orange (later spoken of as yellow or gold) and blue (or, as she said, rather purple).[1] It might have been embroidery for church purposes.

'The man was the opposite type from the one who had passed by me at the beginning of the dream. He was stout, short, and clean shaven with a pale face, and dressed in a black suit, more fashionably than the other (who was poor). He was more like the owner of a shop, possibly a tailor (quite nice-looking), and was showing them how to make folds in a piece of black velvet that was draped over a chair. The way he did this was to gather in one of the strands near the selvedge (at the *bottom* of the cloth) so as to make folds as if for a curtain. It seemed as if he was showing this to the two ladies, but as a matter of fact they were bending over their books with their backs to him. The only person who was watching was Margaret, who sat near to where he was working. The thread he pulled out was black like the rest of the velvet.'

The keynote of the dream is of course 'Fear not', which she realized so fully that there was no need to discuss it. I said, 'If the first man was Christ, who was the other?' She said, 'Could it have been the Devil?' I said, 'He's wearing black, so might be, but didn't you think Christ was the Devil when he first looked over your shoulder with that pointed beard of his?' She said, 'Yes.' So I said, 'They seem to be rather mixed up, don't they? So perhaps, if this tailor is the Devil, he may also be Christ.' She laughed, and I said, 'Christ Himself has a dual

[1] She only saw one corner of the book as she looked over the left-hand lady's shoulder. She later associated the orange and blue with the coloured representation of Christ's robe seen in a picture (p. 77). Though I did not know this at the time, I now know that the two intermingled colours, yellow and blue, represent respectively extraverted and introverted intuition or spiritual perception (see footnote on p. 32 and p. 82, note 1).

Fig. 2. To illustrate Dream 7

Mrs. Wright enters a room, in which a gentleman-tailor in a black suit is showing Margaret (dressed in brown) a piece of black velvet draped over a chair, gathering in one of the strands of the selvedge so as to make folds as if for a curtain. Two ladies seated at a table are studying embroidery books.

character, hasn't he? He is both Son of God and Son of Man.' Then I pointed out all the dualities in the dream.

(1) Feeling of fear, then 'Fear not'.
(2) Two ways.
(3) Two men.
(4) Two women.
(5) Two books.
(6) Each book has two pages open.

We talked about the duality of everything: heaven and hell—light and darkness—day and night—good and evil—each pair composed of opposites necessary and complementary to one another. 'What would you do if it was *always* day? You would work yourself silly and never get any rest.' She said, 'Yes, that's what I've done.' I said, 'And what would you do if it was *always* night?' She said, 'You would get nothing done at all.'

So we discussed all sorts of opposites. I pointed out, and she finally agreed, that evil was necessary (i.e. inevitable) as well as good, so that anyone who tries to do good all the time *must* fail, because the other side has not been allowed for.

Then we talked about the tailor's *black* suit, contrasted with the *blue* (heavenly) suit of the man she realized was Christ. Black represents hell (what we don't know) which is as important as what we do. Christ Himself had to 'descend into hell' before He 'rose again into heaven', and also had to meet the Devil face to face before He entered on His mission. If He had not been to hell He would never have got to heaven, for the way to heaven is and must be *through hell.* This was not only her own problem, but has been mine, and is everyone's, and is a universal law.

At this she expressed huge relief. I said, 'And the black curtain is hell too, meaning what we don't know. And it is in front of Margaret. She is enveloped in it, and so are you with regard to her. But in the dream, because you were not afraid, the tailor (who is the dark side of God) is now showing her how to draw the curtain back so as to let in the light. You know what happens if you go wandering about in the dark. The same things are there as are there in the daytime, only you can't see them, and you go knocking up against them and bark your shins.' She laughed, and I said, 'So what you do is to put on a torch or light a candle, so that you can see. That's what the tailor is doing. He is showing her (and you) how to let *in* the light.'

We talked round and about this subject. Then she said, 'What are my lights [referring to the yellow "lights" she spoke of in our second interview] that warn me of deaths?' and told me of one such 'light' she had had last March, one evening when she was going out to feed her chickens. She saw a long yellow light streak down from the sky and then disappear behind a tree. No death that she knew of had come *from that direction*, so she had wondered whether this was a warning of her own approaching death, so that she might get herself ready. I said, 'It might be, but it might also be that only part of you had to die, as was the case with Saint Paul, so as to make ready the way for a new kind of life'. She said, 'I think it was to tell me of you, that God would send you to me. You are a minister of God.' I said, 'We all are', and she laughed.[1]

She then told me of her very rigid upbringing. She was brought up as a Presbyterian, and her husband was in the Church of England. He had always looked on things differently from her, saying she should take things more easily, but she had not believed him. Now she did, because I had showed her the way. I said, 'Not I, but your dreams.' She said, 'I never knew before that dreams meant anything, but now I know.' I said, 'That is the trouble with us all. I didn't either at one time. It's not only our individual problem, but one affecting our times.' We ended by discussing the decay of the Church and the prospect of its revitalization through contact with the life-giving knowledge vouchsafed through our dreams.

[1] For the importance of disclaiming the Saviour archetype, see p. 82.

SIXTH INTERVIEW

30th August

On arriving, Mrs. Wright said she had four dreams to tell.

8. Dream-vision

Dream-Vision of a woman clothed in a veil-like garment so thin that her form could be distinctly seen. The colour of the veil was a brownish fawn.

Mrs. Wright is a modest woman in the best sense of the word. A superficially more educated woman might have reacted differently, but by her this vision was taken for what it really was—a revelation of herself. When asked what she thought it meant, she said, 'I thought of what Saint Paul said about "seeing through a glass darkly". I could see her form underneath the veil.' She understood so clearly the significance of the vision as symbolizing a meeting with her own spiritual and so psychologically knowledgeable side that I said I had no more comment to make. She then told me the next dream.

9. Dream (*Sacrifice of the Hare*)

'The scene is near my home in Ireland, and I am walking with Margaret up to a square house belonging to a female cousin whom I know very well. The ground was covered with snow. Margaret was in a bit of a fuss wanting to hurry up and get the place dusted, but I told her not to be in such a hurry, as in any case, with the snow lying about, there wouldn't be much dust.

'There was a crowd of people close to the gates, but they didn't come in. As Margaret and I walked up the drive after going through the drive gates the owner of the house appeared, ordering Margaret in rather a bossy way to go into the house to fetch her a glass of lemonade. Margaret went in at the front door to do this, and I never saw her again.

'Then I went round alone into the kitchen at the back of the house. Inside there was a great light and everything was as white as it was outside, though how the snow got in there I cannot tell.

'There were people inside, too, and there, in a white bowl with a little water in it, was a live hare. Someone told me I had got to kill it. This seemed a terrible thing to do, but I had to do it. I picked up the knife (an ordinary kitchen knife) which seemed to have been placed ready for me and which was lying in the water inside the bowl beside the hare, and with a feeling of horror I started cutting into the fur and through to the skin beneath. I had to cut the hare straight down the middle of the back, and started to do this, but my hand trembled so much that, as I cut down, the knife slipped away from the straight line, and ended up by cutting obliquely into the hare's haunch.

'I felt awful doing this, but the hare never moved and did not seem to mind.[1]

'Though the ground outside was covered with snow we had left no footmarks on it.'

I said I would withhold comment on this dream till I had heard the other two.

10. Dream

'A man speaking over my shoulder said [and here Mrs. Wright wept for a moment and then pulled herself together and went on]: "Margaret and her mother may sleep together."

Asked why she wept, Mrs. Wright said that, when Margaret was born and during her childhood, she had, in obedience to instructions issued to nurses, stifled her own motherly feelings and refused ever to have her baby in bed with her except when it was ill. She agreed now that this was foolish. I pointed out the wickedness of man with his puny conceit setting up his own rationalizations with regard to infant feeding against the instinctive knowledge implanted in both mothers and babies,

[1] She later (p. 63) told me of the look of extreme satisfaction and trust that had been in the hare's eyes as it looked back at her when she plunged the knife into its back.

which leads them to do the right thing by one another if only their instincts are allowed to operate in the way desired by both. I pointed out also the premium placed by this rationalized system on illness, as being the only method left open to a child of forcing its mother to give it that motherly attention which is its due, but of which this system has quite artificially deprived it.

What the dream meant was not necessarily that the mother should now take her 16-year-old daughter into her bed—though there was no reason why she should not do so even now—but its real meaning was a spiritual one, namely that as the mother improved, her own improvement would convey itself automatically to her daughter through the channel of the Collective Unconscious, and the daughter would herself get better.[1]

Mrs. Wright then told me her fourth dream in this week's series.

11. DREAM (*Dreamt the night before the interview*)

'Miss Hardacre was conducting an examination in Mathematics, but I could not do the sums.'

Miss Hardacre (a capable but not very sympathetic woman who has in the past been in a position to exert considerable influence over Mrs. Wright's life) here represents the strait-laced part of Mrs. Wright, previously seen in the figure of her sister-in-law in Dream 5. It was thus clear that Mrs. Wright was quite right not to be able to do such impersonal sums.

We now returned to a consideration of the dream about killing the hare.[2] Mrs. Wright had very little idea about the mean-

[1] This was in fact amply proved as the analysis proceeded, since, though during the period with which this volume deals I never saw the daughter again, she did in fact greatly improve. Some of the initial stages of her development are described later in these pages. Her subsequent development will be dealt with in a later volume, and is briefly referred to in the postscript at the end of this book.

[2] I report this conversation just as it occurred. I had at that time no knowledge of the widespread folk-tales and mythological beliefs from many parts of the world in which the hare figures as a self-sacrificing animal and symbol of spiritual insights. These, and in particular the association of the hare in folk-lore with Easter are dealt with in Part II of this book entitled *The Mythology of the Hare*, from which

ing of this dream, except that the snow in her opinion signified 'washing away sin'. I said, 'Surely the trouble is that you've not sinned enough—against your own mistaken ideals. You remember the mistake discovered in our second talk, indicated by the angel's warning against false idealism and the subsequent warning in Dream 4 against climbing the stony mountain. To-day's dream about the hare has another meaning.' Then I said I would like to make a guess, and asked whether there was any relation between the colour of the veil in Vision 8 with that of the hare. She said they were very similar. I said, 'So there's probably something beneath the hare's fur also that you should see. What would happen actually if you *had* killed the hare?' She said, 'I didn't want to kill it, but it seems I had to.' I said, 'It would have bled, wouldn't it?' She said, 'Yes.' I said, 'And the blood would have run into the bowl. I want to talk very carefully about this, because it is a mystery that no man can fully understand and can only be talked about with the greatest delicacy and reserve. You know about the blood of the Lamb which we now drink in the Communion Cup. The bowl is the cup. The whole dream is a preparation for the Communion Rite, in which Christ sheds His blood for the redemption of sin. *Your* sin has been being too "good" in a mistakenly idealistic way, so God sends his blood to correct the too great whiteness of the snow. That's why the hare didn't mind, because he is a willing sacrifice.'[1]

She said, 'It's wonderful that these mysteries still happen. I used to suppose it only happened once. That must be why we didn't leave any footsteps in the snow.'

it will be seen that many of the motives in Mrs. Wright's dream correspond in surprising detail with ancient symbolic wisdom of which neither she nor I had at the time any conscious knowledge at all.

As will be seen, therefore, in my ensuing conversations with Mrs. Wright no special emphasis was laid on the precise meaning of the hare, whose sacrifice was dealt with only in general terms as representing the transformation of blind instinct into spiritual power.

[1] The reader will not fail to notice the similarity between the willing sacrifice of the hare and that of the husband in Dream 3, now recapitulated on this deeper level.

I added, 'If the hare's blood *had* been shed into the bowl, it would have mixed with the water already *in* the bowl, like the mixing of wine and water in the Communion Cup, commemorating and carrying on the symbolism of the blood and water flowing from Christ's side.'

I then said, 'There's one more thing. I don't understand what your cousin has to do with it all. What was your relationship with her?' She said, 'She was one of my best friends. She was a very religious woman.' I said, 'You were a Presbyterian, weren't you? Was she too?' She said, 'Yes, but she was a little bit fierce.' I said, 'Oh, like Miss Hardacre?' She said, 'Yes.' I said, 'So she also may represent a rather restricting influence, like the one that stopped you from taking your child into your bed.' We then talked about the attitude of Presbyterians in Ireland towards the Communion Rite, which they perform (according to Mrs. Wright) only twice a year and which they regard not as a sacrifice but as something more closely resembling a commemorative meal.[1] I said, 'That's why your cousin only wanted lemonade, and why Margaret disappeared from the dream as soon as she obeyed the order to get this very bodiless drink, hardly a proper substitute for the body and blood of Christ. The reason why Margaret disappeared from the dream at that point was because she had been sent on a mistaken errand.'

Mrs. Wright was very silent for a time as the meaning of all this sank in. The analytical process is itself like the Mass, and like all true ritual as well as great works of dramatic art, in that it leads to peaks of emotion from which the participant has to be led back from scenes of glory very gently into the realms of everyday life, lest the sudden contrast damage the soul. For this reason the last five minutes of the interview were spent in talking of more mundane matters: and, instead of turning her out unprotected into the busy town, I was luckily able to leave her alone in my consulting-room for a time to gather herself together before leaving. How long she stayed there I do not know. When I came back after an hour she was gone.

[1] The doctrine of the Church of Scotland is much more Catholic.

SEVENTH INTERVIEW

4th September

Mrs. Wright told me to-day that, after leaving my room and going home, she had that night (30–31 August) had a 'wonderful experience'. She went to bed at the usual time, but woke up with a feeling of things rushing to and fro in her head, with the result that her head was 'like to burst'. This went on for a long time, with a feeling that something was sawing backwards and forwards in her brain, and every time it sawed a voice said, 'O Jesus, I have promised' (a quotation from the hymn continuing '—to serve thee to the end'). This had been the text of a sermon on the Holy Communion preached the previous Sunday by the Vicar who had had the insight to persuade her in the first instance to seek psychological treatment for her daughter. As she lay suffering in this way in her head, the voice repeated itself with even greater intensity, till she heard the clock striking twelve (a thing she rarely hears, as she sleeps soundly), when suddenly she herself started to repeat the words, altered into 'Jesus, I renew my promise'; and then with a feeling of intense relief fell off to sleep. Next morning she woke feeling body and spirit 'light as air', without the slightest sign of fatigue in spite of (really because of) what she had been through the previous night.

She told me also that, since this analysis began, she had found herself frequently remembering biblical texts which she had long forgotten, and had of late found herself inwardly praying as she worked.

There was no need to comment on the general meaning of the night's initiation experience, during which she accepted the pain leading to ultimate release; and I refrained from complicating matters by asking just what was meant by the promise made to Jesus, since its positive nature, whatever it might mean, was quite clear from the resulting feeling the following morning.

Fig. 3. To illustrate Dream 12

Mrs. Wright, 'taking shelter' from an air raid in a great square 'open to heaven' surrounded on three sides by buildings, prays in front of her fowl-house, while others who were there before her pray also. Later, she leaves the square and is now a schoolgirl taking leave, outside it, of an old schoolfriend wearing a square white object as of linen over her breast, who says, 'I am going away.' Mrs. Wright feels desolate, but is relieved when she says, 'I'm only going for three days.'

She then told me a dream she had had the following night (31 August–1 September).

12. Dream

Scene I

'I was in a wide open space (I don't know where) and suddenly noticed there was no-one about. I thought, "There must be an air raid." I felt afraid, and started looking for shelter. Then I saw through a gate some people kneeling down praying. I went in and found myself in a great square surrounded on three sides by buildings and on the fourth side by a wall separating it from the road in which I had been.

'Though the place was "open to heaven" and there was no roof, once inside I ceased being afraid. I did not, however, quite join the praying group, but went off by myself to where stood a caravan rather like one of my own fowl-houses which is on wheels, and there knelt down to pray. No bombs were dropped, and I began to wonder whether there had really been an air raid or not.

Scene II

'Then I came out of the square place, and there met a young girl with whom I used to be very friendly at school. I now seemed too to be a girl, and felt towards her the same warmth that we had felt all those years ago when we had been such close friends. I seemed to have a loose garment on me, which I put round her. She turned to me and said: "I am going away." I felt desolated and lonely, as I had done when we parted as girls, and said so to her, but she said: "Well, I'm only going for three days." There seemed to be a railway station near by, and it seemed she was going away by train, but when she said she was coming back, I felt happy again. I noticed her dress, which was black, with a square patch of dull white (as of linen) reaching from her neck almost to her waist.'

Asked what she thought about this dream, she said she had no idea what was meant by the air raid that never happened, though she quickly realized the relation between the square yard in this dream and the square house in which the incipient Communion Rite had been held in the previous dream about killing the hare.

When asked about the three days' absence of her friend, however, she said outright that it reminded her of the three days which Christ spent in hell before the resurrection, and that her feeling of despair and subsequent relief tallied well with what must have been the feeling of the disciples at that time.

I then pointed out the significance of the supposed air raid as indicating the powerful spirit of God descending out of the clear heavens upon man,[1] which can wreak destruction upon unbelievers—i.e. those outside the square yard—but which is the highest blessing to those gathered together within. Spirit is indeed powerful for evil as well as good, and the feeling of fear followed by one of safety on entering the holy place of prayer is typical of all religious experience once the power of the spirit is accepted. The same alternation of feeling took place when her friend said she was going away but then said she would come back in three days, and also when the man whom she took for the Devil looking over her shoulder in a previous dream[2] turned out to be Christ. I then pointed out that the plan of the yard resembled that of a church, with the fowl-house representing the altar and herself as the officiating priest. It was at first not quite clear why the altar should have been represented by a fowl-house, as she had not stated whether the fowls were reared for their meat or for their eggs. On being asked which, she said 'Eggs', whereon I suggested the parallel of Easter Eggs. She said, awestruck, 'Then it must all be about Good Friday and Easter.'[3]

I said, 'Yes, your girl friend whom you wrap round with your garment is your spiritual part whom you are now taking to yourself in the sense meant by a former voice saying that Margaret might henceforth sleep with her mother.[4] As you withdraw this projection into yourself the real Margaret will become free.' She said, 'She is becoming so already. Last week of her own will she kissed her aunty good night for the first time for years.'

I then pointed out that the square patch of white clothing on her friend's breast was like the square yard—a patch of consciousness surrounded by unconsciousness (the black dress), corresponding with the area of safety in the bosom of God *in-*

[1] This is a frequent motive in dreams, about which a whole volume could be written.

[2] See Dream 7.

[3] For the meaning of Easter Eggs and their connection with the hare sacrificed in Dream 9, see pp. 171 sqq.

[4] See Dream 10.

side the yard surrounded by the region of fear and danger outside. To my surprise this concept presented no difficulty.[1]

She then said, 'Why was I represented in the dream as being a child?' I said, 'Because it takes you back to a time when you still had a *childlike belief*. It means what Christ meant when He said, "You must become as a little child", believing the inner voice that so many adults have lost.'

I then asked whether the girl friend was at all like the veiled female figure in a former vision, and she said, 'Yes. She was taller than me, and would have grown into a woman like that one.'

She then said she thought she might have been remiss in not going to communion more often. I pointed out that the church in her dream was an open-air one, and square, unlike the church she goes to, and that the communion referred to was a communion inside herself, complementary to the external celebration which might complete and aid the inner process, but lacking which the inner process would still continue.

I did ask, however, what was the colour of the fowl-house in her dream, and she said, 'A reddish colour'. As she was showing signs of having had enough for one day, I refrained from pointing out the symbolic aspect of this as referring to the wine and to her husband's blood in the first dream, which is now clearly seen to refer on one level to the blood issuing from Christ's side when pierced on the Cross.

Nor did I point out that the number of worshippers she had indicated in the square yard was 8, which is the number signifying completion.[2]

[1] It may be noted that there is also an interesting parallel to the ephod, a piece of cloth worn apparently in this position by the Jewish high priest over his dress, and from which hung a pocket containing the oracle—the Urim and Thummim, by means of which the priest ascertained the divine will. Such symbols crop up in dreams, and the divine setting of this dream cannot be in doubt. As will be seen in the sequel, moreover, Mrs. Wright's dreams did indeed contain a markedly prophetic element.

[2] The number 8 is a reduplication of 4, representing the 4-square earth, the 4 cardinal points, the 4 psychological functions and innumerable other quaternities of psychological and religious import. In

As last week, the whole interview which I have described lasted less than three-quarters of an hour, and the remaining quarter of an hour was taken in again coming down to earth by her description of her career in America (where she had gone as a young woman to look after her brother) and of her subsequent experiences as midwife.

dreams it is often represented by 4 couples—4 men and 4 women. See C. G. Jung, *Psychological Types*, London, 1924, and John Layard, *Stone Men of Malekula*, London, 1942, pp. 643–8.

EIGHTH INTERVIEW

11th September

Last time there had been a symbolic representation of Easter and Good Friday, in this reverse order,[1] but no crucifixion, and in each case the human representatives had been female. To-day this lack was made good in a dream representing the sacrifice in which both victim and sacrificer were male.

Before this, however, there was one other matter that had to be cleared up, or 'way' that had to be opened. This was dealt with in the first two of the three dreams she now related as having taken place since the last interview.

13. DREAM

The scene was in a small room at the back of the Wrights' cottage, near the kitchen, which was too damp to be used for a sitting-room and was therefore used as a store. The Rev. Mac X (Presbyterian Minister at the Wrights' former home in Ireland) was coming to tea, and the meal was to take place in this room. Bertha (Mrs. Wright's sister) was in a great state of mind because the floor was all over crumbs such as might have been swept carelessly off the table. She was working herself into a temper about these, and accusing Mrs. Wright of having caused the mess, and then suddenly collapsed into a swoon. (Mrs. Wright here explained that this is the time of year when

[1] It is characteristic of dreams in an early stage of analysis that certain archetypal situations such as a psychological death and resurrection are as it were broken up and experienced only in snatches, not always in their normal order, and sometimes missing out certain essential elements. This indicates that the patient is at the time not far enough advanced to appreciate their full meaning. In a successful analysis they are invariably lived through later on a deeper level involving a fuller awareness of their significance and having consequently a more integrating effect. This particular sequence of psychological events was in fact lived through at a later stage by Mrs. Wright in a manner that will be described in another volume.

Bertha in fact is in the habit of swooning, and that she [Mrs. Wright] has up till now always felt her sister might die and she might be to blame, and has therefore always been careful to lay her on her back and later get her up to bed where she has usually stayed for several days.) In the dream, however, she did not lay her down, but propped her up in a chair, where she left her leaning her head over the table. Mrs. Wright felt it was very unlike herself to do this and that it might be very wrong, but her husband said, 'Don't worry. Bertha will soon be all right'.

We first talked a bit about Bertha and these seasonal attacks always taking place in this month of the year. I said, 'This is what happens also in epilepsy. The fits are as a rule also preceded by something resembling anger, which is suppressed, so that the attacks are then turned against the subject.' I told her how these attacks were often seasonal in the same way as her sister's, and represented the re-enacting of the original drama causing the fit. I said I did not suggest that her sister was an epileptic, but did suggest that something of the same nature was taking place, and that it might very well be that this was the time of year at which the abortive love affair which had so soured Bertha had taken place. Mrs. Wright did not know whether this was the case, but said she would try and find out.

We then turned to the question of the crumbs, which were like those used in the Communion Rite as observed in the Presbyterian Church and regarded as being simply a commemorative meal. On the manifest level the event so commemorated would be Bertha's own personal trauma, but on the deeper level it was the Mass. The fact that the crumbs had been carelessly swept off the table signified on one level the disregard of the sacrificial nature of the rite as performed by the Presbyterians. On another level, it represented the crumbs falling from the master's table, through acceptance of which on the part of the Tyro-Phoenician woman in Matthew xv, 21–8 her daughter who had been vexed with a devil became healed. Her sister was too proud (one aspect of this pride had been the rejection of the lover and her consequent lifelong disappointment), and had to humble herself to the dust in order to lick up the fallen crumbs. That's why she swooned. The deep knowledge in Mrs. Wright's unconscious was therefore quite right in not treating the swooning as a disease, but in raising her to the communion-table to eat in company with all others who were sufficiently humble to partake.

The husband's voice saying 'Bertha will soon be all right' indicated on the one hand that Bertha *would* be all right if treated in this way (either in life through not having herself fussed over, or else in death which would be better than a living death ruled over by pride). On the other hand, Bertha represented the pride aspect of Mrs. Wright, in thinking that she was really her sister's keeper. More vitally still did the dream mean that, like the Tyro-Phoenician's daughter, Margaret would automatically recover in proportion to the extent to which Mrs. Wright herself could humbly accept the crumbs of revelation now being given to her in her dreams.

Mrs. Wright said that Margaret was already immeasurably better, and now kissed her aunt good night every night, so that she (Mrs. Wright) no longer had any hesitation in leaving them together after a lifetime spent in guarding them against contact lest something dreadful should befall.

She also said she now realized why the scene of the dream had been set in the store-room, since this represented the store of spiritual sustenance now coming into its own.

The next dream formed a bridge between this one and the next but one.

14. Dream-vision

This was more in the nature of a vision, in which she entered a square room which was a draper's store-room, where were displayed four bales of material, which she described as being respectively 'fawn, green, white, and flesh-pink'. They were arranged as in the illustration.

Asked what she thought of this, she said she thought it was a kind of ethereal counterpart of the store-room in the last dream, and gave her great comfort. What she particularly noticed was the lovely flesh-pink.

I did not at this point make any mention of the four functions,[1] nor of colour-symbolism in general, but I did note the contrast between the bright colours she now saw and the black cloth displayed to Margaret in Dream 7. The meaning of the flesh-pink became immediately apparent when we proceeded to a discussion of the following sacrificial dream, to which it clearly led up.

Fig. 4. To illustrate Dream Vision 14

Mrs. Wright enters a draper's square store-room displaying four bales of material of the colours indicated.

15. Dream

She first said that this dream was about a new butcher who had recently arrived at her village, and with whom she now dealt. His name was Abrahams, so he was presumably a Jew. He was good-looking and a fine figure of a man, quite young, and 'in the pride of his life'.

She dreamt that this butcher was there, and that an unknown doctor arrived and said, 'Well, he's a nice fellow', and

[1] See p. 57, note 2.

then said, 'This man must go through an operation'. The operating table was an ordinary kitchen table, on to which, to her astonishment, the patient got all by himself as if in the best of health, and fully clothed. There were no blankets, nor any of the paraphernalia ordinarily used for an operation. She herself had to prepare the bed into which he was to be placed after the operation, but quite forgot to ask the doctor what kind of antiseptic he used.

When asked, she said she had no idea whatever what the dream meant. The whole thing seemed so uncanny she could not make head or tail of it. So I began with the butcher, one who killed animals, as she herself in a previous dream had had to kill a hare.[1] This man, however, was both sacrificer (killer of animals, and I told her how in certain primitive religions the animal was always sacrificed before being eaten), and was himself at the same time the willing sacrifice, just as the hare had been. She then told me of the look of extreme satisfaction and trust that had been in the hare's eyes as it looked back at her when she plunged the knife into its back. This made her think of Christ, and we then realized the meaning of the butcher being a Jew. Still she could not understand why such an apparently fine healthy man should be sacrificed, and said, 'I have never fathomed why Christ, the perfect man, should have to suffer like that'.

We then talked about the nature of sacrifice, that it must be willing, and that it must be of something perfect or of the highest value. We talked of circumcision, the sacrifice of part of man's virile member, a sacrifice to God for the privilege of being redeemed of our animal nature. Beasts may be free to do what they like, but they are not human. Man in a primitive state may have been free to do what he liked, but had no knowledge of God. Being civilized had its advantages, but entailed the sacrifice of the exercise of untrammelled instinct. That's what is meant by sacrifice. By sacrifice we willingly give up part of our primitive natural satisfactions in return for all that is entailed by civilization and the spiritual benefits that true

[1] Dream 9.

civilization confers. Mrs. Wright then re-stated this all in terms of religion, substituting 'Church' for 'Civilization', and I agreed, so she added, 'The trouble is that the Church has not always accomplished its mission, and that's why we've got in such a muddle'. I said, 'Yes, that's why we have now to rediscover inside ourselves some of the truths the Church has still enshrined in its liturgy but has forgotten in its life.'

We then talked of the sacrifice of Isaac, which God commuted because Abraham had been willing to make it, so that the sacrifice of the spirit was now equivalent to the sacrifice of the flesh. That was what Bertha had had to do in the first dream,[1] and why Mrs. Wright was quite right in not treating her swoon as a disease but rather as a sign of redemption. In the last dream also Mrs. Wright was quite right in forgetting the antiseptic. Christ had no antiseptic on the wounds He suffered on the cross, nor had her hare, and if they had had, the sacrifice would have been worthless.

Once more she said, 'I had thought that it was only in olden times that men had had dreams to show them how to live. I never dreamt we had it in us now.'

At this point I saw that the high point of the day's analysis had been reached, and we then talked of more mundane and practical matters such as the greater prevalence of septicaemia in the West End of London than in the East End, because septicaemia was due to lack of spirituality quite as much as to lack of merely physical hygiene. She told me of one of the finest maternity doctors she had known in Ireland who rarely washed his hands and who had got into trouble with medical authorities because of the state of his doctor's bag, but who had never mishandled a case.

[1] Dream 13.

NINTH INTERVIEW

18th September

Today Mrs. Wright brought what she called 'three small dreams' which in fact turned out to be four.

16. **Dream**

'I was driving a black pony harnessed to a cart full of clover.[1] The pony was the one we used to have in Ireland. The clover was in flower—it was being taken to feed animals—and I noticed the threefold nature of the leaves. The countryside was one which I do not know, but I seem to have been there before. I was taking the pony to the blacksmith to be re-shod, though I remember now that I never even looked to see whether it needed it. Margaret was on the cart with me. After a time we met my sister Bertha by the side of the road, outside some house. A woman came out of the house and asked her if she would like some tea. She said yes, and asked Margaret if she would like to have some too. Margaret said she would, and got down off the cart. She asked me also if I would have some tea, but I said I would not, but must go on to get the pony shod. Margaret went into the house, and I did not see her again. I drove on through the lovely countryside, feeling again that it was a country I had been in before.'

17. **Dream**

'I was in a class, in a school. We were all sitting round in a circle, and the teacher (a man) was asking questions from left to right. He asked some girl, "What is a Church?" She answered, "*A Church is a place where we are sanctified and made holy by marriage to God.*" The teacher then skipped over the girls in between and pounced on me, saying, "*Who is higher*

[1] It is to be noted that this was the common purple-flowered clover, and not shamrock. Shamrock appeared later in Dream 37 (to be published in a future volume), which carries the symbolism of this dream a considerable stage further.

than God?" I said, "There is none higher than God." He said, "*Oh yes, there is one higher than God.*" I said, "I've never been taught that", whereon the teacher smiled knowingly, but said no more.'

Fig. 5. To illustrate Dream 17
The teacher in class asks 'Who is higher than God?'

18. Dream

'In the same class-room as the previous dream. Miss Hardacre was taking the class—it was a kind of religious exam—and asked some boy a question which he could not answer. She pressed him again, but he answered, "*I haven't time for lessons. I have to work so hard*". Miss Hardacre said harshly, "That's no excuse", and then turned to me asking a question which I also was unable to answer. The Vicar [who had recommended analysis to her] was there, and he said to me, "*But you do know.*" I said, "I don't know", and he again said, "But you do."'

19. Dream

'I was in a house with my husband's sister Kate, the one who is a nurse and who appeared in a previous dream.[1] The

[1] Dream 5.

house was a strange one. In real life Kate and I always disagree. Among other things I love flowers but she does not like them and despises me for growing them. But in the dream she was as friendly as anything, and said to me, "I have a lovely lot of flowers for you to see. Come and look at my lovely flowers." We were in a room, and in it was a miniature garden composed of two beautiful bowls. They were big shallow bowls with earth in them and beautifully tended grass like turf that covered the earth, and growing out of the grass were some lovely red dahlias, which I looked at with delight. I said, "They are beautiful", and was amazed at her liking the flowers and having planted them, and being so friendly.'

I asked her what she thought about the first dream, and about the unknown countryside seeming familiar. She had no answer, so I pointed out how this meant that the dream referred to a constantly recurring situation always reappearing under some new guise. This was clearly seen also in the fact that she was once more leaving Margaret with her sister, referring to the time when she had so disastrously left her there when a baby. She said, "Yes. I had thought of that, but this time I had no fear. I used to feel I must protect Margaret from her, but now I feel that Margaret is quite safe with her, and won't come to any harm.'

I then asked what she thought about the clover. She said, 'It's three leaves in one. That is the sign of the Trinity. I was very interested in those three leaves, and when I got up next morning I went out to have a look at some.'

I said, 'Then it looks as if this dream had something to do with the Trinity. What do you think it meant when the teacher asked, 'Who is higher than God?' She had no answer to this, any more than she had had in the dream. I then said, 'I want to be very careful about this, as we had to be careful about the dream about sacrificing the hare.[1] It's quite clear, isn't it, that the teacher knew what he was talking about?' She agreed, and I said, 'Yet he thinks there *is* someone higher than God. This sounds sacrilegious, yet the dream says it is so. What

[1] Dream 9.

he clearly means is higher than God as you conceive Him to be. What can it be that you have left out of account?' I asked her to name the persons of the Trinity, and then said, 'Are they the only power in the world?' She said, 'Well, no. There's Evil. There is the Devil. He is a bad power.' I asked her, 'What is evil?' She said, 'What is against God'. I said, 'What is it that is against God?' She said, 'It's not easy to say. I'd like you to tell me.' I said, 'Well, God is Light, isn't he? Then evil is dark, that means, what we don't know. We now speak of the Germans as evil, because we didn't know they were preparing to attack us. Or rather, we did know, but blinded ourselves to it. If we had admitted to ourselves what we in fact knew, and had prepared ourselves adequately against it, the evil would not have taken us unawares. Now that it has come, and that we are neither deluding ourselves as to its existence nor letting it overwhelm us we are recovering the strength that we had lost through our false sense of security, and it is now actually galvanizing our whole life. So there is a use in evil if we know it is there and don't pretend it is not. The trouble about Christianity in recent times is that it has become too falsely idealistic. We have come to think of God as giving us only those things which we regard as good, and have forgotten the Old Testament and that He can be also a God of Wrath. So Christianity has for many become a wishy-washy affair, and has lost the strength that comes from a recognition that God can be a Destroyer as well as a Creator;[1] for all things are possible to Him. He rules over the night as well as the day. But if we say He rules only over the day, what happens to the night? Now let's see what your dreams say about it. What dark object is there in them?'

She could not at first think of any, till she remembered the black pony. I pointed out that in that first dream of to-day's series the threefold symbol was repeated twice, first in the three-leaved clover, and then in the three persons, herself, Margaret, and Bertha, the figure who offered the tea being so shadowy that she hardly counted. I then talked about the symbolism of the cross, with its four arms, of which, on one sym-

[1] Compare, for example, Isaiah xlv, 7, and Hebrews x, 31; xii, 29.

bolic level, the three upper arms represent the Trinity and the fourth, plunged into the ground, represents the Devil who had been sent down to hell, and who for this reason had passed out of consciousness and been lost. Where then was the fourth sentient being in the dream? She said, 'The black pony. That means he is the Devil who is leading me astray.' I said, 'That may be what you have thought. It's certainly true that he is leading, as he is pulling the cart but are you sure he is leading you astray?' She said, 'Well, no. I was taking him to be shod.' I said, 'That means he is the unconscious power that you are preparing to use in your service by giving him the attention he needs. He is the hidden fourth power representing, like all animals, the instinctive reactions that we in our present civilization have tended to lose through our too great concentration on the light side of the godhead, thereby neglecting the dark. You know this already through the success of your dream-treatment of Bertha. It is precisely the instinctual knowledge that has to be resurrected, and that is symbolized here by the black pony. It is as fatal to neglect the powers of darkness as to neglect the powers of light. Both have to function together, for they are two sides of the same coin. That's what is meant by the marriage with God. What did the girl in the next dream (17) mean when she answered that "A Church is a place where we are sanctified and made holy by the marriage to God"? Is that a phrase used in your catechism?'

She said, 'No. I've never heard it before I heard her saying it in the dream.' I said, 'What does it mean?' She said, 'It seemed perfect when she said it, but, now you ask me, I can't say just what it does mean. You know. Will you tell me?' I said I didn't know anything, but could only act as a translator, as best I could, for the word of God revealed to her in her dream, and pressed her again to say what was meant by the word 'we'. How can 'we' be married to God? Who are '*we*'? She could not say, so I went on to point out that 'we' were evidently not sanctified until marriage with God. What things was it that had to be sanctified in us all? It was clearly our instincts. What then did it mean that our instincts had to be married to God? Clearly that they were of equal importance with the 'good' God she already knew, for only equals can be married. It meant that, while in the early days of Christianity an over-developed self-indulgence in the Roman world had to be countered by a move *against* instinctive or animal life, this process had gone too far, and must now be reversed till instinct was given its true place alongside that aspect of the godhead which represented conscious control, and that only when the two were properly balanced together could we live satisfactory lives. But only those things which were known could be controlled. Her instinct was represented by the pony, and it was to the pony that the Teacher referred as being 'the one higher than God', meaning not that he *was* higher than God, for, as we had seen, the two should be equal and married, but that he must for the moment be *represented* as 'higher', because our instincts had been too much neglected and therefore must for the time being be given most honour in order to make up for the dishonour they had of late suffered.[1]

Going on now to the last two dreams, it was clear that Miss Hardacre represented the too great conscious control over instinct, and it was for this reason that the unknown boy who stood for Mrs. Wright's soul was quite right in ignoring her questions, as he was fully occupied with the more important work in which she was engaged during analysis, just as the boy Christ had left his everyday occupation to go to the temple 'about his father's business'. She said, 'The boy in my dream was about twelve years old', which was Christ's age when this occurred. In the dream, Mrs. Wright was also quite right not to answer the irrelevant questions, just as she had not been able to do the sum required of her by Miss Hardacre in a previous dream.[2] But at the same time the Vicar, a representative of Christ, said, 'But you do know', meaning that her instinctive side did, though the true answer that this side of her would make would be quite unintelligible to Miss Hardacre, or to that side of herself which Miss Hardacre represented, and therefore remained unspoken, as the marriage with God referred to in

[1] Compare 1 Corinthians xii, 22, 23, 24; also the Augustinian phrase, 'God permits evil that good may come'.

[2] Dream 11.

the previous dream was there only adumbrated as a future possibility and was as yet by no means fully realized.

The last dréam about Kate, her husband's sister, again represented the marriage under a different form, namely that with her own self-criticizing self, and was a comment on the dream about Miss Hardacre, whereby that part of herself became assimilated under the aegis of the sacrament represented by the two bowls, one for each side of herself, in which, growing in the green grass of simplicity, were the red flowers representing the blood of the hare she had been willing to sacrifice in a previous dream,[1] and of which the last dream represented the fruit.

[1] Dream 9.

TENTH INTERVIEW

2nd October

A fortnight had elapsed since the last interview, owing to my having been away.

20. Dream

'I was going with my husband along a lane towards my old home in Ireland. There was an air raid, though the curious thing was that the aeroplane I saw in the sky was not like an ordinary aeroplane, but had its wings in the middle. I was afraid, and started hurrying home to warn my own people. But my husband caught hold of my arm and said (as he often does in real life), "No need to worry". I obeyed him, and the aeroplane seemed to descend till it came down close to the gate leading up to the house, and stayed propped up against the low wall, just as one might prop up a bicycle. There it stood, with one wing touching the ground and the other sticking straight up into the air, with the fuselage parallel to the ground. Out of it came a German in a light blue suit, who seemed in no way to want to attack us, but just busied himself with repairing the middle part of the 'plane. I said to my husband, "This is a friendly German after all." I felt we had no need to fear. There was no need any more to warn my people, so we just went on walking together past the house.'

Mrs. Wright had already realized when waking that the supposed aeroplane was in fact an equal-armed cross, and that that was why her husband had told her there was no need to worry. We noted the now regular pattern of many of her dreams beginning with the motive of fear and ending with that of 'fear not'. She was, however, a little puzzled about the 'friendly' German till I pointed out to her that almost everyone was now having dreams about friendly Germans, this representing the esoteric complement to our overt defence against their attack.

The spirit called forth by their attack and our defence against it was regenerating an England that sorely needed regeneration, and in this sense the Germans, by attacking us, were indeed proving our best friends. I pointed out also the close parallel between the figure of the German in her drawing and that of Christ on the Cross. This meant that salvation came through our acceptance of the Shadow or 'other' hated or despised side

Fig. 6. To ILLUSTRATE DREAM 20

The raiding aeroplane in the form of a Cross descends, propping itself against a wall. The blue-suited pilot, instead of being hostile, quietly repairs the engine situated in the middle of the 'plane.

of ourselves, and that it was the acceptance of this Shadow and its resuscitation out of the unconscious that had caused the long lower limb of the Latin Cross to become shortened in her dream so as to make a balanced equal-sided union of complementary opposites, and that this in turn corresponded with the new balance she was finding in her life. The light blue colour of the German's suit, representing the sky or heavenly understanding, recalled the blue suit worn by the Christ-figure in Dream 7.

She said that, after having this dream, she woke up singing

Holy, Holy, Holy! Lord God Almighty!
Early in the morning our song shall rise to thee.

In singing this, she realized that, though for years she had not been able to sing, she was now singing like a lark. She said also that her whole health was better than it had been for years, that she no longer suffered from the acidity, rheumatism, and headaches that had constantly troubled her before this analysis began. The only physical disability now left to her was her eyesight. She still had to wear spectacles.

I asked her how Margaret was getting on. She said she was much better and more independent than she had ever been, that she was now able to stand up to her Aunt Bertha's bad tempers in a way she had never been able to do before, and that Mrs. Wright herself now felt the wells of friendship rising again towards her sister after all these years of trouble.

She then said that her second dream was about Bertha.

21. Dream

'The scene was in an unknown house. Bertha was preparing herself for marriage. I looked round, and was surprised to see nothing but women. I thought she must have someone to go to church with her to give her away. Then I thought, "Where is my father?", and went to look for him. I found him in some other room. He said, "I'm ready." I went back to tell them so, but found Bertha in a swoon. There she was, not even in her wedding-dress, but dressed in cream, with three other women round her, also dressed in cream instead of white, who should have been her bridesmaids, one on each side and one near her head. Unlike what I would have done in real life, I let her be.

'I then thought "Where is Margaret?" Someone said, "Margaret has gone to take a bath." I called out to her, and she called back, "Mother, I'm taking a bath." I called back, "All right, carry on."

'Then I went out into a corridor. There were two unknown ladies sewing. They were making a bed quilt, made by stitching together the tartans of all the Scottish clans. I said, "What a pretty covering for a sick bed", and the two ladies smiled.'

Mrs. Wright's first comment on this dream was, 'Does Bertha not being ready for the marriage, mean me?' We came to the conclusion, however, that, in view of the extremely positive nature of the first dream it could not mean her, but quite literally referred to her sister Bertha, who indeed was not ready.[1] She told me that Bertha had not yet had her customary

FIG. 7. TO ILLUSTRATE DREAM 21

Bertha, too late for her wedding, lying in a swoon surrounded by the three women who should have been her bridesmaids, who stand looking at her prostrate body.

[1] I have been criticized for not accepting Mrs. Wright's own suggestion that Bertha's unpreparedness for the marriage really referred to Mrs. Wright's own unwillingness to deal with her own shadow-problem (see p. 87) by still projecting it upon Bertha, unless, my critic adds, Bertha 'undergoes a remarkable but most improbable conversion'. There is indeed some theoretical validity in this, but the

autumn swooning fit which she usually had in September, but had been terribly bad-tempered—the kind of temper that usually led to the swooning fits but rather worse. I pointed out that the swooning could be taken from at least two angles. On the one hand it meant (as in the previous dream about the crumbs swept from the table)[1] that she must humble herself to the earth before any kind of salvation could come her way. On the manifest level, on the other hand, the swooning was a method of escape from her own tempers, by means of which she could temporarily forget her own annually recurring problem. I pointed out that, just as Mrs. Wright's own spiritual recovery was influencing her sister as well as Margaret, this was probably the cause of her sister no longer being able to find this illusive way out. I warned her, however, that for this reason her sister's tempers would for the time being almost certainly get worse, but that this was a necessary crucifixion that she would have to put up with, and that it would actually lead in the long run to an improvement, so long as Margaret, and Mrs. Wright herself, were not made to suffer too much on account of them. Mrs. Wright said that both she and Margaret were no longer seriously affected by them, and would put up with them cheerfully if it would do Bertha any good. I said there was no hope, in my opinion, of Bertha ever being ready for marriage, but that there was a distinct hope that she would become calmer and more tolerant as the general family situation improved.

Mrs. Wright herself remarked at this point that the position of the two women on either side of Bertha corresponded to the two wings of the aeroplane, and added that their dresses were almost the same colour as the wings, which were the colour of unbleached linen. Bertha thus represented the vertical bar of

whole subject of Bertha had to be handled with great tact and, as will be seen in a later volume, Mrs. Wright did accomplish her own spiritual union on a much deeper level than that seen in this dream, and Bertha's 'conversion' is at the time of publication far from being beyond the bounds of probability and in fact shows distinct signs of being realized.

[1] Dream 13.

the cross and the two 'bridesmaids' its arms. The symmetry was spoilt, however, by the third 'bridesmaid' standing near her head, thus indicating the seat of Bertha's trouble.

It had by this time become quite clear that the unpreparedness for the marriage was indeed Bertha's, and not Mrs. Wright's,[1] whereon the latter said, 'Then what does it mean about my father being ready when Bertha was not?' I pointed out that it was Mrs. Wright, and not Bertha, who had found out the father, and to whom he had said, 'I am ready', and that it was not only her earthly father, but also the Father in Heaven who thus told her that *he* was ready. There was no need to discuss what he was ready for (i.e. the marriage to God referred to in a previous dream[2]). The symbolism spoke for itself.

I then asked her why she thought Margaret had gone to take a bath. She said she did not know, but when I hinted at baptism she said, 'Yes, I had been thinking that myself. I used not to know what rebirth meant, but now I do.'

The only thing left to discuss was the tartan quilt made by the two unknown ladies. She first said, 'Does this mean the Scottish Church?" But this suggestion had no content, and she then said, 'My family came originally from Scotland', whereon it became clear that, having made spiritual contact with her father and through him with the Father of all men, the joining of the tartans of all the Scottish clans symbolized the gathering together of all the innate forces which, arising from the branching family tree, had gone to build up her own individuality, the origins of which were thus traced back through an endless series of links to the dim distant past represented by the emergent godhead.

I said the two ladies reminded me of the two ladies looking at their books of embroidery patterns in Dream 7, and asked whether the tartans were of the same colours as those. She said, 'No, but I saw a picture the other day which showed me what those embroidery colours were. It was a picture of our Lord, and those colours were the colours of His robe.'

She said, 'Why should I think the tartan covering was for a

[1] But see footnote on p. 75. [2] Dream 17.

sick bed?' We came to the conclusion that this might partly refer to her profession as a nurse, but that it probably had a deeper meaning to the effect that all sickness was due to a break in the continuity of spiritual life which this gathering of the clans was designed to heal. Her last question was, 'Do I do wrong, then, to go on giving the village people the simple remedies they come to me for? Is this serving two masters?' I said, 'No. You can't advertise your own conversion like that. That is your own private matter. If it eventually affects them as it is already affecting Margaret and Bertha, well and good. But you won't do that by talking, and meanwhile, if these accustomed remedies give them comfort, there's no reason why they should not have them.'

She then told me she had had another snatch of a dream.

22. Dream

'I was surrounded in my own house by children, and the Vicar came in and asked if he could help. I said, "No", but he went on moving in and out among them.'[1]

As it so happened, I met the Vicar that afternoon, and he told me what an improvement he had noticed in Margaret, and that for the first time in her life she had actually answered some of his questions with something more than a plain 'Yes' or 'No', and had actually had a short conversation with him about the work she was doing.

[1] Mrs. Wright's rejection of the Vicar's help is in line with Bertha's rejection of marriage in the previous dream. (See footnote on p. 75.) The solution of this problem of the rejected *animus* as it occurred after the events here dealt with will be described in a later volume.

ELEVENTH INTERVIEW

9th October

Mrs. Wright started the interview by saying once more how immensely the whole family situation had improved. The whole village was remarking how much better Margaret was. She would now return the villagers' greetings out loud with a 'Good morning' or 'Good afternoon' instead of mumbling these to herself so that she could not be heard and was often thought to have made no reply at all. She had also started to knit quite well instead of dropping half her stitches as she had always done before, and had even begun to tend, mend, and iron her own clothes and for the first time in her life generally to take an interest in her personal appearance. She had also for the first time begun to say her prayers. When asked, 'What prayers?' Mrs. Wright said, 'The Lord's Prayer', and told how hitherto Margaret had been unable to struggle through it, but could now say it all through.

Then followed a brief discussion on the Lord's Prayer, including the fact that the words 'daily bread' have in this context an obvious spiritual meaning as well as a material one.

Mrs. Wright said also that she herself had never felt better in her life, that instead of the rheumatism and indigestion from which she had suffered for years and had accepted as inevitable, she now had 'neither ache, raik, nor pain'. For years all sorts of food had disagreed with her, but this week she had found she could eat anything—so much so that she had deliberately been eating all those things that had formerly upset her, and found she sustained no harm but on the contrary doubly enjoyed and profited from everything she touched.

The same, though in not quite so exuberant degree, was true of her sister Bertha, who not only had not swooned this autumn at all (though to compensate for this her tempers had at the time lasted a trifle longer), but was now far less bad-tempered than usual and was also enjoying food she had 'never had in years'. She then described a whole meal her sister Bertha had had of things that formerly she had refused to touch.

Even her husband, always good-tempered and placid, had become if possible yet more so than before.

After this panegyric, which was repeated at intervals throughout the session, Mrs. Wright said rather shyly that she had not done much dreaming, but had had one dream into which I and my wife came.

23. Dream

'The dream was of a hospital, but there were no beds in it. It was a large building with many rooms, all filled with a bright light similar to the light in the kitchen in Dream 9 [in which she had sacrificed the hare]. You [the analyst] and your wife were both in it. There were lots of people there and you seemed to be entertaining. You walked about quietly among the guests, but what I most noticed was your wife, who moved more quickly among the people, as women do, and whose eyes shone like stars. She said to me, "I will show you your room". Then she took me into one of the rooms, in which there was a bed, and on it a night costume finely embroidered with lace. I said, "That costume is too fine for me. A plain one would do." But she said, "That is your costume." I began to undress, but had only taken off two garments when I awoke.

'Your little son was not there, but I noticed a little boy about five years old wearing a blue suit and a blue tam-o'-shanter.'

When asked what was the pattern embroidered on the lace, she made the drawing reproduced in Fig. 8, in which the squares represent the gathered-in lace and the curved lines the fronds of the palm leaf spreading on both sides of a central stem. Below this were a few tucks, whence downward the costume was plain.

Asked what she thought this meant, she said she had woken up repeating the words of a Rescue Mission hymn which ran,

Palms of victory, crowns of glory,
Palms of victory I shall wear.

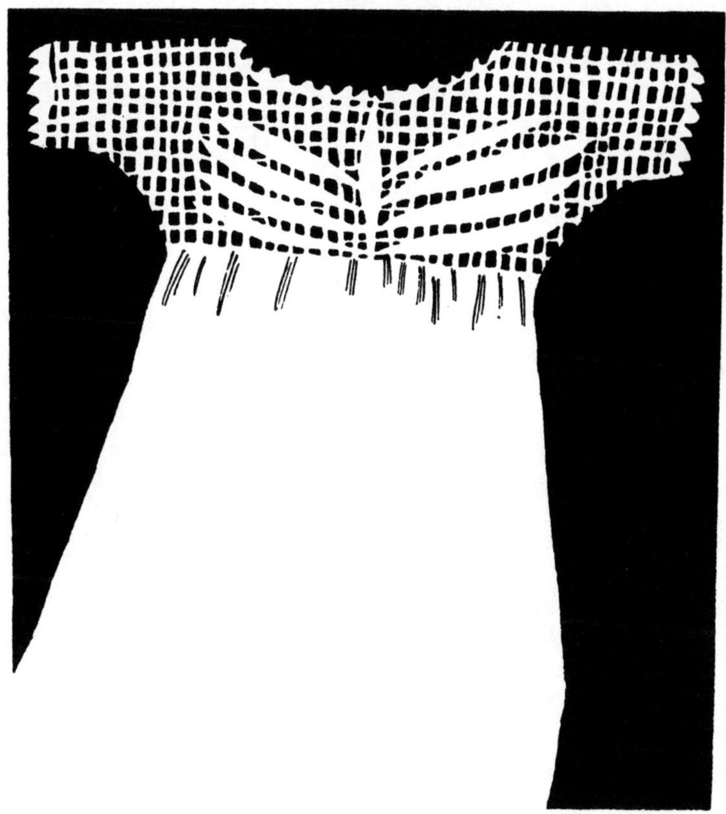

Fig. 8

The 'night costume' offered to Mrs. Wright in her dream by the analyst's wife.

These words were said with utter modesty indicating heartfelt acceptance devoid of any kind of inflated pride.

No word from me was needed to point out that the blue suit the boy was wearing was the same colour as that of the German airman in Dream 20 who turned out to be the crucified Christ, here reincarnated after the victory of Palm Sunday in the form of her own rejuvenated soul. I only added that 'blue' was the colour of heaven and meant understanding[1]—the understanding her dreams had brought her. Asked what was the exact shape of the boy's tam o'shanter, she said it was not worn, as some are, on one side, but was flat on his head, more like a child's sailor hat, had a central knob and resembled a halo.

I pointed out that the fact that the dream showed her this Christ-child and not my own son meant that what she took to be me and my wife were in fact not us but dream representations of the divine family. She agreed that no human eyes shone as did my wife's eyes in the dream. I had, however, taken great care throughout the analysis to deal with the danger of her transferring the Saviour archetype on to myself by disclaiming it on every occasion when it arose (cf. page 47), and took this opportunity of further emphasizing the obvious unsuitability of any such personal projection.

The brief survey of the dream then showed that it was in reality a visual representation of the opening phrases of that very Lord's Prayer she had been teaching her daughter, and which (now that, in terms of a previous dream,[2] 'Margaret and her mother may sleep together') her daughter was for the first time absorbing through the mediumship of her mother. Thus the bright light clearly set forth the setting of the opening phrase, 'Our Father which art in heaven', to which the blue of the Christ-child's suit and his halo also contributed. No direct allusion was found to 'Hallowed be thy name', unless it were the feeling of awe with which she regarded the dedicatory costume (in which the symbol of the spreading palm leaf as well as the shape of the garment itself closely resembled a

[1] In other words, introverted intuition (see footnotes on pp. 32, 44).

[2] Dream 10.

cross). 'Thy kingdom come' was, however, clearly represented by the hospital in which no beds were needed since the whole problem of everyday disease had now lost for her its material character and was seen as a result of her own analysis to depend on spiritual and not physical factors. Here she herself alluded to the phrase 'In my father's house are many mansions' as being represented by the great number of rooms the hospital contained. 'Thy will be done' was in turn represented by the now proven efficacy of believing in God's will as revealed in her own dreams. Perhaps most striking of all, however, was her reaction when I pointed out the significance of the phrase 'in earth as it is in heaven', whereon she said 'Yes, and the carpets were brown, the colour of the earth. They don't have carpets in real hospitals, do they?'

That ended the stage of the Lord's Prayer to which the dream took us, and we then wonderingly looked forward to how the second half would be dealt with in future dreams and what these would reveal.

The interview ended with her mentioning a neighbour, Mrs. R, a married woman having trouble with her husband (which, as Mrs. Wright put it, was her own fault) and who, attracted by Mrs. Wright's new-found stability, had confided in her, and asked her advice.

TWELFTH AND LAST INTERVIEW

16th October

Mrs. Wright came to-day saying that she had had a dream clearly referring to Mrs. R., but possibly also to herself.

24. Dream

'I was walking along the village street and met a woman covered from head to foot with a thick shroud of brown stuff darker than the brown tissue covering the lightly veiled form seen in a former dream.[1] This figure I felt to be that of Mrs. R. She was seeking the way into a field, but, being shrouded, stumbled and could not find her way because she could not see. One of the village women, Mrs. Smart, who had a sharp tongue and a sarcastic nature, jeered at her for stumbling, and made no offer of help. But I took her by the arm and led her towards the field. There was a green hedge (possibly a privet) higher than a man's head surrounding the field, and in it a gate, through which I saw the sun shining. I led her through the gate, and just inside it there was a man, who took her from me. I looked into the field, and saw a man ploughing. He was using an old-fashioned plough, not a tractor, and was getting the field ready for sowing. It was springtime (not autumn as it is now), for he had his coat off as if the weather was warm. He was probably going to sow spring oats'.

This dream just related occurred during the night. Next morning she had a brief vision.

25. Vision

It was the same field, in which green blades of corn were now showing above the earth. She woke up thinking to herself 'A sower went forth to sow', and as soon as she had time re-read the parable of the sower in Matthew xiii.

[1] Dream-Vision 8.

TWELFTH AND LAST INTERVIEW

There was little comment to make on this dream, except to ask whether the ploughman was in any way like the figure of her husband in Dream 3. She said it was not, and that both the ploughman and the man into whose hands she delivered the shrouded figure were quite impersonal figures.

This dream clearly marked the end of a phase. Mrs. Wright said she felt this was the case, and that for the next few weeks she must get busy with her garden, pulling the weeds and getting it ready for the winter. So we parted for the time being, wondering what the next phase, especially in Margaret's development, would be.[1]

[1] The subsequent development, both of Mrs. Wright and her daughter, are summarized in the Note on p. 96, and will be dealt with in a later volume.

BRIEF THEORETICAL DISCUSSION

and summary of the dream-process

The reader may wonder what was the nature of the process by which the results here outlined were achieved. Was it by consciously readjusting her outlook that Mrs. Wright managed so to improve both her own condition and that of those immediately depending on her or was it by some other means unknown to the ordinary man?

The answer, so far as it can be given in logical terms, is that the conscious part of the process consists not so much in an effort of will as in a redirection of attention towards psychic factors of great power with which men and women nowadays are apt to lose contact owing to a lack of understanding of the problems involved.

Certain concepts are useful as tools by means of which these powers may be assimilated into the conscious mind and so made available for the conduct of life. Analytical Psychology does not think of that vast psychic field so glibly called the 'unconscious' as being in any way homogeneous, but conceives of it as being composed of two main parts not divided by any rigid line but which are nevertheless sufficiently distinct to merit separate names. Nearest the surface is what is termed the *personal unconscious*, which differs in each individual and contains those personal contents of the psyche that were once conscious but have been repressed out of consciousness for one reason or another, together with those personal potentialities which, thwarted by misconceptions, have become turned in on themselves and so, by failing to find expression, have taken on a negative character. The chief element in this personal unconscious is what is technically called the *Shadow*, which is the mirror image of our conscious evaluation of ourselves and is commonly represented in dreams by persons of the *same sex* as the dreamer.[1] This is the personal aspect, beneath which lies

[1] In a later stage in the integration process the Shadow often appears as a guide, either to warn or help.

the deep well of what is called the *impersonal* or *collective unconscious* which contains, on the other hand, all those driving forces of which the individual can never be fully aware, including those non-personal aspirations which in religious terminology have to do with the soul. These, belonging as they do to the 'other side' of life, appear, so far as the dream symbolizes them in human form, commonly as persons of the *opposite sex.* The technical term used for this soul phenomenon thus symbolized in men's dreams by women is the Latin word *anima* meaning 'soul' or 'breath',[1] while in the case of a woman, for whom it appears as something male, it is called the *animus.* In the present dream-series, therefore, in which the dreamer is a woman, various aspects of the *Shadow* (the repressed personal side of her character) are represented by women, and those of the soul or *animus* by men.

These are the main characters in the drama dealt with in the foregoing account, a brief summary of which will help to epitomize the analytical process so far as it has progressed at this stage of Mrs. Wright's development, showing to what extent personal misconceptions which had obscured the essential pattern of the psyche were removed and its harmony thereby restored.

The series starts off with a clear adumbration of opposites by the Angel's paradoxical warning against seeking heaven in the sky where the dreamer has been brought up to seek it. This play of opposites is carried a step further in highly dramatic fashion in the first two 'pregnancy' dreams.

In the first of these (Dream 3) her soul or *animus*, here projected on to the figure of her husband, is seen lacerated, owing, as the angel had indicated by its gesture, to her putting 'the cart before the horse', in other words the husband in front of instead of behind the plough. This would be equivalent to regarding God as a vague ideal to strive towards, rather than as the cause from which all life sprang and whom it is necessary to seek first in the past—this was the meaning of the ancestral tartan representing the roots of her being. The first need in tending a plant is to see that its roots are properly cared for and

[1] Compare p. 166.

watered, since without this all care lavished on its superstructure will be without avail. In the same way, a small child must first have its body and emotions nourished before any attempt is made by transforming them to develop its soul.

In the second pregnancy dream (Dream 4) the opposites are stated more clearly still in the contrast between, on the one hand, her mistakenly idealistic striving upwards towards the mountain crest on the right (or conscious) side, and on the other hand, the real starting place represented by the green pasture to the left which must be returned to before conscious effort can build anything other than castles in the air.

Her first task was to accept the 'shadow', in her case the falsely idealistic side of herself represented in the first place by the other nurse in Dream 5, indicating the sin of personal pride which always stands in the way of real communion with the soul or *animus* here represented by the concealed lover. Being a wise woman, she did accept, and as a reward her positive *animus* then appeared to her in the form of the young bridegroom in Dream 6.

But the soul is a very terrifying thing, partaking of the numinous ambivalent quality of God. Hence the inevitable conflict introduced by the concept of fear. What was it that Mrs. Wright had 'not to fear'? She certainly did fear. We all do, for fear is a part of nature, seen at its lowest in panic, and at its highest in the fear of the Lord. What she, like all of us, needed was to learn not to be afraid of fear. It was precisely this fear of fear that she overcame in Dream 7 when the man overtook her, and fear in the physical sense became transmuted into the numinous feeling of awe, or in psychological terms the *negative* (because unconscious) *animus* became transformed into a potent *positive animus* through the conscious performance of an act of faith. This act of faith overcoming fear was repeated in Dream 9 when she sacrificed the hare and in her subsequent experience the following night; in Dream 12 in which she overcame the lonely terror of the air raid by translating it into communal worship and awe; and finally in Dream 13 in the conquest of the self-righteous conceit that she was her sister's keeper.

All this time the 'shadow' had been becoming more and more absorbed, this process reaching its peak when in Dream 8 she saw the veiled form of her naked self, and during the same week (in Dream 10) accepted the identity of her own problem with that of her daughter Margaret, expressed by the voice saying, 'Margaret and her mother may sleep together', whereby she acquired a sense of oneness with fate, while at the same time refusing in Dream 18 the false intellectual knowledge which the reverse side of her 'shadow' represented by Miss Hardacre attempted to impose.

It will be noted that the culmination of her experience—her real conversion—was represented in purely symbolical terms in the dream sequence (Dreams 9, 12, 13, 14, and 15) following the sacrifice of the hare. A point not discussed in the analysis was just why the sacrificial animal appearing in Mrs. Wright's dream should have been a hare. At that time I was not aware of the mass of extremely relevant mythology from many parts of the world dealing with the hare as a self-sacrificing animal and as a symbol of spiritual insight, which I have since summarized in Part II on *The Mythology of the Hare*. I was then aware only of the hare as one of the animals into which witches were often said to transform themselves, and as a well-known witch's 'familiar', but since the significance of this was at the moment far from clear I refrained from calling attention to it, thinking it safer to concentrate purely on the more general significance of animal sacrifice as representing the transformation of unredeemed instinct into spiritual value.

What was, at any rate, quite clear was that this sacrifice represented the conquest over some pre-Christian and therefore deeply unconscious element that joined Mrs. Wright in that kind of unconscious tangle with destructive primitive forces that is technically called negative *participation mystique*, and which invariably leads to the projection of negative psychological contents on to some object. It was equally clear that the object upon which these negative contents were fixed was Margaret, since the very next dream (Dream 10) brought the welcome announcement that 'Margaret and her mother may sleep together'. This meant that the negative contents that Mrs. Wright had previously projected upon her daughter were now withdrawn, and that she could now do her daughter nothing but good. In other words the era of negative *participation* was at an end and a new era of positive *participation mystique* had dawned. It was this message that brought the relieving bitter-sweet tears to Mrs. Wright's eyes, and it was from this moment that Margaret began to improve.

A point worth the attention of theologians is the evidence that the dream process affords with regard to the relative values of ritual symbolism and dogma. It will be noted that it was not till after the symbolic sacrifice of the hare in Dream 9, subsequently repeated by that of the Jewish butcher in Dream 15, that the intellectual question as to the nature of God arose in Dream 17. In the same way the intellectual concept of the sacred marriage between God and Man followed the much earlier emotional experience expressed in purely human terms in the union of the non-nubile bride and bridegroom in Dream 6. This precedence in time and depth sequence of feeling over thought is of fundamental importance to the whole theory and teaching of religion. The fact that feeling precedes and *underlies* and provides the dynamic force for thought is of fundamental importance to all spiritual progress. Just as the body of the unborn babe miraculously developing within its mother's womb in nine months recapitulates all the stages of biological evolution, so also does it recapitulate all psychic evolution from the amoeba to man, including man's history up to the moment when the child breaks away from the maternal matrix and first sees the light of day. This is the basis of the whole concept of the collective unconscious. The child's first act of emancipation from the matrix is birth, when it achieves individuality in the body. Its second act of emancipation is when it becomes re-born by returning to the mother in a spiritual sense through full participation in Mother Church, the mystical *body* of Christ. During the interval between birth and rebirth it once more recapitulates, this time as an individual, the psychic development of the race, and *must* follow that development planned by God for each individual as well as for the race as a whole. Short cuts to heaven do not exist, but are offered at almost every turn by religious teaching that ignores this inevitable process and thus, instead of providing a short cut to heaven, furnishes all too easy a one in the opposite direction. Premature intellectualizations provide this very nicely! The world to-day is full of theory and of a vicious kind of pseudo-spirituality that kills life because it is not founded *on* life.

The world to-day does not believe in miracles because it forestalls them with an attempted miracle that is impossible, namely, the attempt to make a child into a man or woman before he or she has been a child. How can we as adults 'become as little children' if we have never *been* children, and thus have never known what it is to be a child? To be as little children we must live through the ordinary emotions of childhood. Margaret had not done this in the fullest sense, owing to circumstances that Mrs. Wright now bitterly regrets. But there is no human life, however mistakenly begun, that cannot be retrieved. So Christ taught, and so the Church professes to believe, though through pride due to its own impatience it does not always act up to this profession. There is a maxim that says 'More haste less speed'. Those who want to make children into good Christians before they are ripe and without going through the necessary preliminary stages cut off the very spirituality they hope to impose. Spirituality cannot be imposed. It can only grow. It has, moreover, its own laws of growth, which are divine laws not depending on the logic of men.

The same laws apply moreover to the individual as apply to the race. The race did not begin by formulating dogma. Dogma was, doubtless, latent from the beginning, as the adult is latent in the child. It is the aim (and perhaps even the prime cause) but it is not the Way. Christ was the Way, but was not unduly concerned with dogma. What he did say which is relevant here is that he came not to destroy the law, but to fulfil it. He certainly therefore had the concept of growth. The law, in so far as he conceived it in human terms, was the law of the Old Testament, which had to be absorbed and transformed, which is the opposite of being destroyed, since what is destroyed cannot be either absorbed or transformed. There are two parts of the Bible, the gradual Growth from early beginnings, and the Fulfilment which was Himself Who in His own person, incarnate through the medium of the Holy Ghost, joined the two opposites God and Man.

Now both the Old Testament and anthropology show that man's early development was far from being regulated by dogma, but proceeded by a system of trial and error, always guided in the long run towards higher things, but groping its way by means of symbolic beliefs of all kinds and by ritual practices expressing and gradually crystallizing these beliefs. Nor can anyone who has lived with primitive peoples, as the writer has, have any doubt as to the vivid nature of these beliefs and practices or of their immense value as indispensable vehicles of the nascent comprehension by mankind of the truths later expressed by dogma.

Nor has any psychologist who recognizes the significance of the 'other side' of things, nor any person having true spiritual insight, any doubt that each individual has to re-live in his own psychic development the same process. The Tree of Life is strong to save, but woe betide him who plucks the fruit of the Knowledge of Good and Evil before the time is ripe. We adults have a social duty towards the child. We have plucked of the Tree of the Knowledge of Good and Evil. That is our thorn, and the thorn is the thorn of consciousness which is at once our burden and our salvation, though being the latter only if we have the wit to unite it with the Tree of Life.

Childhood is the time of the Tree of Life, and we should tamper with it only if we have a very clear idea of what we are doing. Primitive peoples know this so well that they often deny that the child has a soul before Initiation. This means that they honour the child by not attempting to tamper with its spiritual development till the time when it is finally taken from its mother and is then introduced with tribulation into the tribe's concept of Good and Evil, at which period it is deemed to have become a man. This is the real meaning of Confirmation, 'When I was a child, I spake as a child, I understood as a child, I thought as a child, but when I became a man,

I put away childish things.'[1] Saint Paul knew that a child's thought was not a man's thought, and Christ says 'Suffer little children to come unto me, for of these is the kingdom of heaven.' The kingdom of heaven is at the beginning and at the end, but it must begin at the beginning. As we grow up we overlay the kingdom with worldly cares and misconceptions. These form the upper layers of consciousness. The child lies buried ever deeper in the unconscious levels. The child has unerring instinct and thinks in symbols. The profound efficacy of play therapy proves the immense curative value wrought by the release of this symbolic activity when it has been repressed by the false superimposition on it of adult thought. I have myself known a child's life altered overnight by an adult simply listening to its dreams without even commenting on them, and so joining the child's symbolic dream material with its conscious life. So long as the dream symbolism had been repressed owing to adult misconceptions about the child's spiritual life, it was engaged in actively destroying that life, but the admission of this dream material into consciousness turned the child from a morose, self-centred, and anti-social creature into a co-operative and happy human being.

The application of this to dogma is that dogma is true as an intellectual expression of what has been previously experienced through a combination of all the four functions of sensation, feeling, thinking and intuition by the most advanced adults of our race in closest contact with God. It is the flower of all these, and it may also be—and probably is—the root. It is a static truth which, on account of its very rigidity, may in practice actually stultify growth unless handled with the utmost care and with due and reverent regard for the growing organism which, in so far as the dogma fulfils and amplifies the stage of development to which that organism has attained, expands and enriches it. But in so far as the teaching of dogma jumps too far ahead or seeks to lead by intellectual argument into formulations which the living organism is not yet sufficiently evolved to follow, it deadens or retards the very development it seeks to foster.

[1] 1 Corinthians xiii, 11.

Thus Mrs. Wright's difficulties had all been due to such an imposition of quite proper ideals too early in life before the emotional background of experience had been lived through, and the success of the analysis rested on the precise re-living by means of symbols of the experience which a too early teaching of dogma had partly killed.

The key to this aspect of her analysis lay in the phrase attributed in Dream 18 to the Vicar as representative of God saying '*You* know'. 'You' here refers to the inner knowledge of the dreamer as brought to the threshold of consciousness, not by dogma, but by the experience of her own childlike inner nature.

The rest follows automatically. In the next dream (19), to resume psychological terminology, the negative 'shadow' representing the superimposed attitudes, hostile only because they *were* superimposed, becomes reconciled to beauty, that is to say to the creative urge of Mrs. Wright's own nature; and in the next dream (20), fortified by the *animus* represented by her husband, the dreamer sees the cross descend from heaven to earth, signifying among other things the descent of truth out of the clouds to a level at which Mrs. Wright can understand it in terms of her own life-process. From here onward the dream series is mainly occupied with consolidating the gains already won.

This answers, I think, in so far as we can answer it at present, the question posed at the beginning. The first part of the analytical process is to show what we are. The issue depends on whether we can accept this new knowledge or not. The great hindrance is pride, a pride based on the belief that men know better than nature. Pride is a necessary thing, but it has to be kept in its proper place. We may well pride ourselves on our material or moral achievement, but if this pride is not balanced by true humility it will have a fall. Like true religion, analysis shows us our faults as hindrances to the attainment of our heart's desire, the Tree of Life. It is up to us whether we accept the revelation or not. Freedom is the acceptance of truth, however that truth may hurt our pride. Acceptance brings wisdom. Wisdom brings power over ourselves, and opens the way for the operation of forces that no self-will can touch. It is this kind of will power that psychological analysis aims to reinforce, the will to submit one's personal will to the pattern of life which is the will of God, whose service is perfect freedom, freedom to act, live and love without the trammels of misconception based on false ideals. God has two aspects. On the one hand he includes all the forces of nature striving for life against every obstacle. On the other hand he is the Moral Law of which the purpose is to control nature. To serve God is to serve Him, not by opposing nature, but by transforming it in obedience to its own hidden laws which it is the purpose of psychology as the handmaiden of religion to reveal. Religion means a joining of these two principles. There is nothing that man cannot achieve within the limits of human frailty, will he but recognize that every material or moral advance opens beneath his feet a chasm of outraged nature which, if he ignore it, will drag him down; but which, if he give it due honour, will, transformed by this act of faith, prove an inexhaustible well of inner knowledge (the wisdom of the serpent) capable of fortifying him against all dangers, by enabling both sides of him to attain equal balance for the successful conduct of life.

Nor is this a selfish quest for purely individual salvation, for just as the branches of forest trees intermingle, so also do their roots. The psyche, which in the conscious is self-contained, also has roots that interpenetrate with those of others, whether we will it or not, and, nature seeking always a balance, increase of poise anywhere affects the whole circle in which we live, witness the family circle of Mrs. Wright.

Everything depends, not on the amount of will power available, but on its direction. Will power is fettered only when occupied with the manifest content. Free will is that which results from a recognition of the opposite or mirror-image of the manifest cast up out of the unconscious depths, and, recognizing it, obeys. The difficulty is, of course, to see it, and where formal religion may fail to reveal the inner light through lack of recognition of the individual way by which each one of us must find his own salvation within the framework of the universal redemptive process, there Analytical Psychology may help, always hoping that one day religion may once more be broadened and deepened, as in the early days of Christianity, to embrace the wayward path traced by the prodigal who reached the goal no less surely than his less wayward brother.

Perhaps a word may be put in here for science, for while modern Christianity tends to teach faith as a duty, Analytical Psychology has arrived at a similar faith through that same process of inductive reasoning by which the best scientists work, the main difference between this and the other sciences being that it applies methods hitherto used exclusively for the examination of material nature, to the nature of spirit. Analytical Psychology thus claims to have a foot in both camps, for while on the one hand it works in the same field of collective symbolism as does religion, on the other it does so with a sense of inquiry into these mysteries that emboldens its followers to think of it as the first modest attempt at a Science of Introversion, by means of which they hope that one day medicine, philosophy and religion may once more, as of old, find common ground for the pursuit of common aims.

SUBSEQUENT DEVELOPMENT OF MARGARET

The reader may well wonder, what, in the three years' interval since the analysis ended, has become of Mrs. Wright and her daughter, and of the aunt to whom so much of Margaret's apparent trouble was due. I say *apparent* trouble, because the sequel has been yet one more demonstration of the truth that God sends evil that good may come, though good does not come unless we know how to find it. This doctrine of the 'positive purpose of evil' has been amply vindicated in Margaret's case, no less than in her mother's.

After the last interview described in this book, which took place on the 16th of October 1940, I saw nothing of the Wright family for almost a year apart from a few fleeting calls at their village, in the course of other duties, to inquire how things were going on. Mrs. Wright showed every sign of continued well-being, and Margaret slowly continued to improve. After the lapse of just under a year, that is to say on the 8th October 1941, Mrs. Wright came to see me to report progress, and told me three outstanding dreams that had somewhat puzzled her but which she felt were important. These dreams, which will be published in a later volume, were of quite a different character from those hitherto recounted, and all pointed to the continued operation of the redemptive process on a considerably deeper level than she had hitherto plumbed. As was the case with her former dream about the hare, one of these dreams raised issues of a historico-mythological nature that at the time I was quite unable to fathom, but which I have since investigated and which I hope to discuss in a third volume completing this series.

Nevertheless, though conscious understanding lagged behind, the dreams had their effect in maintaining her contact with the healing forces welling up out of the collective unconscious and so helping her on her way.

After this brief interlude, I had no further contact with the family till, in April of the following year (1942) the manuscript for this book was accepted for publication and the publishers asked me to write a postscript describing the state of affairs in the Wright family, at an interval of what was then a year and a half after the formal analysis had ended. This proved a notable date, for from this renewed contact sprang a new phase in the development of the whole situation remarkable enough in itself and with possibilities still unforeseen.

Mrs. Wright then said that her dream-life had settled down into a rhythmical pattern consisting of alternating periods of intense dreaming, which, far from interfering with the normal activities of everyday life, enriched and intensified them, and were then followed by fallow periods in which the insight gained from her most recent dream-series was assimilated and made available for practical use.

I spent several days with long intervals between them (owing to wartime difficulties of transport) analysing the contents of the latest of such dream-series, and in August left for my brief annual holiday in Cornwall. While there, I had a letter from her saying that Margaret was about to be called up for National Service, and asking me, as Margaret was still quite unable to fend for herself, what she should do. A medical colleague who is a psychiatric expert kindly took the matter in hand and, after examining her, obtained exemption for her on the grounds that she was a High Grade Mental Defective. Mrs. Wright, in writing to thank me for having arranged the interview and expressing her gratitude for the sympathetic and understanding way in which the psychiatrist had handled the matter, added, 'I am sure you will be delighted to know that Margaret is doing very well and is very bright and happy, and not the Margaret that we used to know'.

I little suspected all that was behind these words, for, though I had every confidence that Margaret would improve greatly, I had not expected the degree of improvement which, on my return, I actually found. The above-mentioned letter reached me on the 8th of August. It was not till I had returned home and till Mrs. Wright had found time to come and see me that I learnt, on the 8th of September 1942, almost two years since the mother's formal analysis ended, the real extent of what had happened.

She told me that during the past month Margaret had completely altered. The first indication of this was when Margaret had started having daylight visions which were in effect the continuation and extension in a still deeper sense of Mrs. Wright's own night-time dreams. These visions quickly developed into what can only be termed 'second sight' combined with knowledge of certain aspects of her mother's past history obtained through visionary and auditory contact with her mother's father, who had died when Margaret herself was only three years old. This visionary perception of her maternal grandfather soon became merged with the traditional figure of Bonnie Prince Charlie who for the loyal Northern Irish Wright family with its Scottish descent was a legendary hero, and this concept in turn merged into or was replaced by a higher concept still, that of the Heavenly Father, under whose direct guidance she now believes herself to be.

A further development is that, without prompting of any

kind, Margaret has now taken to interpreting her mother's dreams, and even knows quite often what her mother has dreamt before she is told. She has, alongside this, acquired what her mother regards as a nascent power for spiritual healing, which it is too early yet to comment on, apart from the brief statement that the barrier of so-called mental deficiency that has cut her off from so many of the good things of this world, has had also as its positive purpose that of protecting her from many of its illusions, and especially from one of the subtlest illusions of all, namely, the belief that disease of the body is anything other than a disguised disease of the soul.

A detailed account of the mother's dream-process leading up to this result and of Margaret's own development will be described in the later volume to which reference has already been made, and into which, on account of the large quantity of new material, the postscript originally asked for by the publisher has now been expanded.

Part Two

THE MYTHOLOGY OF THE HARE

INTRODUCTORY

In any analysis there are certain key dreams which mark conspicuous turning-points in the dreamer's development. One such key dream dreamt by Mrs. Wright was, as we have already seen, Dream 9 in which she sacrificed the Hare. It will be remembered, however, that the form which the analysis of this dream took was one applicable to any kind of animal sacrifice, as representing the transformation of untutored instinct, through sacrifice, into spiritual value. Mrs. Wright being a devout Christian, I used the simile of the sacrifice of the Lamb to bring home its essential meaning. This treatment of the dream was efficacious beyond expectation, but left out of account the whole question of just why the animal chosen by her dream-mind to sacrifice was not a lamb but a hare.

This was because I was myself at that time completely ignorant of the immense role the hare has in fact played as a symbol in the complex mythological systems of many nations, including that of our own ancestors.

It was in fact not till more than two years later, and after the remarkable further development both of Mrs. Wright and of her daughter Margaret, referred to on page 96 and to be described fully in a later volume, that I became aware of the peculiar significance of the hare in the world's mythological systems, and of the reason why just that animal and no other offered itself for sacrifice at this juncture in Mrs. Wright's dream-life. The evidence, culled from religious records of some of the world's most ancient civilizations and from the folk-lore of some of the less advanced, is so striking, not only as an explanation in general terms of why Mrs. Wright's unconscious should have chosen precisely this symbol, but also on account of the light it sheds on certain details of the dream that had so far been only tentatively interpreted, that I feel no hesitation in setting the facts before the reader, partly in order to elucidate the dream material still further, and partly as one example among many of how the dream-mind is in fact a storehouse of ancient symbolic wisdom unsuspected by the most learned scholars of our time, and also, incidentally, quite unknown consciously to the dreamer.

THE HARE AS ARCHETYPE

In other words, the Hare is an Archetype in the sense used by Jung, who, after describing the personal unconscious as the repository of those purely personal experiences that have been repressed, says: 'Yet this personal unconscious appears to rest upon a deeper layer that does not derive from personal experience and achievement but is inborn. This deeper layer I call the *collective unconscious.* I have chosen the term 'collective' because this part of the unconscious is not individual, but universal; in contrast to the personal psyche, it has contents and modes of behaviour that are more or less the same everywhere and in all individuals. The collective unconscious, so far as we know, is self-identical in all Western men and thus constitutes a psychic foundation, superpersonal in its nature, that is present in every one of us. . . . The contents of the personal unconscious constitute the personal and private side of psychic life. They are chiefly the so-called *feeling-toned complexes.* The contents of the collective unconscious, on the other hand, are the so-called *archetypes.*

The term 'archetype' derives from Saint Augustine, and deals with 'ancient or, better yet, with primordial types—that is to say, with images impressed upon the mind since of old. . . . Primitive tribal lore treats of archetypes that are modified in a particular way . . . , changed into conscious formulas [*sic*] that are taught according to tradition, generally in the form of esoteric teaching. . . .

'Another well-known expression of the archetype is myth and fable. But here also we are dealing with conscious and specifically moulded forms that have been handed on relatively unchanged through long periods of time.'[1]

An archetype 'designates the psychic content that has as yet been subjected to no conscious treatment and so represents an immediate, psychic actuality'.[2] Thus, 'myths are related to psychic happening',[3] and, as such, continue to present themselves actively in dreams to express and actually bring about what the conscious mind alone is incapable either of understanding or of achieving.

Those who have read the foregoing narrative will have recognized already a number of such archetypes, which are familiar to them through their common heritage of Christian symbolism. Such were the Angel of Vision 1, the deep water and green pastures of Dream 4, the 'opener of the way' symbolized by the Vicar in several dreams, the various Christ symbols occurring throughout the dream-series, the sacrificial motives adumbrating the crucifixion in Dreams 9 and 15, the number 3 representing the initiation process in Dream 12, the bread-crumbs representing the Host in Dream 13, the Cross represented by the descending aeroplane in Dream 20, the palms of victory in Dream 23, the ploughing of the field in Dream 24, and the appearance of the growing corn in Vision 25, and many others.

The most efficacious archetype of all, however, and of greatest import perhaps for the very reason that archetypes have their strongest effect when not watered down by vain repetition, was one that is not recognized as a symbol at all by official Christendom, namely the Hare. And since this archetype has not, so far as I know, yet been taken note of by psychologists, I propose now to trace its history in such measure as is possble from available sources.

Since this inquiry covers four continents and includes mythological beliefs current in India, China, Ancient Egypt, and in

[1] C. G. Jung, *The Integration of the Personality*, London, 1940, pp. 52, 53.

[2] ibid., p. 54. [3] ibid., p. 55.

the classical periods of Greece and Rome, some of which are still held while others are recoverable only from ancient texts, and in North America where beliefs strikingly similar in essentials were held till the advent of the white man by the Algonkin and by the Aztecs of Mexico, as well as modern folk-tales from many parts of Africa and a mass of medieval and modern folk-lore from Europe, it has not been possible except in certain cases to establish anything like a historical sequence, and the aim has been rather to chronicle the various beliefs regarding the hare wherever they occur, and to attempt tentatively to interpret them in a psychologico-religious sense.

This task has been the easier in that, as the mass of evidence unfolded itself, the beliefs accompanying the use of the hare as a mythological symbol showed such remarkable similarity throughout the world as to leave no doubt whatever about its fundamental meaning. It would be anticipating the evidence to describe here just what the various gradations of meaning are, which are to be found summarized on pages 222–9. The full flavour of the psychologico-religious process cannot, however, be communicated by means of conclusions only, since psychology does not consist in cut-and-dried and pigeon-holed conclusions, but in a living growth, which, as in the case of the foregoing analysis of Mrs. Wright, can be appreciated only by following the facts in the order in which they present themselves.

The value of a knowledge of archetypes is well illustrated by the fact that, since this study of the Mythology of the Hare was completed, I have in daily practice come across many occurrences of the hare-symbol in the dreams of other patients, the significance of which I should otherwise largely have missed, all showing similar features, through the resulting understanding of which the patients have greatly benefited and their comprehension of the forces involved in the individuation process has been correspondingly deepened. It would be out of place to give these here, and I have therefore recorded a selection of them in Part III, and will begin this inquiry into the mythology by reminding the reader of the relevant features of Mrs.

Wright's Dream 9 of sacrificing the Hare from which it started, and from which it will be seen, after the inquiry has been concluded, that the Hare is indeed a living archetype still wielding its old power in the deeper levels of the psyche of Modern Man.

EXTRACT FROM MRS. WRIGHT'S DREAM OF SACRIFICING THE HARE

It will be remembered how, after approaching, in company with her daughter Margaret, a square house near her former home in Ireland, over ground covered with snow, and how Margaret then went in at the front door, the dream in Mrs. Wright's words went on:

'Then I went round alone into the kitchen at the back of the house. Inside there was a great light and everything was as white as it was outside, though how the snow got in there I cannot tell.

'There were people inside too, and there, in a white bowl with a little water in it, was a live hare. Someone told me I had got to kill it. This seemed a terrible thing to do, but I had to do it. I picked up the knife (an ordinary kitchen knife) which seemed to have been placed ready for me and which was lying in the water inside the bowl beside the hare, and with a feeling of horror I started cutting into the fur and through to the skin beneath. I had to cut the hare straight down the middle of the back, and started to do this, but my hand trembled so much that, as I cut down, the knife slipped away from the straight line, and ended up by cutting obliquely into the hare's haunch.

'I felt awful doing this, but the hare never moved and did not seem to mind.

'Though the ground outside was covered with snow, we had left no footmarks on it.'

It will be remembered also that Mrs. Wright later (p. 63) 'told me of the look of extreme satisfaction and trust that had been in the hare's eyes as it looked back at her when she plunged the knife into its back', and that this made her think of the willing sacrifice of Christ.

INTRODUCTORY

THE HARE AS SACRIFICIAL ANIMAL
THE GROWTH OF SYMBOLS

Since Mrs. Wright draws her immediate cultural heritage from the British Isles, and lives in an epoch in which for almost twenty centuries all symbolic wisdom has been suspect other than that sanctioned by a Church who regards herself as the exclusive channel of divine revelation and is therefore highly suspicious if not actually jealous of unmediated religious experience, it is not surprising that such symbolic wisdom should often present itself under the guise of pure superstition. I will therefore reverse the proverbial order and proceed from the apparently ridiculous to the sublime, by first quoting the well-known memorandum of Dr. White Kenneth. Bearing in mind the willing sacrifice of the hare in Mrs. Wright's dream, this memorandum is of no little interest in that it asserts that 'when one keeps a hare alive, and feedeth him till he have occasion to eat him, if he telles before he killes him that he will doe so, the hare will thereupon be found dead, having killed himself'.[1]

This apparently fantastic statement would at first sight appear to bear no possible relation to fact until we begin to compare it with other legends from more than one part of the world in which the hare figures as sacrificing itself, always in a very peculiar way. That is to say, that the special way in which it sacrifices itself is invariably, so far as I know, by leaping into a fire. Such an act recalls that of the phoenix, the mythical bird that burnt itself, whereon a new and rejuvenated bird sprang from the ashes. This motive of rejuvenation is so applicable to Mrs. Wright's case that it is worth while considering in the first place how such a story about the hare voluntarily leaping into the fire can ever have been invented, and in the second place the meaning of some of the legends that have grown up around this theme.

Now it is a truism that no symbol has ever been invented; that is to say that no one has ever successfully 'thought out' a symbol and used it to express a truth. Such artificial efforts

[1] Aubrey's *Remains of Gentilisme*, pp. 101–2, quoted by W. C. Black, *The Folk-lore Journal*, vol. i, p. 86.

are doomed to failure, and never succeed in drawing to themselves the power of real symbols, since they are no more than similes based on a mental process that never touches the depths of human personality. Such are the 'didactic' similes we know so well and react against so wisely. True symbols, on the other hand, are those that leap to mind without conscious effort. Symbols of this kind vary immensely as to their applicability, some being of purely individual significance, while others have a far deeper meaning. Those that go to build up mythology and folk-lore are those that leap simultaneously to many minds, or, being first expressed by one find ready soil in others, so that they become a common language. Some symbols are universal, such as the four elements, earth, water, fire, air. Others are more restricted, such as the particular symbols of the various world religions, like the cross or crescent, the Mithraic bull or the Jewish and Christian lamb. No one invented them. They grew out of the life of the people, and drew their symbolic value from what men thought to be their chief characteristics, the bull from its procreative power and the lamb from its gentle innocence. In this way the Egyptian scarab drew its symbolic value from its prolificness, and its habit of rolling its eggs in dung pellets that resembled the sun, the hawk from its swift soaring flight symbolizing power ascending upwards towards the sky, and its successor the dove from its soft sweetness symbolizing the power of love descending from heaven to earth. Other characteristics doubtless joined to these to produce other symbolic attributes, for no symbol is a simple thing.

The Hare also has more than one attribute, as we shall see, but one attribute well known to all farmers is its habit, when scrub is being burnt, of not running like a rabbit does before the fire comes too close, but of clinging till the last moment to its hiding-place until the flames close in on it, and then wildly rushing out with fur blazing so that it burns to death.[1]

[1] Compare among other references the account given by R. R. Clarke, *In Breckland Wilds*, Cambridge, 1937, p. 16, of a heath fire, in which he writes of 'a hare which remained in its form so long that when it at length fled its fur was ablaze. Maddened by the pain it tore off at tremendous speed, doubtless to die a lingering death somewhere among the bracken.'

This, doubtless, is the material or physical fact that gave rise to the notion of the hare as a willing victim leaping into the fire. The symbolic meaning of this is another matter, which will be discussed after we have briefly noted some of the legends in which it occurs.

THE HARE IN INDIA

THE BUDDHA, IN ONE OF HIS REBIRTHS, TAKES THE FORM OF A HARE AND IN A FERVOUR OF RENUNCIATION LEAPS INTO A FIRE. THE HARE IS UNSCATHED AND ITS IMAGE IS TRANSLATED INTO THE MOON

The best-known of such legends is probably that according to which the Buddha himself, in one of his rebirths before attaining full Buddhahood, took the form of a hare. The following account is an abridged translation, by the present writer, of this tale as rendered into German by Elsie Lüders[1] with certain modifications taken from the English translation of the same tale as edited by Professor E. B. Cowell.[2] It is one of the so-called Jātaka stories forming part of the lore of Southern (Hinayana) Buddhism, which are said to have been told by Buddha himself of his own earlier existences while still a Bodhisattva[3] (that is to say, a being that is destined to develop, in a future existence, into a Buddha), and contains one of the numerous references to the belief held in many parts of the world of the connection with the hare and the moon, a connection which will be explained later.

The tale relates how the Bodhisattva was in one of his incarnations reborn as a hare, and had three friends, a monkey, a jackal, and an otter. This 'wise hare' was in the habit of instructing his three friends in the teaching that 'a man should give alms, obey the law, and observe the regulations regarding the keeping of holy day'. One day the Bodhisattva looked at the moon, and seeing from this that the following day was a holy day,[4] said to the other three, 'To-morrow is a holy

[1] *Buddhistische Märchen*, translated by Elsie Lüders, Jena, 1921.

[2] *The Jātaka*, or stories of the Buddha's former births. Translated from the Pāli by various hands, under the editorship of Professor E. B. Cowell, Cambridge, 1895–1907, vol. iii, no. 316.

[3] This is the Sanskrit form of the word which in Pāli is spelt Bodhisatta. Its literal meaning is 'one who is on the way to the attainment of perfect knowledge'.

[4] Buddhism observes the new moon and full moon as holy days.

day. Observe it in that you make an oath to obey the law. . . . If therefore a beggar comes to you, give him of your food and do not think of eating till he has fed.' Each of the three animals then managed by trickery to steal from some human being its appropriate foodstuff, the otter some fish, the jackal two meat puddings, a newt, and a bottle of sour milk, and the monkey a bunch of mangoes. But the Bodhisattva (in the shape of the hare) thought to himself, "I will not bother to get any food for myself till the time comes. . . . If a beggar comes to me, I will give him the flesh of my own body.' Through the power of his renunciation, however, the stone seat covered with a white woollen blanket, on which the god Sakka[1] habitually sits in his heaven, began to grow very hot. On turning over in his mind the reason for this heat, Sakka at last perceived its cause, and decided to put the king of the hares to the test. After appearing in the form of a Brahman to the other three animals in turn, and being offered food by them but having refused it, he went to the hare, who asked, 'Why do you stand here?' The Brahman answered, as he had done to the others, 'Wise one, if I could get something to eat I would observe the holy day and so be able to fulfil my priestly duties'. The Bodhisattva, delighted at his words, answered: 'Brahman, thou hast done well to come to me for food. Now I will make you a gift such as I have never given before. But, following the law, you must destroy no life. Go, friend, fetch wood and make a fire, and tell me when it is ready. I will offer myself by leaping into the fire. But when my flesh is roasted, you must eat it, so that you can then go and fulfil your priestly duties.'

Then with his supernatural power Sakka created a fire of burning logs, and told the Bodhisattva. Then arose the hare

[1] Sakka is the king of the gods. *Sakka* is the Pāli form of the Sanskrit *Sakra*, 'strong', 'powerful', the usual epithet of Indra. Early Buddhism did not believe in gods, but reckoned with the fact that simple people could not do without them. The stone seat on which Sakka sits always grows hot by magic whenever an earthly being, through the power of its penance, or renunciation, or virtue, endangers Sakka's position as the king of the gods. Sakka feels the heat through the blanket and descends in disguise to put some temptation in the way of the pious being in order to save his own position.

from its form of *kusa* grass,[1] and said, 'If any small insects are in my hair they should not be destroyed', saying which he shook himself three times (so as to let them escape) and, offering his whole body as a free gift, leapt up, and, like a royal swan alighting on a lotus bed, threw himself in an ecstasy of joy into the burning fire. But the fire was powerless to heat so much as the pores of a hair on his body. It was as if he had leapt into snow. Then he turned to Sakka, and said, 'Brahman, the fire which thou hast made is too cold. . . . What is the meaning of this?' The other said, 'Wise one, I am no Brahman, I am Sakka, who came to put thy virtue to the test.' The Bodhisattva then bellowed like a lion,[2] 'though not only thee but the whole world should test my generosity, it would not find me unwilling'. Sakka replied, 'Wise one, thy virtue shall be known for a whole aeon.' Then he squeezed the mountain, and with the essence thus extracted he painted the hare's image on the moon's disk. Then Sakka returned to his heavenly seat. The four wise ones continued to live in amity, fulfilling the law, observing the holy days, and each fared according to his merits.

The Hare-Moon as symbol of Intuition, signifying the transformation of unredeemed instinct into spiritual power

This legend is one of a large number found in many parts of the world, in which the hare is connected with the moon, and in particular it is identified with the markings on the face of the moon, and becomes the 'Hare in the Moon', corresponding to our own 'Man in the Moon'.

It may be wondered what the connection between the hare and the moon can be. The answer lies, in my opinion, in the character common to both of apparent 'surprise' or 'fickleness'. The moon is traditionally 'fickle' in that it never appears two

[1] The word 'form' is of course the technical term for a hare's bed. *Kusa* grass is the sacred grass (*Poa cynosuroides*) of Brahmanic ritual since Vedic times.

[2] The 'lion's roar' is a conventional expression sometimes used in Buddhist literature for recital of the Buddhist doctrine. For this and other footnotes to this tale I am indebted to the kindness of Dr. H. Meinhard.

nights running in the same place or even in the same shape, and the same characteristics of surprise and variability are traditionally and actually associated with the hare, which pops up here and there among the shrubby undergrowth of woodland country or from the tall grass in which it has made its form, to be gone next moment, fleetly running till it appears again unexpectedly in some quite different direction. This is of course the reason why, in Europe and elsewhere, the hare is so closely associated with witches, who are popularly believed to have a similar habit of appearing from nowhere, and of riding on broomsticks at great speed from one place to another. This association of hares with witches will be discussed later in greater detail,[1] and is mentioned here only because, whatever witches may really be like, they are undoubtedly accredited in popular fancy (which is what myths are made of) with a strong negative intuition of a kind that knows just when, where, and how to carry out their devilish mission. This is of course a thoroughly negative aspect of intuition, due to the repression of witchcraft and its consequently being driven to practise only in secret, owing to which, though there are white witches as well as black, witchcraft came to be regarded as wholly bad.

Now the moon also is *par excellence* a symbol of intuition,[2] that is to say of the 'light in the darkness' which guides the

[1] See pp. 194 sqq.

[2] The word 'intuition' is here and throughout this work used in Jung's sense to designate a definite psychological function, which he deals with at some length on pp. 461–8, 505–10, and 567–9 of his *Psychological Types* (translated by H. Godwin Baynes), London, 1924.

In his general definition on pp. 567–8 he describes it as 'that psychological function which transmits perceptions *in an unconscious way*. Everything, whether outer or inner objects or their associations, can be the object of this perception. Intuition has this peculiar quality: it is neither sensation, nor feeling, nor intellectual conclusion, although it may appear in any of these forms. Through intuition any one content is presented as a complete whole, without our being able to explain or discover in what way this content has been arrived at. Intuition is a kind of instinctive apprehension, irrespective of the nature of its contents. Like sensation it is an *irrational* perceptive traveller through the limitless spaces of that uncharted country which, for want of a better word, psychologists refer to as the Unconscious. Like all psychological functions, intuition may be used either for good or evil. It always appears as it were, 'out of the blue' in the form of complete certainty, a certainty that may bear the mark of highest spiritual knowledge, or on the other hand of machiavellian destructiveness.

There is no doubt which of the two is implied in the tale of the Buddha just quoted, which deals with precisely the same problem as was implicit in Mrs. Wright's dream, namely the transformation of untamed instinct into spiritual value. In Mrs. Wright's dream the hare representing instinct was a willing victim. The Buddhist story also demonstrates the deep truth, with which psychological findings agree, that instinct *wants* to transform itself into spirit, and will do so (as it has in fact done in the history of the human race) if not hampered by false ideology. This is of course the prime lesson to be drawn from Mrs. Wright's history, namely that when the artificial

function. Its contents, like those of sensation, have the character of being given, in contrast to the 'derived' or 'deduced' character of feeling and thinking contents. Intuitive cognition, therefore, possesses an intrinsic character of certainty and conviction which enabled Spinoza to uphold the *scientia intuitiva* as the highest form of cognition. Intuition has this quality in common with sensation, whose physical foundation is the ground and origin of its certitude. In the same way, the certainty of intuition depends upon a definite psychic matter of fact, of whose origin and state of readiness, however, the subject was quite unconscious.'

'In contrast to sensation, which deals with things as they are, [p. 463], intuition tries to encompass the greatest *possibilities*, since only through the awareness of possibilities is *intuition* fully satisfied. Intuition seeks to discover possibilities in the objective situation; hence as a mere tributary function (viz., when not in a position of priority) it is also the instrument which, in the presence of a hopelessly blocked situation, works automatically towards the issue, which no other function could discover.'

Intuition may be extraverted or introverted. Extraverted intuition is (p. 464) 'orientated by the object', but (p. 505) 'intuition, in the introverted attitude, is directed upon the inner object, a term we might justly apply to the elements of the unconscious. For the relation of inner objects to consciousness is entirely analogous to that of outer

clutter of mistaken thinking is removed, this process follows as automatically as the sun rises at dawn, the flowers bloom in the spring, or death follows life, and as death itself is followed by new life.

Fire the transforming medium

In all cases, however, some transforming influence has to be at work. In the case of the sun rising it is the movement of the earth, in the case of the flower it is the spring. In the case of the hare in this story, it is the fire. In this tale there are two kinds of fire, the internal fire of faith leading to the renunciation which so heated the stone seat that it activated the god, and the external fire of burning logs which the god made, into which the hare leapt.

Fire is, of course, one of the prime transformers. It transforms cold into heat, it transforms raw food into digestible meat, it breaks down compounds into their respective parts, and above all in spiritual language it is the fire that burns but does not

objects, although theirs is a psychological and not a physical reality. Inner objects appear to the intuitive perception as subjective images of things, which, though not met with in external experience, really determine the contents of the unconscious.'

In this way (p. 506) 'introverted intuition perceives all the background processes of consciousness with almost the same distinctness as extraverted sensation senses outer objects. For intuition, therefore, the unconscious images attain to the dignity of things or objects.'

Since it is with this introverted intuition that the mythological images dealt with in this book are concerned, one further quotation will give perhaps a pointer to what is to follow. As Jung says on pp. 507–8, 'Introverted intuition apprehends the images which arise from the *a priori*, i.e. the inherited foundations of the unconscious mind. These archetypes, whose innermost nature is inaccessible to experience, represent the precipitate of psychic functioning of the whole ancestral line, i.e. the heaped-up, or pooled, experiences of organic existence in general, a million times repeated, and condensed into types. Hence, in these archetypes all experiences are represented which since primeval time have happened on this planet. Their archetypal distinctness is the more marked, the more frequently and intensely they have been experienced. The archetype would be—to borrow from Kant—the noumenon of the image which intuition perceives and, in perceiving, creates.'

consume. So God appeared to Moses in the burning bush, and so Shadrach, Meshach, and Abednego passed unscathed through the fiery furnace prepared for them by Nebuchadnezzar, a fire so hot that it consumed those who cast them into it, but, as for those three, the king saw them come out 'upon whose bodies the fire had no power, nor was an hair of their head singed'.[1] So also with the Buddha in the form of a hare, 'the fire was powerless to heat so much as the pores of a hair on his body'. This means that the material body had been transformed into a spiritual one capable of resisting all evil or disintegration.

But fire has one more characteristic feature. It produces smoke, and smoke ascends to heaven. This is the meaning of burnt sacrifice, namely, that the smell and spiritual essence thereof ascend to heaven. Burnt sacrifice during the daytime therefore ascends to the sun, the sun ruling the social order and conscious life. But this is not Buddha's intention. Buddha desires Nirvana, that pregnant nothingness that is of the spirit only. So he sacrifices himself to the moon.

Sakka is one of the names given to Indra, who as a sky-god of lightning, thunder, and rain, and also as war-god, could be compared with the German Wotan or the Norse Thor, and with the more terrible aspects of Jove such as Jupiter Fulgur or Jupiter Tonans. Indra is moreover one of the eight guardians of the world whose place is in the East, which will be found to be of interest when we come to examine the connection of the hare with Easter.[2] It is presumably in his capacity of god of lightning that he spontaneously kindles the fire in which the Hare-Buddha sacrifices himself. It is thus the violent Sakka to whom the hare offers its body to eat, while he translated its spiritualized aspect associated with the self-sacrificing Buddha into the moon.

Further tales regarding the Hare-Buddha and the Moon

In this story, it is true, the hare's image is only painted on the moon, but in another version the hare is itself put in the moon. There is a tale told in Ceylon of how Buddha was wandering through a wood and met a hare, whom he told, in

[1] Daniel ix. 27.

[2] See pp. 170 sqq.

answer to his question, that he was poor and hungry. 'Art thou hungry?' said the hare; 'make a fire then; then kill, cook, and eat me.' Buddha made a fire, and the hare leapt into it. Then Buddha exercised his skill as a god, rescued the benevolent hare from the flames, and placed it in the moon.[1] Here it is not the Buddha who changes himself into a hare, but it is for him that the hare sacrifices itself. The roles are reversed again in the statement that 'it was into a hare that the highest lord of heaven, according to the Mongolian belief, changed himself to feed a hungry traveller, and does not therefore the hare sit in the moon?' In all these versions it is clear that the hare represents the material part, or unredeemed instinct, of the Buddha, Bodhisattva, or god which is transformed into spirit by being translated to the moon, whence it shines down to earth in the form of divine intuition.

Steiner quotes yet another version, this time in the form of a Kalmuck legend to the effect that 'in the moon there lives a hare; it came there because the Buddha sacrificed himself and the spirit of the earth himself painted the picture of the hare upon the moon. The great truth is here expressed of the Bodhisattva who became Buddha and sacrificed himself, bestowing upon humanity, for its nourishment, the content of his own being, so that it now rays forth from the hearts of men into the world.'[2]

FOLK-TALES ILLUSTRATING THE HARE'S INTUITIVE FACULTY

The theme is taken up in innumerable folk-tales, in which the hare's intuitive faculty is shown in his ready wit and power of triumphing over the sheer weight of material might.

One of these clearly indicates the victory of intuition, as represented by the hare in conjunction with the moon, over

[1] W. G. Black, 'The Hare in Folk-lore,' *Folk-lore Journal*, vol. i, p. 88.

[2] *The Gospel of Saint Luke*, by Rudolf Steiner, translated by G. Metaxa, London, 1935, pp. 71–2. I am indebted to Mrs. Marcia A. B. Dodwell for calling my attention to this.

brute strength and the power of earth as represented by the elephant, or, in other words, of spirit over matter. It runs:

Tale of the Elephants and the Hares

'There is a great lake abounding in water, called Chandrasaras [which means Moon Lake], and on its bank there lived a king of the hares, named Śilīmukha. Now, once on a time, a leader of a herd of elephants, named Chaturdanta, came there to drink water, because all the other reservoirs of water were dried up in the drought that prevailed. Then many of the hares, who were subjects of that king, were trampled to death by Chaturdanta's herd, while entering the lake. When that monarch of the herd had departed, the hare-king, Śilīmukha, being grieved, said to a hare named Vijaya in the presence of others: "Now that the lord of elephants has tasted the water of this lake, he will come here again and again, and utterly destroy us all, so think of some expedient in this case. Go to him, and see if you have any artifice which will suit the purpose or not. For you know business and expedients, and are an ingenious orator. And in all cases in which you have been engaged the result has been fortunate."

'When dispatched with these words, the hare was pleased, and went slowly on his way. And following up the track of the herd he overtook that elephant-king and saw him, and being determined somehow or other to have an interview with the mighty beast, the wise hare climbed up to the top of a rock, and said to the elephant: "I am the ambassador of the moon, and this is what the god says to you by my mouth: 'I dwell in a cool lake named Chandrasaras; there dwell hares whose king I am, and I love them well, and thence I am known to men as the cool-rayed and the hare-marked; now thou hast defiled that lake and slain those hares of mine. If thou doest that again, thou shalt receive thy due recompense from me.' "

'When the king of the elephants heard this speech of the crafty hare he said in his terror: "I will never do so again: I must show respect to the awful moon-god." The hare said: "So come, my friend, I pray, and we will show him to you." After saying this, the hare led the king of elephants to the lake and showed him the reflection of the moon in the water. When the lord of the herd saw that, he bowed before it timidly at a distance, oppressed with awe, and never came there again. And Śilīmukha, the king of the hares, was present, and witnessed the whole transaction, and after honouring that hare, who went as an ambassador, he lived there in security.'[1]

This tale represents the elephant (earth) as bowing awe-struck before the reflection of the moon which symbolizes intuition. The elephant was wise in that it recognized a superior power.

The Lion and the Hare

The lion, in another story, was not so wise, but, as the following account shows, instead of seeing and honouring the moon, saw only his own reflection and was, in psychological jargon, therefore devoured by his Shadow.

[1] 'The Elephants and the Hares', in *The Ocean of Story*, London, 1924, translated by C. H. Tawney, vol. i, 121 BB. Dr. Meinhard has kindly called my attention to the fact that this story in which the elephants are represented as oppressed with numinous awe of the moon, is quoted by A. W. von Schlegel in *Indische Bibliothek*, vol. i (Bonn, 1820), pp. 216 sq. He mentions that the same motive—elephants worshipping the moon—is also related by the elder Pliny, *Historia naturalis*, liber viii, cap. i: 'In the wooded hill country of Mauretania, at the appearance of the new moon, the herds of elephants come down to a certain river, called Aurilo; they cleanse themselves by solemnly splashing themselves with water; and after having thus saluted the celestial luminary, they return to their forests.'

Another tale connecting hares with water and also faintly echoing the hare's efforts at self-sacrifice, though from a very different angle, is Aesop's tale of 'The Hares and the Frogs', according to which 'the Hares, oppressed with a sense of their own exceeding timidity, and weary of the perpetual alarm to which they were exposed, with one accord determined to put an end to themselves and their troubles by jumping from a lofty precipice into a deep lake below. As they scampered off in a very numerous body to carry out their resolve, the Frogs lying on the banks of the lake heard the noise of their feet, and rushed helter-skelter to the deep water for safety. On seeing the rapid disappearance of the Frogs, one of the Hares cried out to his companions: "Stay, my friends, do not do as you intended; for you now see that other creatures who yet live are more timorous than ourselves."'

'There was in a certain forest a lion, who was invincible, and sole champion of it, and whatever creatures he saw in it he killed. Then all the animals, deer and all, met and deliberated together, and they made the following petition to that king of beasts: "Why by killing us all at once do you ruin your own interests? We will send you one animal every day for your dinner." When the lion heard this, he consented to their proposal, and as he was in the habit of eating one animal every day, it happened that it was one day the lot of a hare to present himself to be eaten. The hare was sent off by the united animals, but on the way the wise creature reflected, "He is truly brave who does not become bewildered even in the time of calamity, so, now that death stares me in the face, I will devise an expedient".

'Thus reflecting, the hare presented himself before the lion late. And when he arrived after his time, the lion said to him: "Hola! how is this that you have neglected to arrive at my dinner-hour, or what worse penalty than death, can I inflict on you, scoundrel?" When the lion said this, the hare bowed before him, and said: "It is not my fault, your Highness; I have not been my own master to-day, for another lion detained me on the road, and only let me go after a long interval. When the lion heard that, he lashed his tail, and his eyes became red with anger, and he said: "Who is that second lion? Show him me." The hare said: "Let your Majesty come and see him". The lion consented and followed him. Thereupon the hare took him away to a distant well. "Here he lives, behold him," said the hare, and when thus addressed by the hare, the lion looked into the well, roaring all the while with anger. And seeing his own reflection in the clear water, and hearing the echo of his own roar, thinking that there was a rival lion there roaring louder than himself, he threw himself in a rage into the well, in order to kill him, and there the fool was drowned. And the hare, having himself escaped death by his wisdom, and having delivered all the animals from it, went and delighted them by telling his adventure.'[1]

[1] 'The Lion and the Hare', *The Ocean of Story*, translated by C. H. Tawney, vol. v, 84 D.

This tale, like that of the hares and the elephants, shows the hare using a crafty wisdom that is of the nature of intuition in that it works in unseen ways, unseen that is to the lion but clearly seen by the hare. But the lion, far from seeking wisdom and finding it as the elephant did, sees instead only the projection of his own Shadow, which he attacks and so gets drowned in the water of his own unconscious. In other words, the lion leapt to a wrong conclusion and so met disaster.

Psychologically speaking, this disaster would mean madness, since madness consists in mistaking the symbol (the image) for reality and so being overwhelmed by the unconscious.

The Buddha (Ghatapandita) reproves his brother by crying for the Hare-Moon

One Indian tale about the Hare-Moon shows this quite clearly. This is the tale of a great king named Vāsudeva, whose son died and who, 'half dead with grief, neglected everything, and lay lamenting, and clutching the frame of his bed. Then Ghatapandita[1] thought to himself, "Except me, no one else is able to soothe my brother's grief; I will find some means of soothing his grief for him." So assuming the appearance of madness, he paced through the whole city, gazing up at the sky, and crying out, "Give me a hare! Give me a hare!" All the city was excited: "Ghatapandita has gone mad!" they said.

'Having been told of this, the king rose and, proceeding to

[1] Ghatapandita is another name for Buddha. The passage quoted is but the end of a long and involved story dealing with ten brothers, the eldest of whom is Vāsudeva and the youngest but one Ghatapandita. They conquer Dvārakā, the holy city of Krishna (on the west coast of the Kathiāwār peninsula), of which Vāsudeva becomes king.

The word Ghatapandita may mean 'learned (*pandita*) in water-jars (*gheta*)' or, since Indian compounds can sometimes be split up in different ways, perhaps 'the wise one with the water-jar'. The question is also complicated by the fact that this name appears in a Pāli, not in a Sanskrit text, and in Pāli *ghata* has a double meaning: (1) water-jar (as in Sanskrit), (2) clarified (or boiled) butter (corresponding to Sanskrit *ghrita*).

Ghatapandita, he got fast hold of him, and speaking to him uttered this stanza:

' "*In maniac fashion, why do you pace Dvārakā*[1] *all through,*
And cry, 'Hare, hare!' Say, who is there has taken a hare from you?"

'To these words of the king he only answered by repeating the same cry over and over again.'

To the king's offer, however, to make a hare, be it of gold, jewels, brass, silver, shell, stone, or coral, Ghatapandita replied:

' "*I crave no hare of earthly kind, but that within the moon.*" . . .

' "Undoubtedly my brother has gone mad," thought the king when he heard this. In great grief he said:

' "*In sooth, my brother, you will die, if you make such a prayer,*
And ask for what no man may pray, the moon's celestial hare."

Ghatapandita, on hearing the king's answer, stood stock still, and said: "My brother, you know that if a man prays for the hare in the moon, and cannot get it, he will die; then why do you mourn for your dead son?" '

This was, of course, a gentle hint that the king, in immoderately lamenting his dead son, was what we also should call 'crying for the moon'. Ghatapandita went on:

' "I, brother, pray only for what exists, but you are mourning for what does not exist." Then he instructed him by repeating two more stanzas:

' "*My son is born, let him not die!*" *Nor man nor deity*
Can have that boon; then wherefore pray for what can never be?

"*Nor mystic charm, nor magic roots, nor herbs, nor money spent,*
Can bring to life again that ghost whom, Kanha, you lament."

[1] The holy city of Krishna. See footnote above.

'The king, on hearing this, answered, "Your intent was good, dear one. You did it to take away my trouble." Then in praise of Ghatapandita he repeated four stanzas:

' "*Men had I wise and excellent to give me good advice:*
But now hath Ghatapandita opened this day mine eyes.

"*Blazing was I, as when a man pours oil upon a fire;*
Thou didst bring water, and didst quench the pain of my desire.

"*Grief for my son, a cruel shaft was lodged within my heart;*
Thou hast consoled me for my grief, and taken out the dart.

"*That dart extracted, free from pain, tranquil and calm I keep;*
Hearing, O youth, thy words of truth, no more I grieve nor weep."

'And, lastly:

' "*Thus do the merciful, and thus they who are wise indeed:*
They free from pain, as Ghata here his eldest brother freed."

'This is the stanza of Perfect Wisdom.'[1]

The moral of this story is clear, but Ghatapandita's utterance, 'I crave no hare of earthly kind, but that within the moon', also enshrines the truth, already expressed in the story of Buddha's self-sacrifice as a hare which then became translated into the moon, that the symbol taken literally is purely negative, but that taken symbolically it is of the highest spiritual value. It has been said that lunatics and saints both see similar visions, and that the world of difference between the two lies in the fact that when, for example, a lunatic or one suffering from delirium tremens has a vision of a snake he thinks it to be real and is correspondingly terrified, while the saint having the same vision would understand that it was a

[1] *The Jātaka*, or Stories of the Buddha's former births, translated by Rowse, under the editorship of Professor E. B. Cowell, Cambridge, 1895–1907, vol. iv, pp. 54–5.

symbol and would derive from it the wisdom for which this reptile is famous.

Returning to the story of the king's son, the supposed connection of the moon with lunacy is widespread, as witnessed by the word 'lunacy' itself, which is derived from the Latin *luna*, meaning 'the moon'. This is not surprising, for the moon, being the night luminary, represents the 'other side' or unseen aspect of things as opposed to the sun which represents the more conscious. The moon is thus a powerful symbol for the deep unconscious which, if honoured, is the source of all spiritual wisdom, but if dishonoured overpowers the subject and leads to madness.

Thus, though in mythological personification the various races of mankind differ remarkably in the sex which they attribute respectively to the sun and moon (the Latin peoples, for instance, regarding the moon as female and the sun as male, while the modern Germans regard the sun as female and the moon as male), the moon nevertheless in dreams almost always represents the contrasexual aspect of things, so that for a male the moon represents the mother (or wife) and the sun the father.

Dream of a modern child of the Moon as a negative mother-symbol

An instance of this occurred quite recently in my practice. I had in my house a small boy of about eight whose mother was one of the worst types of devouring woman. One night I heard him shouting, 'Don't, don't'. I went in to him and said, 'Have you been having a bad dream?' He said, 'No.' I said, 'But you've been shouting.' He said, 'I know, but I was awake.' I asked, 'Then what's been frightening you?' The moon was shining in at the window as he replied, 'I thought Mummy was with me, but she got smaller and smaller and went right up to the moon. Then the moon started getting bigger and bigger, and bigger and bigger, and came right at me, as if it were going to swallow me up.' This was the first dream-vision he had told me. I did not tell him what it meant, but the very fact of his reciting it released something in him that, along with the narration of many subsequent dreams of the most vivid character, changed him from being a frightened doormat to becoming an open-hearted and happy child.

Though we do not ourselves speak of the hare in the moon, the hare is for us nevertheless on occasion a symbol of madness as in the expression 'March hare', derived from the wild careering of hares during the mating season.

Philological connection between Sanskrit and Teutonic words for the Moon

Nor is the cultural distance between the British Isles and India so great when we reflect that, as Max Müller points out, our very word 'hare' (Anglo-Saxon, *hara*) is directly related, through the medium of the modern German *Hase* and the Old High German *haso* (all of which belong to the comparatively small group of words including relationship nouns, names of domestic animals, etc., which have cognate forms throughout all Indo-European languages), to the Sanskrit *śaśa* used for the same animal.[1] This word is also used in at least a dozen Sanskrit words for the moon, such as *Śaśin*, literally 'having the hare', and *Śaśānka*, 'having the marks of a hare'. Other Sanskrit compounds used to designate the moon which

[1] Max Müller, *Biographies of Words, and the Home of the Aryas*, London, 1880, p. 145, and cf. p. 164. Compare Anglo-Saxon *hara*. Le Page Renouf (see below, p. 151) says that the Sanskrit *çaça* (*śaśa*), like the Ancient Egyptian *unnu*, the appellative of 'a hare', and the Greek λαγῶς, all mean 'a leaper'. Mayers, discussing the hare-moon in China, says, 'In Sanskrit the *çaças* means properly the leaping one, as well as the hare, the rabbit, and the spots on the moon (the *saltans*), which suggest the figure of a hare'. (Mayers, *The Chinese Reader's Manual*, p. 235, quoting de Gubernatis, *Zoological Mythology*, ii, 76.)

N.B. It will be observed that in this brief philological discussion three different transliterations, *ś*, *ç*, and *sh*, are used for the same Sanskrit sibilant, according to the different authors quoted. The same sibilant *ś* is variously recorded by yet other authors as *ṡ* or *ś*, but it should be noted that they all represent the same Sanskrit sound, which differs from that of the *sh* in Vishnu, which may be written *ṣ*. In Pāli the three sibilants, *ś*, *ṣ*, and *s*, fall together, so that Sanskrit *Śakra* becomes Pāli *Sakka* and Sanskrit *śaśa* becomes Pāli *sasa*.

my friend Hari Prasad Shastri has told me of, and which are of interest to us here, are *Himkar*, which he translates 'the Creator of Snow' (but which may be otherwise rendered as *himakara*, 'causing or producing cold'), and *Shītānshu*, literally cool-rayed,[1] which he translates 'Essence of Coldness'.

The Hare-Man makes the best sexual partner

Finally, in the systematized *Kāmaśāstra*, or science of sexual love (*kāma*), men are divided into four types named after animals, of which the best, described as being mild and easy to live with, is the Hare-man (*śaśa*, the hare), and the other three are associated respectively with the horse (*aśva*), the antelope (*mṛiga*), and the bull (*vṛishan*).

[1] See p. 116.

THE HARE IN CHINA[1]

The Hare-Moon is found also in China. Whether this is through direct influence from India cannot at present be stated with any certainty, although the possibility cannot be ruled out. It is, however, believed by more than one authority that Indian influence reached China as early as the fourth century B.C., owing to the close similarities found between the teachings of Taoism which arose in that century in China, and those of Buddhism which arose during the previous century in India.

Vision of the Han Emperor regarding the introduction of Buddhism

Buddhism did not receive official sanction in China, however, until the time of the Han Emperor called Ming Ti,[2] who reigned from A.D. 58 to A.D. 75, of whom it is said that he saw in a dream a tall male figure having a bright light on the summit of his head. He asked his ministers to interpret the dream, and one of them said, 'There lives in the west a god called Fo [the Chinese name for Buddha]. He is sixteen feet tall and he is the colour of yellow gold.' The Emperor then sent a mission to India to procure, so the legend runs, the image of the god he had seen in his dream. The mission took six years, from A.D. 61 to A.D. 67, over its task, and returned bearing sutras and images of the Buddha on a white horse. The missionaries were suitably lodged, and settled down to translate Buddhist texts into Chinese. After their death the place was consecrated as a Buddhist monastery, and after many vicissitudes Mahayana Buddhism became one of the recognized religions of China.

Whether the Hare-Moon symbolism in China is due to early Buddhist influence or not is uncertain. What is certain, how-

[1] This not being a learned treatise on China, Chinese names are throughout spelt according to the transcription of the authors quoted.

[2] Not to be confused with the Ming Dynasty.

ever, is that there are no known records of it before the fourth century B.C. (that is to say in the late Chou period) when Buddhist and other Indian influences were beginning to be felt. From this date onward there are frequent references to it, though, as might be expected, it developed in a way quite peculiarly Chinese.

The Hare derives its vital essence from the Moon where it compounds the Elixir of Life

Thus in China the mythical hare is not only seen in the moon's spots, but, according to Mayers,[1] from whose account much of the following information is taken, the hare (*lepus sinensis*) itself derives its origin from the vital essence of the moon, and is therefore at all times subject to its influence.[2] One Chinese authority actually asserts that the hare conceives by gazing at the moon, though earlier writers have alleged that the female hare becomes with young by licking the fur of the male.

In China, as in India, the hare is said also to inhabit the moon. I know of no legend of how it got there similar to the Indian legend of its self-immolation in fire and its subsequent translation by the god into the moon,[3] but the miraculous healing element in the Indian story is replaced in China by the belief that the hare lives in the moon eternally compounding

[1] William Frederick Mayers, *The Chinese Reader's Manual*, Shanghai, 1924, pp. 234–5.

[2] According to S. C. Nott (*Chinese Jade*, London, 1936, p. 86), this information is derived from the records of the Han dynasty, which flourished between 206 B.C. and A.D. 220.

[3] It is just possible that a faint recollection of its self-immolation is to be found in the Chinese proverbial phrase, 'sitting beside a stump on the watch for a hare', based on the legend narrated by Han Fei-tsze, to the effect that a husbandman of the state of Sung was ploughing one day when he saw a hare dash itself against a stump which stood in his field, and immediately fall dead. The foolish peasant, thereupon abandoning his plough, seated himself beside the stump to wait for another hare to come and do likewise.' (Mayers, *The Chinese Reader's Manual*, p. 235.) This may, however, have quite a different origin more closely connected with what we refer to as the 'March madness' of hares when they career wildly about during the mating season (referred to on page 123).

FIGURE 9. T'ang Mirror showing the Hare pounding the Herb of Immortality in the Moon

Left to right—Heng O [Ch'ang O] the Moon Queen; a Frog; the Lunar Tree; the Lunar Hare pounding the Drug of Immortality. From *Arts and Crafts of Ancient Annam; Discoveries at Lach-Truong*, by Professor O. Janse, *Illustrated London News*, 7 March 1936

FIGURE 10. Jade Amulet in the form of a Hare

(late Chou period, 4th century B.C.) from *Chinese Jade*, by C. S. Nott, London, 1936, Pl. LXIX

the elixir of life. Thus Werner refers to the moon as symbolized by a hare on its hind-legs pounding rice in a mortar,[1] and Mayers refers to a later Taoist fable depicting the 'gemmeous' hare[2] as the servitor of the genii who employ it in pounding the drugs which compose the elixir of life.

Werner further refers to Chinese paintings depicting, associated together: (*a*) the moon-palace of Ch'ang O [the Moon Queen] who stole the pill of immortality and flew to the moon; (*b*) the fragrant tree which one of the genii, who are the Moon-Queen's servants, tried to cut down; and (*c*) a hare 'pestling medicine in a corner' (see Fig. 9). He says that these refer to a certain court functionary who, together with the then Emperor, went to a well-known holy mountain with the object of being initiated into the doctrine of immortality. The Emperor was instructed in the secrets of the doctrine by the spirit of this famous mountain who, when the Emperor was about to take his departure, begged him to allow the court official to remain with him. The new hermit (the court official) went out every day to gather the flowering plants which formed the only food of his master (the spirit of the mountain), and he took also to eating those flowers, so that his body gradually became spiritualized.[3]

The White Hare called 'bright eyes'

The Taoists claimed that the white hare was Ch'ang O's (the

[1] F. I. C. Werner, *Myths and Legends of China*, London, 1922, p. 176. He says the moon may be symbolized also by a three-legged toad.

[2] The word 'gemmeous', meaning 'relating to, having the nature of, or resembling gems', is interesting in this connection, since one of the most important dreams in Mrs. Wright's later dream-series (to be described in a later volume) centred round the representation of a bishop's mitre, and on examining the mitre of William of Wykeham, preserved in New College, Oxford, which he founded, I found to my surprise that among the jewels with which it is furnished are a number of small cameos representing hares in various postures.

[3] Werner, *Myths and Legends of China*, p. 179. These tales were written down in the late Chou period, but almost certainly go back to a much earlier time, the tales belonging to which were now first committed to writing.

Moon Queen's) servant. Mayers tells us that, like the fox, the hare lives a thousand years, and becomes white when half that period is completed. Another writer[1] on Chinese matters tells us that the white hare has from ancient times been thought of as divine, and is therefore always regarded as an auspicious omen, portending the reign of a beneficent and just ruler. Thus it is said that during the golden age of the Chou Dynasty white hares played in the streets of the capital city.

'The hare is also one of the animals sacrificed in the temple of the Imperial Ancestors. When so used it is known by the name *ming shih*, "bright eyes", because it is said that the hare's eyes, unlike those of any other animal, grow larger and brighter with age. The eyes of the hare were regarded by the Chinese as significant of the beginning of events and periods, and particularly of pubescence.'[2]

The whiteness of this hare and its bright eyes, together with the belief in their association with new life, is particularly interesting when we remember the snow covering the ground both outside and inside the kitchen in Mrs. Wright's dream, a snow in which no footprints were seen, as well as the accompanying white light, the whiteness of everything inside the room, and the white bowl in which the hare sat. It will be seen later how frequently in all parts of the world the mythical hare is represented as being white, and how often, as in the case of the Buddha legend, myths connected with the Hare include references to snow. All these symbols are undoubtedly connected with the white light of the moon, which represents direct intuitive knowledge.

The Red Hare

In China, however, not all the divine hares are white. The author mentioned above refers to ancient writings describing a red hare which, in company with the phoenix and the unicorn, appears as a harbinger of peace and prosperity. Mayers also refers to the red hare as 'a supernatural beast of auspicious

[1] S. C. Nott, *Chinese Jade*, pp. 86–7.

[2] Ibid. Note the Roman belief that the hare sleeps with its eyes open, cited on pp. 190 and 221 of the present work.

omen, which appears when virtuous rulers govern the Empire'.[1]

The Black Hare

One Chinese writer tells also of a black hare, saying, 'The black hare is more uncommon than the white hare. It comes from the North Pole bringing greetings from the moon goddess, and is auspicious of a successful reign. Now may the magic medicine be pounded with jade pestle and the divine nectar be prepared in a crystal cup.'[2]

Colours and Animal Deities of the Four Cardinal Points

All these references are rather obscure, but some light may be thrown on them by the fact that, in early Chinese beliefs found flourishing in the fourth century B.C. when the Hare-Moon makes its first recorded appearance on the Chinese historical scene, the Four Cardinal Points are represented by colours which are at the same time associated with four mythical animals and the four seasons, symbols representing the Deities of these four cardinal points. They are arranged as follows:

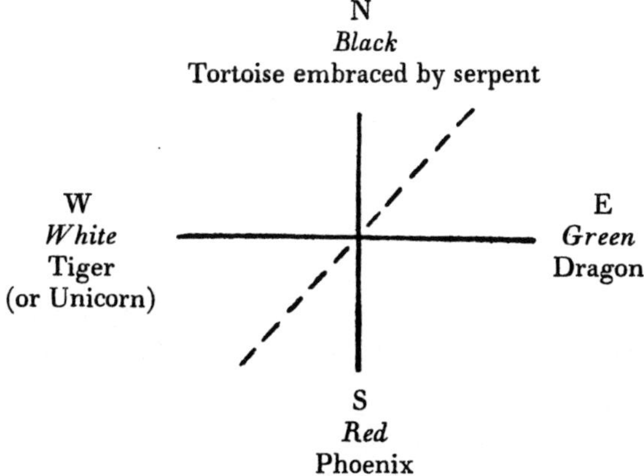

It will be noted that East and South are represented by the

[1] Mayers, *The Chinese Readers' Manual*, pp. 234–5.
[2] Quoted by S. C. Nott, *Chinese Jade*, p. 87.

complementary colours green and red, while North and West are represented by the complementary opposites black and white. This is a very interesting configuration, since it would appear that for the Chinese mind East (whence the sun rises) and South (which represents warmth and passion), through their association with colours, represent different aspects of Instinctual Life; while North (representing darkness) and West (the quarter of sundown and so signifying death), which have no colour at all, represent two aspects of Spirit.

This fits in with the concept of the moon as a white luminary shining in darkness, since it is precisely the moon that symbolizes the spiritual or 'other side' of life, the 'light in the darkness' as opposed to the sun that rules the conscious day. This is clearly the reason why the black hare comes from the North Pole with greetings from the moon-goddess.

The association of the red hare with the phoenix is equally clear, since the phoenix (which burns itself and rises rejuvenated from the ashes) belongs to the South, of which the colour is red. More obscure, however, is the association (cited above) of the red hare also with the Unicorn, which belongs to the West and of which the colour is white. I do not pretend to explain this.[1] But I would point out that the animal

[1] It is of interest to note that the unicorn is mentioned by Greek and Roman writers as a native of India (the earliest known reference is by Ctesias of Cnidas, physician to Artaxerxes II, Mnemon of Persia in about 400 B.C.), and that they describe its body as being white, its horn as being white at the base, black in the middle and tipped with red, while its head is red and its eyes blue. It is used frequently in medieval heraldry, and the sinister supporter of the insignia of the United Kingdom is a unicorn argent. The *Physiologus*, written in the first half of the second century A.D., describes the unicorn as being similar to a small white kid, so swift-footed that the huntsmen cannot catch it. It can only be caught by a trick. An untouched virgin is placed in its way, and as soon as the unicorn sees her, it runs straight towards her and throws itself into her lap, abandoning all fierceness. This is used as an allegory of the Immaculate Conception. Later the unicorn is conceived as a kind of white horse with a goat's beard, and as a symbol of chastity. The horn is said, already by Ctesias, to be a prophylactic against poison, and is used as a symbol of the cross. The Unicorn mentioned in various parts of the Old Testa-

symbol of the North is a tortoise coupled in sexual embrace with a serpent, from which embrace, that is to say out of the union of opposites (the tortoise being held to be female and the serpent male) in the black night of the soul, arose at a later date (in the Sung Dynasty, 960–1279) a deity in human form. Not one of the other three animal deities thus gave rise to a human god, and the god which thus arose out of the embrace was the Dark Emperor, who was the Supreme Lord of the Dark Heaven (i.e. of the soul). The revelation of this transformation came in a vision to the Emperor Hui Tsung, who was himself a great painter, and the Dark Emperor of his vision 'rose here to life at a time when animals as deities no longer had any meaning'.[1]

So also did Mrs. Wright's dream of sacrificing the hare lead directly to the darkest night of her life, when for three hours she suffered agony and was not only reborn herself, but also, through her acceptance of the revelation, released the bonds of her daughter Margaret, thus conferring rebirth on her also.

The Hare, as Resurrection Symbol, pounds the Herb of Immortality in the Moon

It is of interest further to note one final observation by Carl Hentze regarding the 'hare in the moon' as a resurrection symbol. Referring to the well-known Chinese mythical motive of 'Spittle flowing out of a vessel', he says: 'This is a widespread mythical motive, whose connection with the New Moon is

ment is frequently interpreted as an anticipatory symbol of Christ, whose resurrection at Easter, as symbol among other things of the rising sun, connects him with the East (see pp. 180–2). In China the hare is connected with the second lunar month corresponding to the Equinox, and is associated with Equality, and corresponds to the trigram ☳. There are eight such trigrams forming the basis of the system known as the Yi King, said to have been founded by Fu Hsi in 3322 B.C. The association with equality is interesting, since the main symbolism of this purely fabulous animal seems to rest on the concept of two horns joined into one, in other words of a union of opposites such as is the basis of all mystical phenomena.

[1] William Cohn, 'The Deities of the Four Cardinal Points in Chinese Art', *Transactions, Oriental Ceramic Society*, 1940–1, p. 72.

often quoted. . . . The connection of the vessel with the New Moon in China is due to the fact that the Chinese "Hare in the Moon" pounds the "Herb of Immortality" in a mortar. . . . Since the hare belongs to the moon, "immortality" can here only refer to the new rising (or resurrection) of the moon, so that the mortar is evidently the New Moon in which the "Herb of Immortality" is prepared, that is to say from which rejuvenation springs.'[1] (See Fig. 9.)

On this analogy, the white bowl in which Mrs. Wright's hare sat would represent the Full Moon with the Hare in it, preparing the 'Herb of Immortality'; 'immortality' here representing, of course, that new and deeper life that comes from renewed contact with the life-giving forces of the Impersonal Unconscious, which Mrs. Wright at this moment acquired and began to transmit to her daughter through the as yet unsevered spiritual umbilical cord still joining them, in the manner already seen in this volume and to be demonstrated more fully in its sequel.

The Hare Garden

While contemplating this humble mother and daughter in their joint search for spiritual truth, it is pleasant to think, at the other side of the world, in times gone by and at the other end of the social scale, in a society that still valued wisdom, of the 'Hare Garden' which was 'the name given by Prince Hiao of Liang to the pleasure grounds in which he sought recreation, surrounded by a retinue of scholars'.[2]

Moon Festival

In view further of the Easter associations of Mrs. Wright's dream, the following quotation from Billson may not be out of place. He says: 'There is a similarity also between the customs

[1] Author's translation from *Frühchinesische Bronzen und Kultdarstellungen*, by Carl Hentze, Antwerp, 1937, p. 100. He adds, 'This is why, in the Chinese myth of Yi Yin, it is again a "mortar" that rises out of the flood, . . . clearly that same "mortar" in which the hare prepares the "Herb of Immortality", that is to say the New Moon'.

[2] Mayers, *The Chinese Reader's Manual*, p. 235.

of the great Chinese Moon Festival and those which are still observed in England and Germany at the season of Easter. "This festival, known as the Yué-Ping (loaves of the moon), dates from the remotest antiquity. Its original purpose was to honour the moon. . . . On this solemn day all labour is suspended; the workmen receive from their employers a present of money; every person puts on his best clothes; and there is merry-making in every family. Relations and friends interchange cakes of various sizes, on which is stamped the image of the moon; that is to say, a hare couching amid a small group of trees."'[1]

The hare is also one of the Signs of the Zodiac in China, though I am not aware which constellation it represents.

PLASTIC REPRESENTATIONS OF THE HARE

I will close this brief summary of the beliefs connected with the Hare in China with a still briefer reference to some of its plastic representations. The most ancient of these known to me are the small jade carvings from the late Chou period (fourth century B.C.) figured in Berthold Laufer's fine book on *Archaic Chinese Jade.*[2] They range from about three or four inches in length and represent hares in all kinds of postures, all pierced as if for use as amulets. Laufer does not believe that they have any mythological significance, but my friend Dr. William Cohn (formerly Keeper of the Far Eastern Department of the Ethnological Museum in Berlin), who kindly called my attention to them as well as to other matters referred to in this section, thinks that they certainly had, as they are found so often in graves.

An outstanding example from the same period, called that of the Warring States lasting from 481 to 221 B.C., in the collec-

[1] C. J. Billson, 'The Easter Hare', *Folk-lore*, vol. iii, p. 460, quoting T. Harley, *Moonlore*, London, 1885, pp. 104–5.

[2] Berthold Laufer, *Archaic Chinese Jade, collected in China by A. W. Bahr, now in the Field Museum of Natural History, Chicago*, privately printed in New York, 1927. Plate xxiv and p. 38.

tion of the late Mr. Oscar Raphael, is figured by Nott[1] (see Fig. 10). This also is pierced, as if for use as an amulet.

There are also numerous Chinese representations of the Hare in the Moon depicted in pottery and on silk.

Buddhism also spread to Japan, and an outstanding example of painting on silk (based, like most Japanese Buddhist paintings, on a Chinese motive) is the Japanese Buddhist painting in Sung style executed by Takuma Shôga in A.D. 1191 as one of the screens depicting the Twelve Devas. It is of the Moon-goddess Gwatten holding in her hands a crescent moon, in the dark portion of which is seated a white hare.[2] (*See* Fig. 11.)

[1] *Chinese Jade*, plate lxix.

[2] H. Minamoto, *An Illustrated History of Japanese Art*, Kyoto, 1935. Illustration 110, p. 134.

FIGURE 11. The Moon-goddess Gwatten holding in her hands a crescent moon, in which is seated a White Hare

Part of a Japanese painting in Buddhist style executed by Takuma Shôga in 1191 A.D. as one of the screens depicting the Twelve Devas

THE HARE IN NORTH AMERICA

The Hare is a religious symbol not only in the Buddhism of Ceylon, India, China, and the surrounding lands, but was also worshipped as such on the other side of the Pacific by many of the pre-conquest inhabitants of North America. Not only so, but the myths of the New World correspond remarkably in main details with those of the Old.

Legend of the Déné Hareskins, who worship a Moon God, and of a white Hare's head thrown into a fire causing the Dawn

We have already met with the hare as a divine animal leaping with self-sacrificing ecstasy into the fire, and thence being translated into the moon. We have seen also the importance of the white hare in China. It is therefore of no little interest to read of a tradition among the Déné Hareskins, who worship a Moon-God who is a god of hunting, plenty, and also of death (death being, of course, a symbol of the 'other', that is to say the 'spiritual' life), to the effect that one of their number, who was beguiled into the underworld in which all paths were serpentine and where profound darkness reigned, effected his escape by throwing the head of a white hare into a fire, whereon it immediately became dawn.[1]

This points to a yet further extension of the idea already seen both in India and in China of the hare as a symbol of the 'light in the darkness'. Whereas the hare is there conceived of as being translated through sacrifice into the moon whence it casts its beams into the dark night of the soul, here it appears, through a similar sacrifice, to be the creator of dawning consciousness, whereby the soul's contents are brought into the light of day.

[1] Petitot, *Traditions Indiennes du Canada Nord-Ouest*, Paris, 1886, p. 173, quoted by Andrew Lang, *Myth, Ritual, and Religion* (first edition), London, 1887, vol. i, p. 184, note 2.

THE MYTHOLOGY OF THE HARE

THE GREAT HARE OF THE ALGONKIN

One of the great students of North American mythology is Dr. D. G. Brinton, who sums up the evidence regarding the beliefs centring round the Divine Hare as conceived by the Algonkin of North America in no uncertain terms. He begins by citing the more degraded late forms of belief, which only serve to throw into yet higher relief the vitality of the earlier and truly inspired myths. He says:

'From the remotest wilds of the north-west to the coast of the Atlantic, from the southern boundaries of Carolina to the cheerless swamps of Hudson's Bay, the Algonkins were never tired of gathering around the winter fire and repeating the story of Manibozho or Michabo, the Great Hare. With entire unanimity the various branches, the Pawhatans of Virginia, the Lenni Lenape of the Delaware, the warlike hordes of New England, the Ottawas of the far north, and the western tribes perhaps without exception, spoke of "this chimerical beast", as one of the old missionaries called it, as their common ancestor. The totem or clan which bore his name was looked up to with peculiar respect. In many of the tales which the whites have preserved of Michabo he seems half a wizard, half a simpleton. He is full of pranks and wiles, but often at a loss for a meal of victuals; ever itching to try his magic arts on great beasts and often meeting ludicrous failures therein; envious of the powers of others, and constantly striving to outdo them in what they do best; in short, little more than a malicious buffoon delighting in practical jokes, and abusing his superhuman powers for selfish and ignoble ends.

'But this is a low, modern, and corrupt version of the character of Michabo, bearing no more resemblance to his real and ancient one than the language and acts of our Saviour and the Apostles in the coarse Mystery Plays of the Middle Ages do to those recorded by the Evangelists.

'What he really was we must seek in the accounts of older travellers, in the invocations of the jossakeeds or prophets, and in the part assigned to him in the solemn mysteries of religion. In these we find him portrayed as the patron and founder of the meda worship,[1] the inventor of picture-writing, the father and guardian of their nation, the ruler of the winds, even the maker and preserver of the world and creator of the sun and moon. From a grain of sand brought from the bottom of the primeval ocean, he fashioned the habitable land and set it floating on the waters, till it grew to such a size that a strong young wolf, running constantly, died of old age ere he reached its limits. Under the name Michabo Ovisaketchak, the Great Hare who created the Earth, he was originally the highest deity recognized by them, "powerful and beneficent beyond all others, maker of the heavens and the world". He was founder of the medicine hunt in which after appropriate ceremonies and incantations the Indian sleeps, and Michabo appears to him in a dream, and tells him where he may readily kill game. He himself was a mighty hunter of old; one of his footsteps measured eight leagues, the Great Lakes were the beaver dams he built, and when the cataracts impeded his progress he tore them away with his hands. Attentively watching the spider spread its web to trap unwary flies, he devised the art of knitting nets to catch fish, and the signs and charms he tested and handed down to his descendants are of marvellous efficacy in the chase. In the autumn, in "the moon of the falling leaf", ere he composes himself to his winter's sleep, he fills his great pipe and takes a god-like smoke. The balmy clouds float over the hills and woodlands, filling the air with the haze of the "Indian summer".

'Sometimes he was said to dwell in the skies with his brother the snow, or, like many great spirits, to have built his wigwam in the far north on some floe of ice in the Arctic Ocean, while the Chipeways localized his birthplace and former home to the island Michilimakinac at the outlet of Lake Superior. But in the oldest accounts of the missionaries he was alleged to reside towards the east, and in the holy formulae of the meda craft, when the winds are invoked to the medicine

[1] The *meda* worship is the ordinary religious ritual of the Algonkin. A *jessakeed* is an inspired prophet who derives his power directly from the higher spirits, and not as the *medawin*, by instruction and practice.

lodge, the east is summoned in his name, the door opens in that direction, and there, at the edge of the earth, where the sun rises, on the shore of the infinite ocean that surrounds the land, he has his house and sends the luminaries forth on their daily journeys.'[1]

This account is so full of symbolic truth that it would take pages to discuss at all fully, so I will content myself with calling attention only to a few salient points.

Childlike aspect of Tales

In the first place, the tales of the hare as a kind of buffoon are partly degraded, but also the kind of tales children are told at a stage when they can enjoy humour but are not yet capable of consciously understanding the more esoteric knowledge of their elders; tales also repeated by adults in lighter vein much as a devoted Catholic may tell, from sheer familiarity, humorous stories about the saints which might shock his more puritanical brethren. At the same time they do indeed show the mischievous and often selfish aspect of intuitive behaviour when not balanced by common sense.

Inventor of Picture-writing

In the second place, the reference to the hare as the inventor of picture-writing is important, because this means that kind of symbolic wisdom which forms the whole subject-matter of this book. As will be seen later, the divine hare was closely connected with the Egyptian god Thoth, the Greek god Hermes, and the Roman Mercury, all of whom were supposed to have similarly invented writing which, in the case of the oldest of them, Thoth, was also picture-writing.[2]

Ruler of the Four Winds

Thirdly, as ruler of the four winds he shows himself to be the uniter of the four psychological functions, and as creator of the sun and moon rules also the zenith and nadir (the zenith

[1] D. G. Brinton, *The Myths of the New World*, New York, 1868, pp. 161–4.

[2] See p. 157.

below the earth), which represent the two spiritual elements added to the material fourfold creation, with himself the supreme seventh element uniting them all.

Grain of sand comparable to 'firmament'

Fourthly, the grain of sand brought up from the bottom of the primeval ocean, out of which habitable land is made, is a worldwide symbol of the establishment of conscious life amidst the chaos of surrounding unconscious forces. It is comparable to the creation of the firmament in the midst of the waters in the first chapter of Genesis, and, among innumerable other myths, to the dry land that the Polynesian god Mauwi fished up from the sea at the end of his fishing-rod. The 'growing' of the habitable land brought up by the Great Hare represents of course growing consciousness and the yeastlike quality of the Holy Spirit, which is itself so closely allied to balanced intuitive knowledge.

Medicine Hunt and appearance in Dreams

Fifthly, there is the medicine hunt, recalling the elixir of life mixed by the Hare in the Moon in China.

Sixthly, there is the reference to the Hare Michabo appearing in dreams telling the hunter where he may best kill his game.

Connection of the Hare with Snow and Whiteness

Seventhly, there is the remarkable reference to the hare's 'brother, the snow', recalling so vividly to mind the snow which in Mrs. Wright's dream not only surrounded the house but also penetrated into the kitchen in which she sacrificed her hare, and which was also filled with white light. White light symbolizes direct knowledge unadulterated by the intrusion of defiling elements, and it will be remembered how, in Mrs. Wright's dream, the divine nature of the snow was demonstrated by the fact that it showed no footprints. The connection of the hare with snow and whiteness in general is remarkably constant in all these accounts, from that of the white hare in China to many other references to snow throughout this narrative.

Connection with the East and Dawn

Eighthly and lastly, we are told that in the oldest accounts the hare was alleged to reside towards the east, that in the most sacred ritual the east is summoned in his name, that the door of the medicine lodge opens in that direction, since it is at the place where the sun rises, on the shore of the infinite ocean that surrounds the land, that the hare has his house. In dreams a door commonly represents a gateway leading to or from salvation. East is proverbially the white quarter,[1] and white is, moreover, the colour ordained to be worn by officiating priests at Easter, when the Son of Man rises in glory to rule men's hearts. The Dawn is met with again as one of the hare's attributes in Ancient Egypt, as will be seen below. Moreover, the hare is the sacred animal of Easter all over Europe, as will also appear later. Dawn also signifies the dawn of that superconsciousness which is commonly called rebirth, which is again what Mrs. Wright experienced as a result of her own hare-dream.

Andrew Lang further quotes Strachey as saying, '"The godly hare's house" is at the place of sun-rising; there the souls of good Indians "feed on delicious fruits with that great hare", who', Andrew Lang adds, 'is clearly the Virginian Osiris' whose attributes and whose connection with the Hare are discussed below in the section on 'The Hare in Ancient Egypt'.[2]

There is no need here to go into the long discussion by Andrew Lang of Brinton's arguments claiming philological affinity between the second element in the name given to the Great Hare, Michabou (*michi* 'great', *wabou* 'hare') and the Algonkin word *wab* meaning 'white'.[3] It is a long discussion

[1] An exception to this is the Chinese association of east with the emergent colour green.

[2] Strachey, *History of Travaile*, pp. 98–9, quoted by Andrew Lang, *Myth, Ritual, and Religion*, vol. ii, pp. 55–6, note 1.

[3] See Andrew Lang, 'Le Lièvre dans la Mythologie', *Mélusine*, vol. iii, cols. 265–6, and *Myth, Ritual, and Religion*, London, 1887, first edition, vol. ii, pp. 54–9, and second edition, 1901, vol. i, pp. xxvii–xxviii.

adding little to our knowledge, since the connection of the hare with 'snow', 'whiteness', 'the east', and 'dawn' is so clearly indicated in the actual mythological accounts. The argument is that on the philological evidence the connection was due simply to an unconscious pun, which Andrew Lang rightly rejects as being not only a quite unnecessary assumption but also irrelevant to the main issue, which is the incontrovertible fact that the hare is indeed accredited with these attributes not only among the Algonkin but also in other places as well, among which he cites Ancient Egypt, to which may now be added India, China, parts of Africa, and even medieval and modern Europe.[1]

The fact is that these common attributes have a deep psychological meaning quite independent of such superficial mechanism as puns, as has been demonstrated once more by Mrs. Wright, who never heard either of folk-lore or of comparative mythology but produced the same combination of symbols out of her own deep union with the collective psyche.

[1] Andrew Lang (*Mélusine*, iii, col. 265) states that the Hare-Moon was known also among the Aztecs, but gives no reference.

Not included in this section on North America, but mentioned later, is the myth of the 'grandmother in the moon' referred to in *Hiawatha* (see p. 171, note 1).

THE HARE IN ANCIENT EGYPT

THE HARE USED AS A HIEROGLYPH FOR THE AUXILIARY VERB 'TO BE'

The symbolic equation of the Great Hare with the Dawn is closely paralleled in Ancient Egypt, where the Hare-deity is connected with ideas of 'opening' and 'uprising', in addition to its more universal connection with the moon. It is to the deep insight of Le Page Renouf into the workings of the human mind that we are indebted for this information, based on a psychological investigation into the reasons for the remarkable fact that an Ancient Egyptian hieroglyph used in writing for the auxiliary verb 'to be' is the hare.

Fig. 12. Egyptian hieroglyph representing the Hare, used in writing for the auxiliary verb 'to be'

After N. de G. Davies, *The Mastaba of Ptahhetep and Akhethetep at Saqqareh,* Part I, Pl. VI, No. 62.

To understand the setting of his remarks it is necessary to remember that in Ancient Egyptian many hieroglyphs, whatever their origin in the representation of natural objects, have in the actual writing a purely phonetic value. It is as if our letter *a,* for instance, once stood for the name of some natural object but had later come to be used for every similar sound, in whatever word it occurred and quite irrespective of its original meaning, in such a way that this original meaning became eventually completely lost through its employment as a purely phonetic symbol.

In this way, the sign representing the hare is used in the hieroglyphic writing of Ancient Egypt for the sound rendered in our notation by Le Page Renouf as *un* and by modern scholars (since hieroglyphic writing does not include the transcription of vowels) as *wn*. As the authorities whom I shall quote in this section belong to the older school which used the transcription *un*, I shall, as this is not primarily a philological treatise, in order to avoid confusing the general reader, adopt this spelling rather than the more modern one though the latter is undoubtedly philologically the more correct.

This hieroglyph representing the hare, of which the phonetic value is *un*, is found throughout Ancient Egyptian writings, in combination with other hieroglyphs, all representing other sounds, in most cases in which the phonetic value of *un* occurs.

There is, however, one word in which this sign occurs alone, and that is the auxiliary verb 'to be', which is mostly written with the hieroglyph of the hare. The question arises as to why this should be the case, particularly as this hieroglyph with the value *un* nowhere in known Ancient Egypt writings *means* 'hare', which is in fact represented by quite a different word having the phonetic value transcribed by modern scholars as *sh't*.

This is the problem which Le Page Renouf set out to solve on the principle that philology alone can never find the solution of this and similar questions unless it enlarges its horizon by attempting to understand the more general workings of the human mind in its use of symbolic values. The obvious nature of this truth may be illustrated by an examination of numerous instances in our own language, of which I will mention one only, namely, our word 'understand', which means quite literally to 'stand under' a thing, in other words to get below the surface in order to gain knowledge of its 'underlying' causes. This happens to be an example of which the meaning is clear once it is pointed out, but numerous other words have become so condensed that the process of tracing them back to their original meaning is by no means so easy.

Some modern philologists have become so specialized that

this kind of symbolic thinking has become difficult for them or even impossible, and these deny outright that, in this case, the hare hieroglyph for *un* meaning 'to be' has any significance other than a purely accidental phonetic one. That such accidents occur in philology is of course patent to anyone who studies the numerous false folk-etymologies of which examples are familiar to all. This does not mean, however, that in innumerable cases the reverse process does not occur, and that original meanings do not get lost and that the use of language thereby does not become sadly impoverished. We have only to observe, for instance, that the Hebrew word translated in the Bible as 'firmament' means a 'hammered-out plate' and, in terms of human life, represents man's character forged out of a play of opposites which it on the one hand resists so that they do not break him, and on the other hand absorbs so that he includes (or should include) in his own person the power and wisdom of both, to realize how language arises out of direct images but loses in intensity as these images get lost and finally becomes an intellectual concept which even intellectuals now commonly fail to grasp.

It is to a similar problem with regard to the purely abstract concept contained in the verb *un*, 'to be' and to its symbolic origin indicated by the hieroglyph of the hare, that Le Page Renouf addresses himself. He says, 'A purely philological inquiry into the primitive meanings of the auxiliary verbs of the Egyptian language has led me to results which throw fresh light upon an interesting question of comparative mythology.'[1]

Referring then to Dr. Brinton's description of the Great Hare of the Algonkin as 'the impersonation of Light, a hero of Dawn' and to certain attempts by the more sophisticated type of philosopher to explain away such symbolism on falsely rationalistic grounds, he says: 'It is now universally acknowledged that the very best classical scholars were till lately utterly mistaken in their etymologies of the languages they knew best. . . .

'No attempt will be made here at a direct refutation of such

[1] P. Le Page Renouf, 'The Myth of Osiris Unnefer', in *Transactions of the Society of Biblical Archaeology*, vol. ix, 1893, p. 281.

explanations as I have alluded to. It will, however, be shown that the ancient Egyptians had myths very similar to that of the Michabo of the Algonkin, and that our knowledge of the Egyptian language enables us . . . to see clearly into the origin of these myths.'[1]

Osiris as 'opener and divider of the ways'

He then refers to Osiris, instancing among his many titles 'Prince of the Unseen World' and 'opener or divider of the ways' of light. Further, with reference to the connection existing in late Egyptian history between Osiris and the Sun-god Rā, he points out their complementary nature by saying "Osiris is the soul of Rā and Rā the soul of Osiris, according to Egyptian orthodoxy. As Rā was the most popular personification of the diurnal Sun, so was Osiris the most popular personification of the nocturnal Sun." Or, rather, as the ancient gloss on the text "I am Yesterday, and I know the Morrow", explains it, "Yesterday is Osiris (of which) the Morrow is Rā". And accordingly Osiris may be considered mythologically either as the father or the son of Rā; the son proceeding from the father, or the father proceeding from the son. The god has twin souls which meet at the heavenly Tattu[2] and are united into one personality.'

'The names of Rā and Osiris are united in prayers addressed to one divinity.'[3]

Osiris Unnefer

Le Page Renouf then refers for the first time to the title Osiris Unnefer, in which the phonetic value *un* represented by the hare occurs, quoting the phrases, '"Rā, Osiris Unnefer, the triumphant, the king of the gods, the mighty Disk whose rays give light". "He showers down light upon the earth at

[1] P. Le Page Renouf; 'The Myth of Osiris Unnefer', in *Transactions of the Society of Biblical Archaeology*, vol. ix, 1893, p. 282.

[2] Tattu (so spelt by Renouf) is the ancient city of Busiris in the Delta. Osiris is regularly called 'Lord of Tattu'.

[3] P. Le Page Renouf, 'The Myth of Osiris Unnefer', in *Transactions of the Society of Biblical Archaeology*, vol. ix, 1893, p. 283.

his rising",' and points out how 'In the Papyrus of Nebseni Horus comes to see his father Osiris, and "sees him Rā, as Unneferu the Lord of Tasert,'"[1] and how 'He is very fre-

Fig. 13. Osiris in the Moon-disk, with the sceptre in his hand and wearing the crown of Upper Egypt. Over him is written his kingly name Unnefer, beginning with the hieroglyph of the Hare

From Lepsius, *Denkmäler*, Section 4, Pl. 31a.

quently called "the king in heaven, the great one upon earth, the mighty sovereign in the nether world"'.[2]

Osiris Unnefer pictured as standing in the Moon's disk

He then goes on, however, to quote from the second chapter of the Book of the Dead the following text: '*Oh thou Only One! shining from the moon, grant that I may come forth at the*

[1] Tasert is a name for the cemetery, especially that of Abydos, and hence is used for the abode of the dead in general.

[2] P. Le Page Renouf, 'The Myth of Osiris Unnefer,' in *Transactions of the Society of Biblical Archaeology*, vol. ix, 1893, p. 283.

head of thy train', and says, 'The best illustration of this ancient text is the picture at Karnak of all the principal gods in adoration of Osiris, who is represented as standing in the moon-disk with the sceptre in his hand, and the royal crown upon his head. Over him is written his kingly name Unnefer.'[1]

Here, then, we find Osiris with his title Unnefer, beginning with the hieroglyphic sign *un* representing the hare, standing in the moon-disk precisely as does the mythical Hare in India, China, and North America (and as we shall see later, in parts of Africa).

Le Page Renouf does not here mention that, as will be seen below, Osiris was originally connected, not with the sun but with the moon, and that the concept of the Nocturnal Sun may well have originally referred to the Moon which in fact shines by night. He is here more concerned with the mythological evidence as throwing light on the original meaning of the syllable *un* as represented by the hieroglyph of the hare used by itself in Ancient Egypt to signify the verb 'to be', and on how and why the apparent transformation in meaning could have occurred.

Philological evidence of concrete images preceding abstract thought

He begins, 'It is a constant fact in the history of language that the name of an object is derived from *one* of its attributes, and the reason why this fact is not more generally recognized is that the languages which we speak have undergone many changes since the time when the names first came into use'.

He then instances many examples, such as 'redbreast' and 'lapwing' from our own language, and others from many other languages, and, referring to the other representations of Osiris under the symbol of a ram or ram-headed personage,

[1] P. Le Page Renouf, 'The Myth of Osiris Unnefer', in *Transactions of the Society of Biblical Archaeology*, vol. ix, 1893, p. 284. Compare the Malekulan myth, according to which Ta-ghar, the creator and god of light, is seen standing in the moon, on which he begets all human children who subsequently enter this world through the portal of their mothers' wombs. *See* John Layard, *Stone Men of Malekula*, London, 1942, pp. 212, 217.

goes on, 'No man, however well educated, can, at the present day, without special inquiry, tell the original meaning of the commonest words in the language which he speaks. It was not so at the time when the names were first adopted. When the Egyptian gave the name *šefit* to the ram, they thought of that powerful action exercised by his head, which has led more modern nations to give the name of *ram* to instruments of powerful energy. And it is an instructive fact that the proper name *Her-Šefit*, "Ram-faced", which is found in the later copies of the Book of the Dead, does not occur in the older copies; the ancient reading is *āa šefit*, "most powerful one".

'The explanation of the Ram-headed god will enable us more readily to understand the symbolism of another form of Osiris.'[1]

Hare-headed Divinity

'A Hare-headed divinity is seen in the temple of Dendera, seated upon an invisible throne, wrapped in mummy clothing, and with the two arms and hands in the position of holding the crook and flail, characteristic of Osiris.[2] The temple of Dendera itself is of recent date, but not so the Hare-headed divinity who appears in the usual vignettes of certain chapters[3] of the Book of the Dead, though here the throne is generally visible, and the hands hold knives.

Hare-headed Goddess

'There is also a Hare-headed goddess in the picture at Dendera, whose name is "*Unnut*,[4] the mistress of the city Unnut and of Dendera".[5] The city Unnut was the metropolis of the 15th nome of Upper Egypt, that of the Hare *Un*, called by the Greeks Hermopolites, on account of their worship of Thoth,

[1] P. Le Page Renouf, 'The Myth of Osiris Unnefer', in *Transactions of the Society of Biblical Archaeology*, vol. ix, 1893, p. 286.

[2] That is to say, with arms and hands crossed, which, without crook or flail would indicate an attitude of humility.

[3] Notably the 146th chapter.

[4] By modern scholars spelt *Wnt*.

[5] E. Lefébure corrects this to 'mistress of Unnu-t, regent of Dendera' (see below, p. 154).

but other chief divinities were worshipped here, especially Osiris. The male divinity would be called *Un* or *Unnu* even when the final vowel is omitted in writing.

'Such a divinity is mentioned at the opening of the 17th chapter of the Book of the Dead.

'"I am Tmu as *Unn*; I am One and only; I am Rā in his first risings."

'And in the glosses upon this opening passage it is spoken of "the sovereignty which Ra exercised as *Unn*" when as yet there was no firmament.'[1]

The name Unnefer or Unnu-neferu

After further discussion he continues: 'What, however, it may be asked, do we know of such a god? My answer is that Unnefer, or rather Unnu-neferu,[2] as a proper name, bears the same relation to Unnu, that Rā-neferu, Tmu-neferu, Hor-neferu, Ptah-neferu, Amon-neferu, Sebak-neferu, Amsu-neferu bear to Rā, Tmu, Horus, Ptah, Amon, Sebak, and Amsu. Unnu is the real name of which Unnu-neferu is a compound.

'The usual interpretation "the good being" of the name Unnefer, which has been current since the time of Champollion, is manifestly erroneous. There is no such noun in Egyptian as *Un* or *Unn* "a being". Mythology does not deal with such names as "good being". "Being" is much too metaphysical, and "good" much too ethical, a notion for names of this kind. A physical sense is the only one admissible. *Nefer*, primarily means *young*, *fair*, *beautiful*, and only secondarily *good.* It is used exactly like the Latin *juvencus*, *juvenca*, in the sense of a youth, a maiden, a foal, a young cow. . . . We also read of the *neferu* in the sense of a youthful troupe of men.

'The sense of beautiful is equally certain. *Nefer ḥra* is a well-known phrase for "of beautiful face". *Neferu* signifies "beautiful raiment, bravery". The wicked wife of the

[1] P. Le Page Renouf, 'The Myth of Osiris Unnefer', in *Transactions of the Society of Biblical Archaeology*, vol. ix, 1893, pp. 286–7.

[2] By modern scholars spelt *Wnn-nfrw*, transliterated as *Wenennofru*,'. The word was by the Greeks further compressed into *Onnophris.*

younger brother in the D'Orbiney Papyrus was *nefert em hāu-set*, "beautiful in all her limbs". *Neferu* is the usual Egyptian word expressing the graces, the beauty, the brightness, the glory of a god. It is said of a goddess in a text quoted by Champollion *meḥ pet ta em neferu-s*, "Heaven and earth are full of her glory"; and it would be easy to quote many expressions of the kind.

Hare-sign signifies 'leaping' or 'uprising', and hence 'being'

'Unnu-neferu signifies the "young, splendid, or glorious Hare". This at least is a signification which in the abstract admits of no contradiction.[1] The question is what is meant by Hare when applied to Osiris or the Sun,[2] and it is a question which can only be solved by an inquiry into the original sense of the Egyptian word signifying Hare.

'As the question has sometimes been raised, it is right to insist upon it that the sign 𓃹 has the value of *un*, and that it has no other value. . . . Now there is a variety of Egypt in words of which the syllable 𓃹 *un*, sometimes written 𓃹𓈖, is the essential part; and one and the same concept underlies the signification of them all, though one of them means a hare, another an *hour* (*unnut*), another a *calf* (*unnui*), another *open*, another *transgress, overleap* (*un*),[3] and the most frequent of all is the very colourless auxiliary verb which we translate "being".

'The fundamental notion is *up, rise, spring up, start up. Un ā*, "up with the hand", expresses the act of the hand rising suddenly, either in adoration of a god, or in the assault of an enemy.

'"Herbs and trees spring up (*her unun*) at thy presence," sings the Poet of the Disk-worshippers.'

After citing a large number of texts, too lengthy to repro-

[1] It must be admitted here that modern scholars do contradict it, but the rest of the evidence in this book culled from all parts of the world lends support to Le Page Renouf's thesis.

[2] For the earlier and more fundamental association of Osiris with the Moon, see below.

[3] There are, of course, many other such combinations having a great variety of meanings.

duce here, in which the word *un* is translated as meaning to 'spring up', 'rise up', etc., Le Page Renouf goes on, 'The connections between the notion of springing up and *un* "open", will be obvious to everyone who knows that our English word "open" is only the verbal form of "up", or who compares the German "auf" and "aufmachen". . . .

'Unnu, then, as the appellative of the "hare" signifies a "springer", "leaper", like the Sanskrit *çaça*, which has its origin in the root *çaç*, implying motion by springing, our own word *hare*, and the Anglo-Saxon *hara*. The Greek λαγώς, which is referred by Pott and other etymologists to the same root as the Sanskrit *laṅgh* "leap", has much the same meaning. *Unnut*, "an hour or moment", is identical with the word signifying "she-hare", and like it signifies "leaper". Our own poets speak of the fleeting hours—"hora agilis, praeceps, fugitiva". In Shelley's *Prometheus*, "The Hours were hounds, which chased the day like a wounded deer". . . .[1]

'But what shall we say of the auxiliary verb *un*? Is not Being a conception prior to all others? It may be so in some systems of Metaphysics, but it is certainly not so in the history of Language. The fact that is an auxiliary verb in the sense of "being" is the very reason why we should look out for the physical sense originally attached to it. All auxiliary verbs in Egyptian, as well as in other languages had originally a physical meaning. We know that *am*, *is*, *was*, *be*, *werden*, were originally verbs of breathing, dwelling, growing, and turning. . . . The case is quite the same in Egyptian. . . .'[2]

'The same kind of idiom is traceable in Hebrew and other Semitic languages. The word "rise" is perpetually used in the Old Testament without an intentional reference to the action of getting up: "rise and go down", "rise and cry", "rise and eat", "rise and sit".[3]

[1] P. Le Page Renouf, 'The Myth of Osiris Unnefer', in *Transactions of the Society of Biblical Archaeology*, vol. ix, 1893, pp. 288–90.

[2] ibid., pp. 291–2.

[3] With regard to the mythical and linguistic connection between the concepts of 'leaping' and 'creation', my friend, W. F. Jackson Knight, calls my attention to the fact that the Greek word θρώσκω, meaning

'And like the Egyptian *un* the Semitic very often acquires the derivative meanings of "being, existing, persisting".

'It is now, I trust, clear enough why *Unn* or *Unnu* should be an appropriate appellative of the rising Sun, who springs forth in glory and triumph.'[1]

Connection of the Hare-deity with Osiris the Moon-god

Le Page Renouf's article from which these quotations are made, though delivered in the form of a lecture in April 1886, was not published till 1893, but an earlier summary had appeared in *Academy* in May 1886 (p. 314) and parts of this summary were quoted by Andrew Lang in an article entitled 'Le Lièvre dans la Mythologie' appearing in the French jour-

'I leap', means also 'emit semen' and so 'beget'. Thus Aeschylus, in lines 658–61 of the *Eumenides*, written a year or two prior to 485 B.C., a play in which the relative roles of the father and mother are a cardinal issue, puts into Apollo's mouth the words, 'She who is called mother is not that one who gives life to the child. She is but one who nurses the swelling embryo. It is he who leaps [*θρῴσκον* 'the leaping one, i.e. the emitter of semen] who gives the life', that is to say that it is the father who is the true originator or creator of the child. In the same way θόρος is 'that which leaps', i.e. the semen. Similarly σπείρω means 'I sow seed' (i.e. cast it upon the ground), from which come σπόρος, a sowing, and σπερμα, the seed, that which is sown, whence our 'sperm', both these Greek words being used in connection with the human act of generation.

[1] P. Le Page Renouf, 'The Myth of Osiris Unnefer', in *Transactions of the Society of Biblical Archaeology*, vol. ix, 1893, pp. 292–3. Le. Page Renouf ends his article by calling attention to the large number of Egyptian porcelain figures in the British Museum representing the Hare, 'emblem of Osiris Onnophris' (the Greek spelling of Unnu-neferu), and to others in the Museum at Bulaq dating from the Saite period. He also quotes Maspero as saying, 'The hare was used frequently as an amulet, either to render the guardians of the other world favourable to the dead or else as representing the incarnation of Osiris'. Dr. Leemans also describes two of the monuments at Leyden as 'the Hare, one of the emblems of Osiris'. Modern scholars say there is no evidence as to what the precise purpose of the hare-amulets was, but it is interesting to compare their existence with that of the hare-amulets already noted from the late Chou period in China.

nal *Mélusine* of 1886–7[1] already referred to, in which he further discussed the evidence, though without apparently having Le Page Renouf's full text to refer to, with the result that he expressed himself unable to pronounce on the rival claims for the meaning of *un*, not seeing that there was in fact no contradiction between the two. Ten years later, in *Mélusine*, 1896–7 (vol. viii, cols. 25–9), Lefébure, having received a copy of the first edition of Lang's *Myth, Ritual, and Religion*, in an Appendix of which his previous article was reproduced under the title 'The Hare in Egypt',[2] took up the cudgels in favour of Le Page Renouf's interpretation, bringing a great deal of further evidence in support, particularly as regards the actuality of a Hare-deity in Egypt and its connection with Osiris in his aspect as Moon-god as being much more ancient than his equation with the Sun.[3]

Lefébure first points out that the apparent contradiction between the view expressed by certain savants following Plutarch and late Egyptian records that the title Unnefer given to Osiris means the 'Good Being' and Le Page Renouf's interpretation as meaning the 'Glorious Hare' is no contradiction at all if we regard the idea of the Hare as being the more primitive, and that of the 'Good Being' as being later, since, as Le Page Renouf intimates, this latter meaning is too metaphysical to be original.

He then proceeds, 'There were in Egypt two main figures capable of bearing the head or title of "hare". . . .

'One of these figures is the goddess *Un-t* or *Unnu-t* belonging to the city of that name, capital city of the fifteenth nome of Upper Egypt, which is also called *Un* or *Unnu*, that is to say,

[1] Andrew Lang, 'Le Lièvre dans la Mythologie', *Mélusine*, vol. iii, cols. 265–9. It is to be noted that in this article the title Unnefer is misprinted as 'Unneter'. This misspelling is corrected in the Appendix to his *Myth, Ritual, and Religion* referred to below.

[2] Andrew Lang, *Myth, Ritual, and Religion*, first edition, London, 1887, vol. ii, pp. 350–5. This appendix was omitted in the second edition published in 1901.

[3] E. Lefébure, 'Le Lièvre dans la Mythologie', *Mélusine*, vol. viii, cols. 25–9. All quotations from Lefébure are translated by the present writer from the original French.

according to several Egyptologists, the Nome of the Hare. The inhabitants of this nome adored a feminine deity called sometimes *Un-t*, sometimes Nehemauai, "she who averts evil", and sometimes Sefekh, "She who inverts the horns (the moon?)"; at Dendera the goddess Hathor was identified with this triple local form, here called also Shepes, "noble". As, from Pyramid times onward, this same city *Unnu* of the South had its parallel in the Northern *Unnu* of Lower Egypt, this goddess became doubled into an *Un-t* of the South and an *Un-t* of the North, which appear together on a monument of the Saite period. Of these the most important was she of the South, who existed in the IVth Dynasty as shown in a fire-lighting formula found in the temple of Unnu-t, the mistress of Unnu.[1] This goddess was, in the Ptolemaic period, represented as having the head of a hare, and was called Unnu-t, mistress of Unnu, regent of Dendera, and not mistress "of Unnu-t or Dendera" as Mr. Lang takes it to be in his discussion of M. le Page Renouf's memoir.[2] With her hare's head the figure of this goddess was used in the late periods [i.e. the Saite period onwards] as the hieroglyph representing the syllable *un*, as, for example, for the word for "hour", *un-t*, and for the word *un*, "to open".

'The other figure having, if not a hare's head, at least a similar name of which the hieroglyph represents a hare, was the god with whom we are concerned here, Osiris *Un-neferu*, whose name is written from New Empire times onward with the last word in the plural, *Un-nefer-u*. This more recent and rarer form of the title brings it into line with that found in the well-known proper names Ptah-nefer-u, Sebak-nefer-u, Ra-nefer-u, together with the honorific inversions Nefer-u-Ptah, and so on. It means therefore "the beauty" or the "splendour of Un". One even finds it in the form Nefer-Un.'[3]

[1] Book of the Dead, Spell 137A. In the rubric to this spell it is stated that 'these things shall be done secretly in the Underworld. They are mysteries of the Underworld.' (See E. A. Wallis Budge, *The Book of the Dead: The Chapters of the Coming Forth by Day*, London, 1898, p. 226.)

[2] See p. 148.

[3] E. Lefébure, 'Le Lièvre dans la Mythologie', *Mélusine*, vol. viii, cols. 25–6.

Lefébure goes on to give reasons for supposing that the name Unnefer may not have come into general use in Egypt till after the Old Kingdom,[1] but adds a warning that absence of evidence does not prove non-existence, since texts of this era are comparatively rare.

He then goes on to point out the further fact that 'Osiris is not exclusively, as M. le Page Renouf thinks, a solar god. [Indeed, the solar attribute of Osiris was a very late one.] The impression given by Egyptian texts indicates, on the contrary, that Osiris was fundamentally a being of the nether world, god of the dead, in other words a god of the underworld having the Nile as his efflux[2] and the moon for soul. The later equation of him with the sun was a secondary phenomenon, as it was with all the Egyptian gods.'[3]

He then cites a text recounting how Rameses IV himself inquired closely into the nature of Osiris according to the sacred books of Abydos, researches which he subsequently commemorated on a stela, and in which Osiris is nowhere confused with the sun. He also cites a royal protocol of Osiris which became popular from the XIIth Dynasty onwards, in which, 'in spite of the solar framework imposed by etiquette', Osiris Unnefer is described as 'the god who opens the womb (?) of the earth, the Nile, the bull of the abyss, a prince in Heliopolis (where he had a temple), the lord of the nether world, the heart's joy (a lunar title)[4] of the gods'.[5] He goes on, 'If Osiris was not the sun, it is apparent that he was often the moon, that is to say, the luminary of the dead, a type of symbolism of which the

[1] That is to say as a divine name, i.e. as an epithet of Osiris, which occurs first in the XIIth Dynasty. It was in use as a personal name already in the Old Kingdom.

[2] The Nile was thought to flow out of the mummified body of Osiris, an interesting parallel to the blood and water flowing from Christ's side and to the blood flowing from the wound of the Mithraic bull, thus causing the fertility of all things needful to man.

[3] E. Lefébure, 'Le Lièvre dans la Mythologie', *Mélusine*, vol. viii, col. 27.

[4] In fairness it must be pointed out that modern scholars deny the special lunar significance of this attribute.

[5] E. Lefébure, 'Le Lièvre dans la Mythologie', *Mélusine*, vol. viii, col. 28.

treatise on Isis and Osiris attributed to Plutarch bears the deepest imprint. There exist also representations and statuettes of Osiris the Moon, not of Osiris the Sun. Moreover, the city of Un belonging to the goddess Un-t was the Hermopolis of the Greeks, the city of the Egyptian Hermes, Thoth, who is the essential personification of the moon, and whose cult became joined with that of this goddess from the days of the Old Empire onward. Osiris himself, who was equated with Thoth had at Un a temple called *Nefer*, the place of his glories, *nefer-u*, probably a pun on the name Un-nefer, which through a further pun is translated "Beautiful Colours". Under these circumstances it is not surprising to find Osiris Unnefer figured inside the lunar disk, as is the case at Karnak,[1] and also the goddess of the Moon-city represented as, *par excellence*, having a hare's head.' He adds, very relevantly to the subject of this article, 'Do not almost all peoples of the earth take the marks on the moon to represent the image of a hare?'[2]

'The concept of a Lunar Hare can thus be traced back to a very remote antiquity in Egypt, since the hare, known on the banks of the Nile from earliest times, had already, in the historical period or at least by the XIIth Dynasty, lost its original name of *un*, which is not found either in Coptic, and which was retained only as a hieroglyphic sign representing the phonetic value of *un* in writing.'

Connection of the Hare-deity with Thoth, Hermes, and Mercury, and the association of all these with writing

After a brief summary, which does not concern us here, of its possible totemic nature, Lefébure ends his article with the words, 'We must not lose sight of the Osirian and Hermopolitan symbolism which has been referred to. . . . It would in fact be a very curious coincidence, that a hare-headed goddess should have been worshipped in the Moon City and that a Hare God called by the same name should have been placed in the moon if each of these was not the Hare-Moon.'[3]

The fact that the city of the hare-goddess Un was also the city

[1] See p. 147.

[2] E. Lefébure, 'Le Lièvre dans la Mythologie', *Mélusine*, vol. viii, cols. 28, 29. (Translated by the author.)

[3] ibid., col. 29.

of Thoth, who is himself the personification of the moon, and who in Greek times was identified with Hermes to such an extent that the city became called Hermopolis, is of special interest on account of what we actually know of Hermes and of his Roman counterpart the god Mercury. Though it is true that the metal we now call mercury was not so named till the thirteenth century A.D., the fact of its being named after the god, together with its adjective 'mercurial', alone gives a clue to what the god stood for. The metal mercury is unique in its versatility in that it is the only metal that is fluid at ordinary temperatures, that is to say that it is symbolically solid and fluid at once. It is thus the only metal that under ordinary circumstances *runs*. So the god Mercury, like his Greek counterpart Hermes, is regarded as the messenger of the gods, and bears wings on his head and feet to indicate his swiftness. The metal mercury is also moon-coloured, which brings it into line with the moon personified by Thoth. The gods Thoth, Hermes, and Mercury, of which the historically oldest is Thoth, are all regarded as personifying 'the external expression of thought, whether human or divine', of which, since he was a god, we may presume that the divine was earliest and therefore the most fundamental.

The chief symbol, both of Hermes and Mercury, was the caduceus or magic wand with twin serpents entwined round it, which is perhaps the world's most famous healing symbol. Hermes, Mercury, and Thoth were also said to be the inventors of writing. In the case of Thoth, this refers not only to written characters but also to literary composition and especially to the so-called 'sacred language'. Words are, of course, the chief messengers between man and man, and the attribution of the invention and patronage of writing to the god Thoth calls inevitably to mind the opening passages of Saint John's Gospel, saying, 'the Word was with God, and the word was God. . . . In him was life, and the life was the light of men. And the light shineth in darkness; and the darkness overpowered[1] it not.'

[1] The Authorized Version has 'comprehended', but 'overpowered' is a more accurate translation. James Moffatt translates the passage, 'Amid the darkness the Light shone, but the darkness did not master it'.

The light in the darkness is among early peoples commonly symbolized by the moon, which brings us back again to the moon-personality of Thoth, and to the fact that, as already seen, the Great Hare of the Algonkin is also credited with the invention of picture-writing, that is to say, of symbolic thought.

Finally, Hermes, under the form of Hermes Trismegistos, or Hermes the Thrice Greatest, came in medieval times to be regarded as the special depository of all magical knowledge. It is he who is said by some to have founded Hermopolis, the city of the hare-headed goddess. His alleged writings were famous throughout the Alexandrine period, and these 'hermetic' works formed the background of most European alchemy, that interesting mixture of early chemical experimentation and symbolic philosophy of which the main preoccupation was in its material aspect the transmutation of base metals into gold, in other words the spiritualization of matter, and in its spiritual aspect the transformation of base natures into divine, in other words the redemptive process of which Mrs. Wright's dream-sacrifice of the hare was a potent symbol.

THE HARE IN AFRICA

THE HARE AS TRICKSTER-HERO

Among the present-day inhabitants of the African continent the hare has no such deep mythical associations as we have seen it to have elsewhere. This does not mean that there are not numerous folk-tales associated with it. Frobenius indeed has constructed a map showing the distribution of folk-tales in which the hare figures as a kind of trickster-hero, a distribution covering the greater part of the Sudan stretching from Senegal on the west coast to the Red Sea on the east, and from thence spreading south to include many parts of East Africa, Rhodesia, whence it branches off into Angolia and also Portuguese East Africa and thence to Bechuanaland and the Transvaal.[1] In these areas the hare plays the role that other trickster animals play in other parts of the Continent. It has not been possible for me to examine all the tales recorded from these areas, but those published by Frobenius from among the Mande-speaking peoples inhabiting northern Liberia and the neighbouring districts, and also the Mossi to the north of the Gold Coast, while depicting the hare as a wise animal and trickster eluding his enemies through the exercise of his great ingenuity and, as such, being in the nature of humorous character-sketches, do not appear to have any mythological bearing which would warrant their inclusion in the present inquiry.[2]

[1] Leo Frobenius, *Erlebte Erdteile*, vol, vi, *Monumenta Africana*, Frankfurt, 1929, map 42, p. 420.

[2] Leo Frobenius, *Atlantis: Volksmärchen und Volksdichtungen Afrikas*, Jena, 1922, vol. viii, *Erzählungen aus dem Westsudan*, Tales 47–58 from the Mande-speaking peoples among whom the hare is called *Sani* or *Sonsanni*, and Tales 98 and 101–7 from the Mossi by whom the hare is callĕd *Samba*.

For similar tales from among the Shilluk, see D. Westermann, *The Shilluk People, Their Language and Folk-lore*, Philadelphia, 1912; from Bari, Anuak, and Moru see *Folk Stories from the Sudan*,

It is nevertheless possible that, among the large number of these tales, some at least preserve in a disguised and humorous form a faint echo of mythological motives already encountered in other parts of the world. Instances of this are the following tales recorded by Madeleine Holland from among the Banyanja of Central Africa.

The Man tries to burn the Hare, but fails

The first, recalling the voluntary sacrifice of Buddha in the form of a Hare by leaping into a fire, relates how 'there was a Man who had often tried to get the Hare and kill him. One day he caught him and said, "Now, I have got you!" and tied him up to a tree and went to get some fire. He wanted to set all the grass round about alight and then the Hare would be burnt too. The Hare sat quiet until he saw a Jackal coming down the road; then he began to call out very loud. The Jackal said, "What is the matter?" The Hare said, "That man *will* go and get meat to feed me; and I don't know how to eat it." The Jackal said, "All right, if you don't like it, come away and tie *me* up where you are, because I am hungry for meat." He loosened the Hare and the Hare tied him up in his place. By and by a crowd came back with the Man shouting, "We'll burn you!" The Jackal says, "What are they shouting?" The Hare says, "They are saying they are bringing a great deal of meat." After the grass was burnt, the people found the body of the Jackal; but the Hare ran away.'[1]

Later, the Hare carried out a similar deception by means of which he caused the Man who tried to burn him in a hut to burn his children instead. The Man, not knowing that the Hare had decoyed his children into the hut and had itself escaped,

vol. iii. Further Anuak stories by E. E. Evans-Pritchard, together with some Moru stories contributed by T. H. B. Mynors, *Sudan Notes and Records*, 1941, vol. xxiv, pp. 69–84; from the Yao and Nyanja of Nyasaland, see Alice Werner, in *Folk-lore*, 1899, vol. x, pp. 282–93; from the Ronga, see H. A. Junod, *Les Chants et les contes des Ba-Ronga de la Baie de Delagoa*, Lausanne, 1897.

[1] Madeleine Holland, 'Folk-lore of the Banyanja', *Folk-lore*, 1916, p. 13.

set fire to the hut, whereon one of the children cried out, "I am not a hare, father; I am your child'; but the Man says, 'No, I know you are the Hare'. The child called out its own name, but the Man would not listen, and burnt them—and the Hare laughed.[1]

There is no indication here of any connection of the Hare with the Moon as in the Buddha story, but in another tale from the same collection there is at least a connection with the sky.

The Man proposes to the Hare that they should kill their mothers. The Hare puts his mother into the sky

'There was a Hare and he was the friend of a Man. One day the Hare said, "Let us kill our mothers, then we shall both be free". The Man thought it would be good, so he killed his mother. The Hare did not kill his mother; he only took his knife and stabbed at a plant with red juice till his knife was red, then he showed it to the Man and said, "With this knife I killed her". The Man thought she was dead, because he never saw her again; but the Hare had put her up in the sky. Every day he used to go by himself and she used to let down a rope and pull him up and give him food. The Man had no-one to feed him. He saw that the Hare was very fat and asked him who fed him. The Hare said, "No-one." Then the Man watched him and saw how he went to a certain place and said, "Cast down the rope", and a rope came down and he climbed up. So the next day the Man went and said, "Cast down the rope", but his voice was too loud. The Hare's mother knew it was not her child. So then the Hare came and the Man hid away and listened. He heard the Hare say softly, "Cast down the rope', and the rope came down and the Hare climbed up. Another day the man went and said very softly, "Cast down the rope", and the Hare's mother thought it was her son, so she let down the rope and the Man went up. He killed the Hare's mother and all the Hare's little ones; only one remained alive. Then he went away. When the Hare came he found the

[1] Madeleine Holland, 'Folk-lore of the Banyanja', *Folk-lore*, 1916, p. 13.

rope hanging: he went up and saw that his mother and all his little ones were dead except one small hare. He asked it, "Who has done this?" and it said, "Your friend the Man." The Hare went to his hut and wept. The Man came in and found him weeping and said, "What is the matter? why do you weep?" He said, "The sun is hurting my eyes." Next day he went and got red stones and heated them in a pot. He told the Man, "I have found a place where there is plenty of game. Lie in the road, open your mouth and shut your eyes and I will throw it in." The Man lay down in the road, opened his mouth and shut his eyes and the Hare threw the stones down his throat and killed him.'[1]

This tale, as well as establishing the hare's connection with the sky world, is deeply significant in view of the fact that of the two sexes the woman is the prime repository of instinct which the man representing society is in the habit of mistakenly wishing to destroy. The hare knows, on the other hand, as we have seen in the case of the Hare-Buddha, that instinct must not be destroyed but must on the contrary be transformed. In tricking the Man to kill his mother the hare thus demonstrates what mankind is always so prone to do to its instinctive life. The hare, on the contrary, transforms his, as symbolized by his putting his mother into the sky and remaining in communion with her there (the rope corresponding to Jacob's ladder which unites heaven and earth). The man, however, still bent on the same mischief, then also destroys the hare's, but suffers for it himself, though it will be noted that his destructive zeal does not entirely succeed, since one small hare still capable of growing up remains in the sky to maintain the hare's own connection with the spiritual world.

The Hare rides the Lion

One other tale is worth mentioning, called 'The Hare Rides the Lion': 'Once there was a Lion, who came to a town and said, "I want this man to be my brother and by and by I will take him to my house". The Man said, "Very well", so every

[1] Madeleine Holland, 'Folk-lore of the Banyanja', *Folk-lore*, 1916, pp. 25–6.

day the Lion came to visit him. By and by the Hare came in and saw this, so he went away and put on nice clothes and came back, saying, "I want this man to be my brother". The Men said, "No, he is the Lion's brother." He said, "The Lion is of no importance; he is my horse." The Man laughed but the Hare repeated it. He went home and the Men told the Lion what the Hare had said. The Lion was very angry and said he would go and get the Hare and make him tell them that he had spoken falsely. He went to the Hare and told him what the Men had said. The Hare denied it and said if he were not feeling so ill he would go and tell the Men themselves that they had said what was not true. The Lion wanted him to come and say so; but the Hare said he was too ill to walk. The Lion said, "Very well, I will carry you." The Hare said, "Very well, because I want to tell them it is a lie." So the Lion took him on his back. By and by the Hare says he is so weak that he will fall off unless the Lion will let him put a bridle in his mouth (a rope made of bark from a tree). The Lion submits and goes on with the rope in his mouth. By and by the Hare says the flies bother him so that he cannot hold on and asks the Lion to give him a little stick to drive them away. The Lion says, "Very well", and gives him a switch. Then they come near to the town and all the Men come out and see the Hare riding on the Lion's back and beating him with a switch. He says, "Hi! hi! didn't I say you were my horse?"'[1]

This, too, recalls the Indian tale quoted on page 117 in which the hare tricks the lion. In that tale the hare tricked the lion into destroying itself, but in this African version the lion (here representing brute force, or unredeemed instinct), is tamed by the hare, representing the power of mind over body, thus bringing it clearly into line, though on a humorous level, with concepts found in the previous tale and elsewhere of the hare as representing transformed instinct or spiritual power.

'The Hare's Skin in the Moon's Face'

While none of the tales from this central area which I have

[1] Madeleine Holland, 'Folk-lore of the Banyanja', *Folk-lore*, 1916, pp. 48–9.

read show the hare as being definitely connected with the moon, others from both north and south of the African continent quite definitely do. One such is a story told by the Abâbde Bedouin in the neighbourhood of the Hamâta mountains near the Red Sea due east of Aswân in Upper Egypt, of which the following is a free translation. It is entitled 'The Hare's Skin in the Moon's Face', and runs: 'Sun and Moon are two sisters. Formerly they were both cold. They walked side by side in the sky. Once they caught a hare, skinned it, and put it in the cooking-pot. While the hare was stewing, the two began to quarrel. They abused one another. In her rage the Sun picked up the hare's skin and flung it into the Moon's face. The Moon, on her part, grasped the cooking-pot and flung the boiling contents into the Sun's face. Since that time hare's skin is to be seen in the full Moon, and since that time the Sun is hot, and since that time they do not any more walk side by side in the sky.'[1]

THE ORIGIN OF DEATH

The other African area in which the hare is definitely connected with the moon is in the extreme south, where it appears in a Hottentot variant of the widespread South African myth dealing with the Origin of Death. The Bantu peoples all have similar myths, in which different animals are represented as taking the chief roles. In all these tales some animal is en-

[1] Hans Alexander Winkler, *Ägyptische Volkskunde*, Stuttgart, 1936, p. 332. Dr. Meinhard, who kindly called my attention to this tale, adds: 'It should be noted that the Fellaheen of the Nile Valley do not seem to have any such beliefs. From Upper Egypt to the Delta they see in the moon either a tree, or a human figure, or face, or a bowl containing flat cakes. The tree is usually a date-palm. The human figure in the moon is described sometimes as a 'man plaïting a basket', or as a 'basket-maker sitting under a date-palm', or else as 'the daughter of the wood-gatherer', or 'the wife of the wood-gatherer', sometimes also as 'the image of the Prophet', etc. See Winkler, ibid., pp. 238–9. The 'basket-maker' calls to mind the 'weaving' or 'spinning woman' in the moon of Indonesia and other parts of the world; in Polynesia, where there is no weaving, this concept is replaced by that of a 'plaiter in the Moon'.

trusted with a message to tell man of Immortality, but invariably gets the message wrong.

The Chameleon and the Lizard

Thus, among the Zulus, Unkulunkulu ('the old-old-one', the most ancient being) sends the chameleon, saying, '"Go, Chameleon, go and say, Let not men die." The chameleon set out; it went slowly; it loitered in the way; and, as it went, it ate of the fruit of a tree, which is called Ubukwebezane. At length Unkulunkulu sent a lizard after the chameleon, when it had already set out for some time. The lizard went; it ran and made great haste, for Unkulunkulu had said, "Lizard, when you have arrived, say, Let men die." So the lizard went, and said, "I tell you, It is said, Let men die." The lizard came back to Unkulunkulu, before the chameleon had reached his destination, the chameleon which was sent first, which was sent and told to go and say, "Let not men die."

'At length it arrived and shouted, saying, "It is said, Let not men die!" But men answered, "O! we have heard the word of the lizard; it has told us the word, 'It is said, Let men die.' We cannot hear your word. Through the word of the lizard men will die."'[1]

The Ronga tell the same story, also of chameleon and lizard.[2]

The use of the chameleon as the animal that really knows is interesting, since owing to its ability to change colour and to the fact that its eyes move independently of one another, it is a fitting symbol of extreme adaptability and of that 'seeing both ways' which is the essence of true spiritual life having one eye on the temporal affairs of men and the other eye simultaneously on the eternal affairs of God. Owing to its habit of living high up among the branches of trees and of inflating itself with air, it was in classical times accredited with the power of 'living on air', which is another symbol of spirit, derived

[1] H. Callaway, *The Religious System of the Amazula*, Natal, 1868, part I, pp. 3–4.

[2] H. A. Junod, *Les Chants et les contes des Ba-Ronga de la Baie de Delagoa*, Lausanne, 1897, p. 137.

from the Latin *spiritus,* meaning 'breath' or 'air'. The fact that its message of immortality was reversed by its biological cousin the lizard which has none of these qualities is a symbol that 'one way' thinking always does get its facts wrong because it is incapable of ever seeing the 'other side'.

The Moon sends the Hare to tell men of Immortality, but he gets the message wrong and the Moon slits his lip.

It must be admitted that in the Hottentot version of the myth the hare also is represented as the half-wit, though it is significant that in this version the hare is sent, not by an anthropomorphic 'old one' but by the Moon which itself every month dies and is reborn. Bleek quotes several forms of this Hottentot myth, one of which runs as follows:

'The Moon, it is said, sent once an Insect to Men, saying, "Go thou to Men, and tell them, 'As I die, and dying live, so ye shall also die, and dying live''.' The Insect started with the message, but whilst on his way was overtaken by the Hare, who asked, "On what errand art thou bound?" The Insect answered, "I am sent by the Moon to Men, to tell them that as she dies, and dying lives, they also shall die, and dying live." The Hare said, "As thou art an awkward runner, let me go" (to take the message). With these words he ran off, and when he reached Men, he said, "I am sent by the Moon to tell you, 'As I die, and dying perish, in the same manner ye shall also die and come wholly to an end'". Then the Hare returned to the Moon and told her what he had said to Men. The Moon reproached him angrily, saying, "Darest thou tell the people a thing which I have not said?" With these words she took up a piece of wood, and struck him on the nose. Since that day the Hare's nose is slit.'[1]

[1] W. H. I. Bleek, *Reynard the Fox in South Africa, or, Hottentot Fables and Tales.* London, 1864, pp. 69–72. According to another version: 'The Moon dies, and rises to life again. The Moon said to the Hare, "Go thou to Men, and tell them, 'Like as I die and rise to life again, so you also shall die and rise to life again'." The Hare went to the Men, and said, "Like as I die and do not rise to life again, so you shall also die, and not rise to life again". When he returned, the Moon asked him, "What hast thou said?" "I have told them,

We have already met in China with the hare pounding the Herb of Immortality in the moon. 'Immortality' is, by the way, like the 'eternity' of Christian belief, no mere hope for the future, but refers to that basic reality at the very centre of the psyche—the divine spark within—which *is* immortal and eternal, because it is universal, common in all ages to all life. It is the loss of this which, as in the Christian story of the Fall, all peoples on earth in their respective mythologies deplore, which in turn means, of course, that they have got out of touch with that ultimate reality which is eternal, and which all seek through their religions to regain.

The insistence on the splitting of the hare's lip is probably due also to its being used originally as a symbol for the split in men's lives that all these tales refer to, and which is commonly referred to as 'separation from God', that is to say, the separation of temporal values from their creative union with eternal truth.

The Hare kills a monster, but offends the Chief

Finally, W. G. Black quotes from Theal's *Kaffir Folk-lore*[1]

'Like as I die and do not rise to life again, so you shall also die and not rise to life again.'" "What," said the Moon, "hast thou said that?" And she took a stick and beat the Hare on his mouth, which was slit by the blow. The Hare fled, and is still fleeing. ['We are now angry with the Hare,' said the old Namaqua, 'because he brought such a bad message, and therefore we dislike to eat his flesh.']

In yet another version it was with a hatchet that the moon slit the hare's lip, whereon the hare 'raised his claws, and scratched the Moon's face; and the dark parts which we now see on the surface of the Moon are the scars which she received on that occasion'. With regard to a Bushman version of the Moon and Hare story called 'The Origin of Death', see W. H. I. Bleek and L. C. Lloyd, *Specimens of Bushmen Folk-lore*, London, 1911, pp. 56–65.

Dr. Meinhard, who called my attention to these stories, points out that the Tibetans tell similar tales regarding the hare as trickster, quoting Capt. W. F. O'Connor, *Folk Tales from Tibet*, London, 1906. The first tale ends with the hare being so amused by the mischief he had done 'that he leaned back on a handy stone, and laughed to such an extent that he actually split his upper lip. And it has remained split to this very day'.

[1] W. G. Black, *Folk-lore*, vol. iii, pp. 88–9.

to the effect that 'the animals . . . had made a kraal and appointed one after another the coney, the muishond, the duiker, and bluebuck, and the porcupine to keep watch over the fat stored therein, and to signal the approach of the inkalimeva (a fabulous animal). These all failed in the duty and were killed by the other animals. The sixth time that fat is put into the kraal the hare is selected as keeper of the gate, rather against his will. He skilfully makes an end of the dreaded inkalimeva, but as he eats the tail, which should have been reserved for the chief, he has to flee for his life.'

This tale beautifully illustrates both positive and negative aspects of the hare's intuitive power. Its ability to deal successfully with the mythical monster represents its deep knowledge of the world of inner reality, while its failure to satisfy convention provides just that apparent futility which justifies its widespread African reputation as a trickster.

The number 6 is a ritual number used among many peoples to indicate that spiritual knowledge which comes as a result of being able to reconcile 'both sides'. One of the best known symbols of this is the Jewish 'Shield of David', ✡ a six-pointed emblem formed of triangles (a double trinity), one pointing upwards towards the sky and the other downwards towards the earth, representing the union of external and internal realities.

FIGURE 14. Saxon 'Idol of the Moon' in the form of a goddess wearing a chapron representing the head and shoulders of a Hare, and holding a Moon-disk containing a human face

From R. Verstigan, *A Restitution of Decayed Intelligence*, Antwerp, 1605, Chapter 3

THE HARE IN EUROPE

SAXON GODDESS OF MONDAY WEARING A HARE-CHAPRON AND CARRYING A MOON-DISK

Having in a previous section dealt with the hare-headed goddess in Ancient Egypt and her connection with the moon, it may possibly come as less of a shock to the reader to find that our own Saxon ancestors worshipped a similar goddess also connected with the moon.

Thus, in a very interesting work published in 1605, we find a chapter headed 'Of the ancient manner of lyving of our Saxon ancestors. Of the Idolles they adored whyle they were pagans: and how they grew to be of greater name and habitation of any other people of Germany.' In this chapter, which deals with the deities connected with the several days of the week, we read:

'The next according to the cours of the dayes of the week, was the Idol of the Moon whereof wee yet retain the name of *Monday* instead of Moōday, and it was made according to the picture heer following.

'The form of this Idol seemeth very strange and ridiculous, for beeing made for a woman shee hath a short cote lyke a man: but more strange it is to see her hood with such two long eares. The holding of a moon before her brest may seem to have bin to expresse what shee is, but the reason of her chapron with long eares, as also of her shorte cote and pyked shuwes, I do not fynd.'[1]

The accompanying illustration (Fig. 14), reproduced from this work, shows clearly that the 'chapron with long eares' is in fact a headdress representing the head and shoulders of a hare.

[1] R. Verstegan (pseudonym for Richard Rowlands), *A Restitution of Decayed Intelligence: In Antiquities. Concerning the most noble and renowned English nation*, Antwerp, 1605, chapter 3. I am indebted to Professor J. H. Hutton for calling my attention to this remarkable work.

It will be noted, morever, that the moon is held, not, as the writer suggests, before her breast but before her abdomen, thus indicating that the hare-goddess is in fact pregnant of the moon, and that in the moon's disk are delineated the features of what may be either an old woman, recalling the 'grandmother' in the moon of the Hiawathan story referred to on p. 171 (note 1), or else our own 'man in the moon' corresponding to the Malekulan belief referred to on p. 147 (note 1).

Pregnancy is another 'dawn' symbol, adumbrating 'new birth', and indicates almost more vividly than any previously cited myth the spiritually pregnant nature of the mythical hare so clearly seen in Mrs. Wright's dream.

REMNANTS OF WORSHIP OF A HARE-GODDESS IN MODERN EUROPE

THE EASTER HARE

CUSTOMS STILL EXTANT IN EASTERN EUROPE

It may be asked, 'Are there no remnants of this worship of the hare-goddess in modern Europe?' The answer is, of course, that there are. One such faint echo is the fact that children in Swabia may not make shadows on the wall to represent the sacred Moon Hare,[1] which recalls the Hare in the Moon of mythological belief elsewhere. More important than this, however, are the numerous European customs connected with the Hare that lays the Easter eggs. The Easter Hare and its accompanying coloured eggs have only recently been reintroduced into England, but represent a whole series of customs still living in many parts of Europe, where they are evidently a survival of what at one time must have been an organized ritual in honour of the hare-goddess.

Easter is itself of course the great Dawn Festival of Christianity, combining as it does the motive of the Resurrection with that of the springtime rebirth of nature. From the standpoint of nature-myth, it would be expected that it should be

[1] W. G. Black, 'The Hare in Folk-lore', *The Folk-lore Journal*, vol. i, p. 88, quoting Grimm.

most deep-rooted in Eastern Europe where the rebirth of nature after a snow-bound winter is so much more striking than in the more temperate climate of the West.

It was my good fortune, while writing this memoir, to meet an Austrian peasant woman who gave me in graphic terms the following account of what she says still happens in many parts of Austria, Czechoslovakia, Hungary, and other neighbouring lands.

First Easter Egg presented before Sunrise on Easter Day

'On Palm Sunday catkins (representing palms) are brought to church and are there consecrated, after which they are taken home and kept in the garden till Easter. On Easter Sunday a lovely rite commemorating the Resurrection is performed in each home, and takes the form of children rising *before sunrise* [note the dawn symbolism] to bring the catkins into the house. The first child to bring in such a catkin is immediately rewarded with the first Easter Egg.'

'Other eggs, hard-boiled and coloured, chiefly red and blue but also with other pigments, are hidden, in large quantities sometimes totalling several hundred, in "nests" all over the garden, and are searched for by the children when the family returns in the morning from High Mass.'

The Hare that lays the Easter Eggs mimed by child on visit to grandmother

'The hare that lays these eggs does not appear, however, until the afternoon, when the children all visit their grandmothers.[1] It does not seem to matter nowadays which grandmother it is, but it must be a grandmother or a grandmother

[1] This visiting of the grandmother is strangely reminiscent of the large number of cases in which the grandmother is connected with the moon, presumably as the archetype of the Old Woman. The reader will be reminded, among other instances, of the lines in Longfellow's *Hiawatha*:

Once a warrior, very angry,
Seized his grandmother, and threw her
Up into the sky at midnight;
Right against the moon he threw her;
'Tis her body that you see there.

substitute, such as an aunt if no actual grandmother is alive or near enough to receive the visit. Whoever the "grandmother" may be, however, the chief figure in the homely procession to her house (which may be miles away from the children's home) is a child dressed in a cape with head and ears representing a hare, who on his or her back carries a small water butt filled with coloured eggs.'

The reader will not fail in this account to recognize the 'hare-goddess' cited above. Nor will he fail to note that the eggs carried by the hare (albeit on the hare's back, since this is easier than in front) take the place of the moon 'carried' by the Saxon goddess, both being symbols of rebirth. The narrator proceeds:

'Meanwhile, "grandmother" has kneaded special Easter Cake made of fine dough puffed up with yeast and baked so as to give it a lovely golden brown colour. This cake is made in the shape of a platter, and is, too, filled with coloured eggs. Prayers are said, and then the afternoon feast consisting of all sorts of dainty foods is consumed. But the chief event, so far as the children are concerned, is the behaviour of the child dressed as a hare. The first eggs out of its butt are given to grandmother, then others to grandfather, and to the parents. It is now that the fun begins. The children all want eggs too. But the power is with the hare-child, who dodges here and there, in and out and round about the house and garden, chased by the rest, to whom it gives its eggs only at its own sweet will, at times stingily withholding, and at others showering its Easter gifts to favourites or others, who snatch and scramble till all the eggs are gone. Eggs from the Easter cake (which is in the form of a nest) are distributed more sedately, but this scramble is renewed when further nests full of coloured eggs are found and searched for all over the grandmother's garden, as in the morning at home.'

The same symbolism is found in the small coral islet of Vao, off the coast of Malekula in the Pacific Ocean, where the moon is called 'grandmother' and conceives children by the God of Light shining upon her, whence they descend to earth through the portal of their mothers' wombs (John Layard, *Stone Men of Malekula*, pp. 212–13).

Game of stabbing an Egg with a Silver Coin

Games also are played, at least one of which has ritual meaning. This consists in somebody holding a coloured egg, while a child, holding a silver coin of the approximate size of an English florin, has quickly to stab the egg with the coin. If the stabber aims well and manages to pierce the egg in the centre, piercing the shell so that the coin sinks right into the egg, both egg and coin are his.

The symbolism of this is clear. On the one hand, the egg of course represents potential life, but, as in real life, cannot come to fruition without fertilization from outside. The silver coin is clearly the fertilizing element. Silver traditionally represents the moon just as gold represents the sun. It is quite true that the egg itself was a few paragraphs back itself equated with the moon, but degraded symbolism, such as this, is apt to become a little mixed. Here, however, the egg clearly represents the dark matter that is penetrated by the light, just as the light of Christ penetrated the tomb, and so paved the way for the Resurrection. From another angle it also represents spirit penetrating matter, as the light of consciousness penetrates the dark night of the soul.

Sugar Eggs containing Religious Pictures. Live hares given as pets.

The same symbolism is seen in the making of sugar eggs, each hollow and with a little window in it, through which can be seen, inside the egg, a picture of Christ rising from the tomb, or of some other religious subject. The whole ritual calls inevitably to mind the Great Egg which is the central religious symbol in Easter Island, that lonely outpost in the Eastern Pacific with its huge megalithic monuments, where so much religious activity at one time took place.[1] Here in Eastern Europe, however, it is so intimately connected with the hare that not only is the hare supposed to lay the eggs, as symbolized by the hare-child bearing them on its back, but live hares are

[1] See Mrs. Scoresby Routledge, *The Mystery of Easter Island*, London, 1919, pp. 254 sqq.

actually given to children as pets and are let loose on Easter Day to play, so long as they do not altogether escape.

Symbolic play

All this information was given to me by my peasant Austrian friend with that mixture of robust humour and childlike delight that are the essence of such symbolic play, not only in Europe but also among primitive peoples, with some of whom the writer has lived and worked, and whose attitude towards that part of their ritual life is precisely similar.[1] She ended her account with sparkling eyes saying, 'But you know it isn't true. The hare doesn't really lay eggs', almost as if I really believed from her account that it did. This is a typically symbolic-intuitive remark, showing that with one part of herself she thought it was. Indeed, unless one part of the personality believed the make-believe, such play would not be possible. It is of course the spiritual part—that which the French call *esprit* —that in fact knows it to be true on a certain level. For the unconscious is the mirror opposite of the conscious. Thus, no material hare would be pleased to have its back slit open as happened in Mrs. Wright's dream, but in her dream it was, because the hare was in fact that unredeemed part of herself that wanted to be redeemed—i.e. transformed into, or united with, its opposite. Thus, in the spirit, the hare representing intuition does in fact lay the eggs of new life, because, of the four psychological functions, intuition alone is that which does actually bring about such transformations. This is of course akin to the famous saying *credo quia impossibile*, meaning that the apparently impossible *is* true, and only seems impossible if we confuse symbolic truth with its complementary opposite, namely the actual facts of a one-sidedly conceived purely materialistic world. I have no doubt whatever that such play stimulates and tends to actuate the inner knowledge of the incarnation of God in man, that is to say of the vitalizing effect of the re-entry of spirit into matter, far more effectively than many serious disquisitions heard from the pulpit or text books

[1] See John Layard, *Stone Men of Malekula*, London, 1942, part iii, on 'Ritual Life', particularly pp. 382 sqq., 511 sqq., 547.

on religious knowledge. Jung once said that the only divine thing he knew in mankind was humour, by which he meant that joyful sense of the incongruous that joins fact to fiction which is essentially the symbolic aspect of fact. This statement is itself a joke, and not to be taken either as blasphemous or as the final word, but is a symbolic way of indicating that union of opposites which warms the cockles of the heart, whether as secular joke or as the life-giving knowledge of the divine spark in man.

The date of Easter regulated by the Moon

Though there is little direct reference in this account to any connection between the Easter Hare and the Moon, it must be remembered that the date of Easter is itself in all Christian Churches regulated by the moon. Billson further points out that 'the moon's periodic death and revival suggest thoughts of Resurrection and Immortality, and recalls the South African myth already quoted in which the moon sends the hare to men, saying, "Like as I die and rise to life again, so you shall also die and rise to life again", which he refers to as an "Easter Gospel" '.[1]

In this connection it is of interest to note the curious mistake made by one writer[2] in taking the animal figured in Dürer's woodcut of the Last Supper (in his series known as 'The Smaller Passion') as the chief item in the meal to be a hare, whereas its tail bones show it quite clearly to be a lamb. The same writer refers to what he speaks of as a similar representation 'in the east window of the beautiful little chapel attached to the house in Gatton Park, described as being a fine specimen of Flemish or German medieval workmanship'. Mindful of the Mosaic law forbidding the Jews to eat the hare[3] and not having seen the east window in question, I can make no pronounce-

[1] See pp. 165 and C. J. Billson, 'The Easter Hare', *Folk-lore*, vol. iii, pp. 459–60, which gives a large number of references.

[2] T. H. Pattison, 'The Hare in representations of the Last Supper', *Notes and Queries*, 1856, 2nd series, vol. ii, p. 490, quoted by C. J. Billson, *Folk-lore*, vol. iii, p. 451, (note 1).

[3] Leviticus xi, 6.

ment on this, and merely mention the alleged anachronism in passing, in order to introduce the question as to whether the hare ever was a sacrificial animal in Europe.

THE HARE FORMERLY A SACRIFICIAL ANIMAL IN EUROPE

Billson, in a long and very interesting article on '*The Easter Hare*', answers this question in the affirmative by citing a considerable body of evidence, based partly on the European custom of eating the Easter Hare, best known in Pomerania, where hares are caught at Eastertide to provide a public meal,[1] and partly on customs still surviving until comparatively recently in England. One such refers to the custom of killing a hare on Good Friday, recorded in a Calendar of State Papers dated 1620.[2]

'*Hunting the Easter Hare*' and the '*Hallaton Hare-pie Scramble*'

The two most detailed accounts of such customs come from Leicestershire. A custom called 'Hunting the Easter Hare' survived late into the eighteenth century, and, as recorded in Throsby's *History of Leicester*, consisted of a mock hunting of the hare in the form of a dead cat[3] trailed before the hounds. The hunt ended at the Mayor's door, whither the dead cat had been trailed, loudly applauded by the populace, whereon the Mayor 'gave a handsome treat to his friends'.[4] This custom fell into disuse about the year 1767, though traces of it lingered in the form of an annual holiday or fair held on Easter Monday. Though Billson comments that from various other items of information 'the hunting was originally, as

[1] C. J. Billson, *Folk-lore*, vol. iii, p. 443, quoting Elton, *Origins of English History*, second edition., 1890, pp. 390.

[2] C. J. Billson, *Folk-lore*, vol. iii, p. 442.

[3] For the connection of hares with cats, see p. 197.

[4] C. J. Billson, *Folk-lore*, vol. iii, pp. 442–3, quoted from Throsby's *History of Leicester*, p. 166.

might be expected, that of a real hare', its sacrificial nature is not very apparent, but becomes more so when it is compared with another custom still in force in the year 1892 in another part of the same country, called the 'Hallaton Hare-pie Scramble and Bottle-kicking'. The word 'Hallaton' is said to mean 'Holy town', and here, 'at a remote period, a piece of land was bequeathed to the Rector conditionally that he and his successors *continued* annually 'two hare pies, a quantity of ale, and two dozen penny loaves, to be scrambled for on each succeeding Easter Monday at the rising ground called Hare Pie Bank".'[1] This land, before the inclosure, was called 'Hare-crop-leys'. When possible, as in 1885, a hare, in sitting posture, was carried on top of a pole. The band, on the occasion recorded, struck up 'See the conquering hero comes', and the hare-pies were duly scrambled for by the spectators, who amused themselves by throwing the contents at one another.[2] Meanwhile, three men abreast have been carrying three wooden bottles, two full of ale, the third a dummy. After the pie-scramble and band playing, one of the large bottles was thrown into the circular hollow on the mound, giving rise to an organized contest for its possession. Next, the dummy was thrown and similarly fought for. Finally the third bottle was taken in triumph to the Market Cross, and its contents drunk with 'due honours'.[3]

Billson, summarizing the two customs, concludes: 'The leading motive of both processions is a hare. In the one case, the hare is followed to the Mayor's house, where a feast is eaten. Whether this feast originally comprised hare's flesh I have not been able to ascertain, though, from an entry in the Chamberlains' accounts, it appears that at one Easter Hunting a great many hares were caught, and these would presumably be used for the Mayor's banquet. At Hallaton the hare is carried in procession (sometimes in the shape of hare-pies, sometimes also mounted on a pole) from the parson's house to a

[1] C. J. Billson, *Folk-lore*, vol. iii, p. 444. [2] ibid., p. 445.

[3] Elsewhere on the Continent, the hare is sometime offered to the parish priest (*Hastings's Encyclopaedia*, p. 518b, quoting *Ann. Soc. Em. Flandre*, 5th series, i, 436).

sacred spot on the boundary of the parish, where the feast of hare-pie is eaten.

'At the Hallaton festival penny loaves are distributed to the people—a common form of survival in sacrificial customs.

'Both these rites take place on Easter Monday, at a season, that is, of special religious solemnity in the spring of the year.'[1]

From this and other evidence he concludes that these customs 'are relics of the religious procession and annual sacrifice of the god',[2] and later infers that 'one of the greatest festivals observed by our early Aryan, perhaps by our pre-Aryan ancestors, must have comprised a similar public and communal procession, in which a god was carried round the district, and afterwards slain and eaten, and this festival took place in the spring of the year'.[3]

The Anglo-Saxon Goddess Eostre and the Germanic Ostara

On the subject of the connection of the hare with Easter, Billson says: 'It has been suggested by Mr. Elton in his *Origins of English History*, that they are survivals of sacrificial rites connected with the worship of the Anglian goddess Eostre, who is mentioned by Bede as giving her name to the great Christian festival. But as to the very existence of this goddess, the opinions of mythologists are divided; for she is referred to only by Bede, and by him only in one passage, to explain the name 'Esturmonath', given to April by the early English.[4] Not a trace of her existence is left among other Teutonic peoples; but as the Germans also speak of "Ostermoneth", whereas all surrounding nations use the Biblical "Pascha", Jacob Grimm gives the goddess a German name also, "Ostara", and labels her, upon etymological grounds, "the divinity of the radiant dawn, of upspringing light, a spectacle that brings joy and blessing, and whose meaning could easily be adapted to the resurrection day of the Christian God".

'In Holtzmann's *German Mythology* she is also referred to as the goddess of Dawn. "The Easter Hare is unintelligible to

[1] C. J. Billson, *Folk-lore*, vol. iii, p. 463. [2] ibid., p. 448.
[3] ibid., p. 463. [4] See p. 180.

me!" he adds, "but probably the hare was the sacred animal of Ostara."'

He goes on: 'Oberle also concludes that the hare which laid the parti-coloured Easter eggs was sacred to the same goddess. Among other authorities who have no doubts as to her existence are W. Grimm, Wackernagel, Simrock, and Wolf. On the other hand, Weinhold rejects the idea on philological grounds, and so do Heinrich Leo and Hermann Oeser. Kuhn says, "The Anglo-Saxon Eostre looks like an invention of Bede", and Mannhardt also dismisses her as an etymological *dea ex machina*.

'The whole question turns, as Oberle says, upon Bede's credibility, with regard to which one is inclined to agree with Jacob Grimm, that it would be uncritical to saddle this eminent Father of the Church, who keeps Heathendom at arms' length and tells us less of it than he knows, with the invention of this goddess. Moreover, the Christianizing of England began at the end of the sixth century, and was completed about the end of the seventh, and as Bede was born in 672, he must have had opportunities of learning the names of heathen goddesses who were hardly extinct in his lifetime.

'But however this may be, whether there ever was a goddess named Eostre, or not, and whatever connection the hare may have had with the ritual of Saxon or British worship, there are good grounds for believing that the sacredness of this animal reaches back into an age still more remote, when it probably played a very important part at the great Spring Festival of the prehistoric inhabitants of this island.'[1]

Other Teutonic Hare-goddesses

The question of the existence or non-existence of a hare-goddess in Europe is, I think, amply answered in the affirmative by:

(*a*) Holtzmann's statement 'that the goddess Freyja was worshipped by the Swedes and Danes under the name "Astrild"—Austr-hildis; "so that Ostara might be Freyja herself

[1] C. J. Billson, *Folk-lore*, vol. iii, pp. 446–8.

or her daughter". It may be noted that Freyja "was attended by hares as her train-bearers and light-bearers".'[1] The mention of light-bearers once more recalls the motive of spiritual illumination so often met with in connection with the hare.

(*b*) The existence of the Saxon goddess holding the pregnant moon cited at the beginning of this section, who clearly, as there stated, goes back to pre-Christian times, but some of the practices and beliefs regarding whom, as seen in the various European customs I have cited, became incorporated into Christian tradition.

Philological evidence of the connection between Easter and the 'east' and 'dawn'

This raises once more the whole question of the meaning of the word 'Easter' itself. Since the Saxon Easter Goddess does seem to have been connected with the hare, and the hare so widely symbolizes 'dawn', and as dawn comes from the east, and Easter is the festival of the Resurrection symbolizing the birth of new life, it had occurred to me to wonder whether the actual word 'Easter' might have a very simple explanation indeed—so simple that philologists and churchmen alike had missed it—namely, that it was in fact cognate to the word 'east' as symbolizing the dawn from which new light came.

It further occurred to me that such a simple and obvious derivation should be susceptible of proof or disproof on plain philological grounds. I therefore inquired of my friend Mrs. Martin-Clarke to know what the derivation of the word actually was. She, like all authorities, pointed out that our only knowledge of the alleged goddess Eostre came from the passage in Bede's *De temporum Ratione*, chapter xv, dealing with the heathen English Calendar, in which April is said to be called Eostur-monath after the goddess Eostre, whose festival was celebrated in that month, which by Christians was called the

[1] See C. J. Billson, *Folk-lore*, vol. iii, p. 447, note 4 (quoting Henderson). Also W. G. Black, *Folk-lore Journal*, vol. i, p. 89. Krappe, *Folk-lore*, vol. iii, quoting Mannhardt, ascribes this note to the Teutonic goddess Holda.

Paschal month.[1] Now, *eo* and *ea* are interchangeable in the Northumbrian dialect that Bede spoke though he wrote in Latin, and in this context we may compare the Northumbrian word for Easter itself, which has the alternative forms *eastro* and *eostro*.

The question arises: Can the forms *Eostre*, *Eastro*, etc., in any way be connected with the adjective 'east', and so with 'dawn'? The Anglo-Saxon for the Christian festival is generally used in the plural, that is to say, *Eastron* (compare Old High German *Ōstarun*), though the two forms of the word beginning respectively with *eo* and *ea* are known, and the root of these is known to be cognate to the Anglo-Saxon adjective 'east' and with the Old Norse *austr*, with which may be compared the Lithuanian *aušra* and the verb *aušta* which means 'day is breaking', and all these are in turn cognate to the Sanskrit *usra* meaning 'dawn'. The insertion of the sound *t* between *s* and *r* is a well-known phonetic phenomenon arising from the difficulty of pronouncing *s* and *r* together without it.

Thus we get Sanskrit *usra* meaning 'dawn' becoming Old Norse *austr* meaning 'east', which has dropped the *r* in the common English pronunciation of our word 'east' when referring to the point of the compass, but has retained it in the name of the Easter festival.

Nor does the philological evidence end here, for allied to the Sanskrit *usra* is also the inferred Hellenic root ἀωσώς (*ausos*) giving rise on the one hand to the Aeolic αὔως, Ionic ἠώς, Doric ἀως, and Attic ἕως, all meaning 'dawn', and on the other hand to the Old Latin form *Ausosa* which (since Indo-European *s* between vowels turns in classical Latin into *r*)[2] becomes the classical *Aurora*, that word for Dawn so dear to poets, and which, like the Anglo-Saxon *Eostre*, is personified in

[1] *The Complete Works of the Venerable Bede*, ed. J. A. Giles, London, 1843, vol. vi, p. 179. Compare also Jacob Grimm, *Teutonic Mythology*, trans. J. S. Stallybrass, London, 1882, vol. i, p. 289, in which the name is spelt Eostra.

[2] Compare, for example, Attic Greek γένος, genitive γένους, from γένεος, originally γένεσος, with Latin *genus*, *generis*.

the form of a goddess. From this it will be seen that our *east*, *Easter*, and the Latin *Aurora*, are cognate, all referring on the material plane to the 'dawn of day', and on the spiritual plane to the Resurrection.

HARE-CUSTOMS CONNECTED WITH THE AUTUMNAL EQUINOX

It will be noted that all the modern European customs hitherto cited have to do with Easter, that is to say, with the period of the vernal equinox, when winter dies and summer is born. Another set of European customs have to do, however, not with the vernal, but with the autumnal equinox when, at harvest, the fruits of summer are transformed into food for man, that is to say when, in the words of the folk-song, 'John Barleycorn must die' and his body become transmuted into human flesh. Here also the hare appears as an emergent symbol, and indeed takes its place among *The Spirits of the Corn and of the Wild* so brilliantly collected and described by Sir James Frazer in his two volumes called by this name.[1]

'Killing the Hare' and 'Cutting the Hare'

The setting in which these customs take place is at the end of harvest, when the area of standing corn is reduced by the reapers to ever smaller and smaller proportions. Every harvester knows the excitement which rises as, coincident with the joy of cutting the grain, the animals that have taken refuge in it make a dash for freedom, pursued with shouts by the reapers. First of the common animals to attempt escape are the rabbits, which from time to time dash for the surrounding hedge. But last of all, as in the case of the burning heath cited at the beginning of this account,[2] the hares cling to their shelter till the very last moment, and do not attempt to leave it till it is so reduced as to afford no further refuge. Then, as the last corn dies, the hare escapes. As Frazer points out: What can this be

[1] Sir James Frazer, *The Golden Bough*, Part V, 'Spirits of the Corn and of the Wild', London, 1933, vol. i, pp. 279–80.

[2] See p. 106.

but the embodied spirit of the corn itself? All round stand the reapers, ready with sticks or other implements to slay it. Thus arises the phrase 'killing the hare' used in many parts of Europe for the man who cuts the last corn, modified in Ayrshire and elsewhere in Scotland to 'cutting the hare', used for cutting the last sheaf which is itself called 'the hare'.[1]

'Hare's blood', the Spartan 'black broth', and the Irish 'Hares of Naas'

Similar customs are recorded from elsewhere in Europe, in all of which the cutting of the last corn appears at one and the same time as a practical and as a sacrificial act, perhaps the most striking of which is the Norwegian custom that the man who is thus said to 'kill the hare' must give 'hare's blood' in the form of brandy to his fellows to drink.[2]

This rite calls to mind the celebrated 'black broth' of the Spartans which was made of the blood and bowels of a hare, and also, very relevant to Mrs. Wright's Irish ancestry, the 'old and peculiar privilege of the Kings of Tara to be fed upon "the hares of Naas", a diet which, as Billson rightly remarks, probably owed its origin to religious ritual'.[3]

'Chasing the Callyach' in Ireland

One last piece of information regarding the hare as a corn spirit or something like it has just been sent to me by my friend the Irish poet Mr. W. R. Rodgers, who, referring to the Northern Irish custom known as 'chasing the callyach'[4] (callyach = a witch or a hare), writes 'In part of County Armagh almost every other farmer keeps a hound (of the beagle kind), and although occasionally I have heard jokes made about the "uselessness" of the hound (i.e. as a watchdog or for herding cattle) yet I have always noted that the hound is petted more

[1] Frazer, *The Golden Bough*, and *British Calendar Customs*, Scotland (London, 1937), vol. i, pp. 80 sqq.

[2] Frazer, *The Golden Bough*, Part V, 'Spirits of the Corn and of the Wild', p. 280.

[3] C. J. Billson, *Folk-lore*, vol. iii, p. 450.

[4] This is the Anglicized spelling. The Irish spelling is *caileach*.

than other dogs, and is looked after well. The hound is kept for the hunting of hares. The season for hunting the hare begins as soon as the harvest is gathered in. Then any farmer's son who wants a hunt takes the horn and goes out and blows it, and immediately all the hounds within earshot come running to where he is. Often too, a "meet" is held, and packs of hounds will be brought to it from considerable distances. It is always the younger farmers and farmers' sons who hunt. The older and more staid men never indulge in it. And "religious" (Protestant) people (and in particular "religious" women) openly condemn the sport, and not from "humane" motives. They condemn it, they say, because it is a "low" sport, and one in which only the riffraff take part. I suspect by riffraff they mean the Catholics and the indigenous people, though Protestants are just as fond of the sport. The men who follow the hunt do not follow it at close range, but move from hill to hill; indeed, any vantage point which allows them to overlook the hunt is used. Custom allows them access to all land, however private. The hare, they say, runs in a circle when hunted and will come back to the place she started from.'

'To attempt to intercept the hare by heading her off, i.e. cutting across the circle she is making in order to catch her in front, is looked on as a very wrong thing. She must be followed by scent. Nor must the hare be trapped in any kind of enclosure as of stone, brick, or (nowadays) wire-netting, but must have a clear run. In England, for example, gamekeepers will leave holes or gaps at the bottom of brick walls to let her through.'

On this interesting account I will make only two observations: first, that 'scent' and noses (particularly dogs' noses) are world-wide symbols for intuition, that is to say, psychological or spiritual knowledge, the kind of knowledge that works in unseen ways (compare Jung's definition of Intuition as 'that psychological function which transmits perceptions *in an unconscious way*',[1] or as 'perception of relations via the unconscious'[2]) as opposed to logical deduction which works by way of

[1] C. G. Jung, *Psychological Types*, London, 1924, pp. 567–8.

[2] C. G. Jung, *The Integration of Personality*, London, 1940, p. 14.

the conscious; and, secondly, that all spiritual knowledge 'goes in circles', that is to say that it has to do with rebirth which is itself a return to the beginning on a different psychic level, as opposed once more to logical deduction which works in a straight line from premise to consciously demonstrable conclusion, and in which 'arguing in a circle' is the greatest sin. If the hare is, in Northern Ireland, as elsewhere, a symbol of intuition, this ritually circular hunting of the hare is what might be expected.

I may here call attention to one further fact, namely, one well known to all hunters of hares and mentioned to Mr. Rodgers by an Irish farmer in connection with this rite, that when caught the hare 'cried like a child'. Since the object of rebirth is to 'become as a little child', its mention in this context may well represent a similar deeply unconscious intuitive motive.

The Hare 'enjoys being hunted'

Mr. Rodgers adds: 'A farmer of my acquaintance in County Armagh, assured me that the hare really enjoys being hunted. As proof of this he adduced the case of a hare which had reared her young close up against the back of a hounds' kennel on his farm. "It liked," he said, "to be near the hounds."'

What better symbolic image could be found of the basic truth enshrined in all 'willing sacrifice' that instinct *wants to be* transformed into spirit?

The ambivalence of the whole problem of spirit and instinct is well expressed in the following poem, written by Mr. Rodgers long before he was aware of the world-wide symbolic significance of this loved but at the same time hunted animal. It is entitled 'Beagles':[1]

Over rock and wrinkled ground
Ran the lingering nose of hound,
The little and elastic hare
Stretched herself nor stayed to stare.

[1] W. R. Rodgers, *Awake! and other Poems*, London, 1941, p. 9.

Stretched herself, and far away
Darted through the chinks of day,
Behind her, shouting out her name,
The whole blind world galloping came.

Over hills a running line
Curled like a whip-lash, fast and fine,
Past me sailed the sudden pack
Along the taut and tingling track.

From the far flat scene each shout
Like jig-saw piece came tumbling out,
I took and put them all together,
And then they turned into a tether.

A tether that held me to the hare
Here, there, and everywhere.

THE HARE MAKES THE ELIXIR OF LIFE

The recent reference to the Kings of Tara feeding upon 'the hares of Naas'[1] brings us back once more to the function of the sacrificial hare as the purveyor of the elixir of life. We have met with this already in China and North America. It will be noted that it is of course never the hare in its natural state that has this power, but only the hare when it has been sacrificed (as, for example, in India when it has reached the moon) that thus acquires this supernatural gift. This is of course the motive of all sacrifice. Thus, in the Mithraic Mysteries it is not till the bull is sacrificed that from its body spring forth all useful herbs, and from its spinal column the wheat that gives us bread, and from the blood flowing from its wounded side issues the vine that produces the sacred drink.[2] These things are of course to be considered symbolically, that is to say as spiritual

[1] See p. 183.

[2] Franz Cumont, *The Mysteries of Mithra* (translated by T. J. McCormick), Chicago, 1903, pp. 136–7.

fact as well as material fact. The supreme example is, of course, the blood and water flowing from the side of Christ, representing abundant life in body and spirit at once. This motive permeates sacrificial acts wherever they are performed and whatever they are. Among primitive peoples the sacrifice of any one species of food-animal is believed to lead to the increase of all food-animals of the same species, and what this really means is that the act when properly carried out, does in fact, by heightening his own instinctive knowledge and thus at the same time increasing his spiritual energy, put man in communion with the beasts and enable him to track them down and slay and eat them, and thus transmute their baser flesh into the more highly organized flesh and spirit of man. In higher religions the material aspect of prosperity tends to disappear and the spiritual to predominate over all others. Thus through the act of consecration in the Christian Mass, which is at the same time a sacrifice, base bread and wine are transformed into the body and blood of Christ, the effect of which is conceived to be primarily a spiritual one, but at the same time does in fact sustain the body through the power it gives to dispense with much unnecessary material food.

It is doubtless due to this spiritualizing effect of sacrifice that the hare is so frequently represented as being pregnant, as, for example, is the case of the Saxon goddess carrying the moon-image on her pregnant part, and of the child dressed up as a hare carrying the Easter eggs.[1]

Examples from European folk-lore

It is quite typical of the degradation of symbolic truth that, from being a spiritual fact, it gradually descends into the realm of superstition till it acquires a purely supposed material connotation and in the end becomes discredited and entirely disregarded. The process of decay is seen in many items of folklore. Billson thus quotes a belief current among the ancient Romans 'that eating hare's-flesh for seven days would make

[1] Compare also pp. 212 sqq. for the Greek view of the hare as a symbol of spiritual pregnancy.

anyone beautiful', a superstition enshrined in one of Martial's epigrams.[1]

Billson and Black both refer to Cogan's *Haven of Health*, written in 1605, in which he says, 'This much will I say as to the commendation of the hare, and of the defence of the hunter's toyle, that no one beast, be it never so great, is profitable to so many and so divers uses in Physicke as the hare and partes thereof', to which Black adds the quotation, 'The ankle-bone of the foote of an hare is good against the cramp'.[2] Black further cites another account to the effect that 'a Dorsetshire mother in the autumn of 1881 was somewhat troubled with the care of recently born twins. "On paying a visit to inquire after the mother, my wife was consulted as to the desirability of a dose of hare's brains (as a soporific). Mentioning the circumstances to my keeper in the hope of eliciting some information as to the prevalence of the belief, he told me that about a fortnight ago the wife of the keeper of the adjoining manor, who had been recently confined, called at his house and told his wife that she had been down to the squire's house to beg a hare's head from the cook in order to give the brains to her baby as a sedative."'[3] Similarly, Robert Burton, in his *Anatomy of Melancholy*,[4] mentions hare's ears applied to the feet among the many remedies against 'fearful dreams', and adds, 'It is good overnight to anoint the face with hare's blood, and in the morning to wash it with strawberry and cowslip water. . . .'

Billson further calls attention to such plant-names as 'harebell' and 'hare-parsley' as having some possible mythological meaning, though he inclines to think that these names are rather due to such facts as that 'harebell' is so called because it grows in places haunted by hares, and 'hare-parsley' because it is eaten by hares.[5]

[1] C. J. Billson, *Folk-lore*, vol. iii, pp. 456–7. See also p. 217 (note 1) of the present volume.

[2] W. G. Black, *The Folk-lore Journal*, vol. i, p. 86.

[3] ibid., p. 90.

[4] Part 2, sect. 5, member 1, subsection 6.

[5] C. J. Billson, *Folk-lore*, vol. iii, p. 457. Note the myrtle-groves to which the hare flees mentioned on p. 189.

HARES AS OMENS

The subject of folk-medicine leads on directly to a consideration of two further aspects of hare lore, namely the use of the hare as an omen and its more recent connection with witches.

Arnold and Boadicea

With regard to its use as an omen, Billson cites several classical instances. 'Thus, in Pausanias,[1] the priest of the moon-goddess [the Taurian Artemis referred to elsewhere[2]] instructs some exiles, who are searching for a propitious place to found a city, to build it in a myrtle grove into which they should see a hare flee for refuge. When Arnold and his German hordes besieged Rome a hare ran towards the walls, and, the Teutons pursuing, a panic seized the Romans, who looked on it as a fatal omen; they deserted the gates without striking a blow, and the barbarians entered.'[3]

Then he mentions the well-known case of Boadicea given by Dio in his *Roman History* [LXII, b] which I will quote here in full, to the effect that 'When the British Queen Boadicea had finished speaking to her people, she employed a species of divination, letting a hare escape from the fold of her dress; and since it ran on what they considered the auspicious side, the whole multitude shouted with pleasure, and Boadicea, raising her hand towards heaven, said, "I thank thee, Andraste . . . I supplicate and pray thee for victory. . . ."'[4]

Hare as fecundatrix

Not unlike this with respect to the part of the body from which the hare was loosed is the account given by de Gubernatis of how 'Philostratos narrates the case of a woman who had miscarried seven times in the act of child-birth, but who

[1] Pausanias, iii, 22.
[2] See pp. 209, 220.
[3] C. J. Billson, *Folk-lore*, vol. iii, p. 453.
[4] Quoted by Ellen Ettlinger,' Omens, and Celtic Warfare', *Man*, vol. xliii (Jan.-Feb. 1943), p. 13. See also Xiphiline, *Mon. Hist. Brit.*, lvii.

the eighth time brought forth a child, when her husband unexpectedly drew a hare out of his bosom. Although the moon is herself the timid and chaste goddess (or eunuch), she is, as pluvial, the *fecundatrix*, and famous as presiding over and predicting child-birth; this is why, when the hare-moon, or Lucina, assisted at parturition, it was sure to issue happily.' Parturition is, of course, another aspect of 'dawn', that is to say, that it also heralds the creation of new life.

Hare, like Moon, sleeps with eyes open. Blind Hare recovers sight by diving

De Gubernatis adds: 'The moon is the watcher of the sky, that is to say, she sleeps with her eyes open; so also does the hare, hence the *somnus leporinus* became a proverb.'[1] This is yet another way of referring to the moon as the 'light in the darkness' symbolizing inner knowledge.[2]

Black cites a cognate German example from more modern times referring to the hare's 'inner eye', saying, 'A blind hare it was, in the North German tale of "The Blue Riband", which ran before the princess, and by plunging in a brook, diving thrice under water, recovered its sight and scampered off, thus teaching her to lead Hans to the same water, with the satisfactory result that after he had plunged in it three times, he, like the hare, recovered his sight.'[3]

This last example is of great interest since it combines the use of the number 3 representing in ancient times the Initiation Process and since Christian times the Redemptive Process, as symbolized in Our Lord's 3-day passage through Death, with the true knowledge that it is only by trust in the healing power

[1] Angelo de Gubernatis, *Zoological Mythology*, London, 1872, vol. ii, pp. 80–1. A curious echo of the belief that the hare sleeps with its eyes open survives still in the modern medical term 'lagophthalmia', from the Greek λαγώφθαλμος, meaning 'hare-eyed'; used for a pathological condition associated with certain complaints such as meningitis and exophthalmia (goitre) in which, owing to the paralysis of the palpebral muscles, the patient is unable to close his or her eyelids.

[2] See also pp. 128 and 221.

[3] W. G. Black, *The Folk-lore Journal*, vol. i, p. 89.

of the deep Unconscious (here as so often, as in baptism, represented by water) that the spiritually blind can indeed receive their sight.

Omens paralleled by and possibly derived from dream symbolism

The use of omens in general appears to me to represent a kind of half-way house between real spiritual understanding and pure superstition, since on the one hand it recognizes the reality of the 'other side' of things in its use of a symbol, but on the other hand depends upon the chance whim of an actual animal (or whatever may be used as an omen) for the answer given. The whole process is exactly parallel to that kind of dream symbolism common to all peoples and no less to ourselves when we examine our dreams, in which the dreamer is, in his dream, actually led by some animal or another to discover the solution to his problem. One such modern dreamer once dreamt that he was asleep, and that a cat jumped on to his bed and brushed his face. In the dream he seemed to wake up, but, as he would do in real life, just turned over to go to sleep again. A second time the cat brushed his face, and this time he became slightly annoyed, being anxious to get all the sleep he could. However, the cat brushed his face yet a third time, this time so violently that he (still in his dream) could sleep no longer and had to sit up and take notice of what the cat wanted. It seemed it wanted to be let out. So, still in his dream, the dreamer opened his bedroom door, whereon the cat led him down the corridor of the modern house in which he actually was, till it arrived at a non-existent door at the end of the corridor, which it indicated it wanted to go through. The dreamer opened the door, and, lo and behold, in this modern house appeared an ancient spiral stone stairway, down which the cat led and he followed. Arrived at the bottom, another corridor revealed itself leading backwards directly beneath the first, which they both passed down till the dreamer found himself in a dream-room situated immediately below the bedroom in which he actually lay sleeping; and in this lower room representing his own Impersonal Unconscious was revealed to him the information which he needed for the solution of the problem which in fact actually beset him.

I believe this to be the kind of dream experience, which is in fact far from infrequent and still crops up constantly in psychological analysis, that gave rise among ancient peoples to the use of animals as omens. It is of course far superior in its efficacy to the observation of external omens, which may be quite fortuitous, because in a dream the dream symbols arise from the dreamer's own unconscious knowledge, or, shall we say, unconscious intuition of what his problem is, whereas external omens do not, unless we think that the human psyche does in fact influence actual animals in their behaviour, which is, of course, not impossible but for which I know of no proof. In any case, it is undoubtedly true that the more we trust to external objects instead of trusting to ourselves, that is to say, to the divine spark in us, the less likely we are to find any solution either for practical or for spiritual problems; and it is presumably for this reason that external omens have now lost all validity, and that we are now being forced once more to find truth in the depths of our own psyche, of which the ultimate centre is the divine spark that is the individual's mirror-image of the divine as approached through revealed religion.

Hare as bad omen

Omens are by no means only *directly* positive, as in the case cited above, but may also be *indirectly* so by pointing to some disaster which may be avoided. Thus, Billson refers to numerous examples from many parts of the world showing that 'to meet a hare is a very bad stroke of luck'. He goes on 'and many people, if they meet a hare when going to work, will return home, and not venture out again until the next meal has been eaten'.[1] The reference to eating is interesting, as in some obscure way referring to a sacrificial meal.

Running Hare portends fire. Impersonal Unconscious the mirror opposite of the Conscious

Gomme also refers to a belief found in south Northampton-

[1] C. J. Billson, *Folk-lore*, vol. iii, p. 454.

shire that 'the running of a hare along the street or mainway of a village portends fire to some house in the immediate vicinity'.[1] Billson refers to a similar belief recorded from Ely and also from Hungary, and says that in the Wheal Vor mine the appearance of a hare presages fatal accident.[2] The particular reference to fire cannot fail to call to mind the Buddhist legends of the hare sacrificing itself by leaping into a fire, and is a typical example of the complete reversal of values when symbolic understanding becomes lost, and is replaced by purely material concepts. For it is a psychological fact of universal application that the unconscious (that is to say, the collective, not the personal unconscious, in other words the spiritual world) is the mirror opposite of the conscious. The outstanding example is, of course, the symbolic interpretation of the death on Calvary as being the necessary precursor of the resurrection, and the Cross being the Tree of Life. The same principle permeates all spiritual understanding, and lies at the base of sacrifice. Fear is itself half of life. This is inevitable and unavoidable. What matters is our attitude towards fear. It will be remembered how 'fear' of the man coming up behind Mrs. Wright in Dream 7 was transmuted by Our Lord's words 'Fear not' into 'awe', whereon the feared stranger turned into a vision of Christ; how she had been horrified at the prospect of sacrificing the hare in Dream 9, but had nevertheless done it and received illumination; and how a similar conquest of fear took place yet again in Dreams 12 and 13; and how, on page 88, it was pointed out that fear is 'seen at its lowest in panic, and at its highest in fear of the Lord'. So, in the case of the Buddha as a hare leaping into the flames, fear was translated into divine knowledge. This was because the act was understood as a symbol, as was the Pentecostal fire descending upon the Apostles' heads, whereas the superstitions just cited, such as that of a hare portending disastrous fire, are due to precisely the same symbolic action conceived through ignorance as representing material fact. That a material outlook of this

[1] G. L. Gomme, 'Totemism in Britain', *Archaeological Review*, vol. iii (March–July 1889), p. 239.

[2] C. J. Billson, *Folk-lore*, vol. iii, p. 454.

kind does actually lead to disaster is seen in the innumerable floods, lightnings, plagues, wars, and other acts of destruction which the God of the Old Testament visited upon His Chosen People whenever they disobeyed Him, and the same fate has now overcome a Europe that has forgotten wisdom and still thinks in terms of economics or national pride of what are in fact the deeply spiritual problems that call for solution all over the world to-day. The individual problem facing Mrs. Wright in Dream 9 was, 'Is this a real hare, or is it a symbol of my own unredeemed nature?' She did not, of course, think in these terms, because it was a problem not of thinking but of intuitive knowledge brought out by the analytical process working in conjunction with a devout nature. But the choice was nevertheless there. Had Mrs. Wright thought in material terms, her gentle soul would have revolted from the sacrifice and her problems would have remained unsolved. But wisdom prevailed. She knew by this time that all things appearing in her dreams were symbols expressing spiritual truths. Trembling with numinous awe, she obeyed the voice which told her to commit what would in material fact have been a crime, but what in a spiritual setting was the highest act of self-sacrifice she could perform, and she had her reward. We in Europe shall not have our reward till we cease thinking in exclusively material terms, as the peasants referred to might think of a material fire caused by the running hare, and till we return to sanity by knowing that the real fire is the spiritual fire which burns but which does not consume, or alternatively that burns out the dross of illusory material values and leaves behind it the essence of truth, as does a wood fire that separates the transitory matter from the essential salts.

THE HARE AS WITCH'S FAMILIAR

Better known than the hare's use as an omen is its notorious role as one of the 'familiar' animals into which witches transform themselves when prosecuting their alleged nefarious designs.

'Participation mystique'

With regard to this kind of supposed transformation, Frazer quotes some relevant passages referring to similar beliefs among still living peoples. Thus, he says, 'The Malays believe that "the soul of a person may pass into another person or into an animal, or rather that such a mysterious relation can arise between the two that the fate of the one is wholly dependent on that of the other"'.[1] This he expands by further references, notably one taken from Codrington to the effect that the Mota word for soul is *atai*. 'The use of the word *atai* in Mota seems properly and originally to have been to signify something peculiarly and intimately connected with a person and sacred to him. . . . Whatever the thing might be the man believed it to be the reflection of his own personality; he and his *atai* flourished, suffered, lived, and died together. But the word must not be supposed to have been borrowed from this use and applied secondarily to describe the soul; the word carries a sense with it which is applicable alike to that second self, the visible object so mysteriously connected with the man, and to this invisible second self which we call the soul. There is another Mota word, *tamaniu*, which has almost if not quite the same meaning as *atai* has when it describes something animate or inanimate which a man has come to believe to have an existence intimately connected with his own. The word *tamaniu* may be taken to be properly '*likeness*', and the noun form of the adverb *tama*, as, "like". It was not everyone in Mota who had his *tamaniu*; only some men fancied that they had this relation to a lizard, a snake, or it might be a stone. . . . It was watched but not fed or worshipped; the natives believed that it came at call, and that the life of the man was bound up with the life of his *tamaniu*, if a living thing, or with its safety; should it die, or if not living get broken or be lost, the man would die.'[2]

This idea of 'sameness' or 'likeness' between a person and

[1] Frazer, *The Golden Bough*, Part VII, 'Balder the Beautiful', London, 1936, vol. ii, p. 197, quoting from Matthes.

[2] R. H. Codrington, *The Melanesians*, Oxford, 1891, pp. 250 sq.

his or her soul-image as externalized in a thing or animal is very relevant here, since it forces us to ask what quality in a witch would persuade her, or those observing her, to associate her soul or second self with a living hare. We must, I think, be careful to distinguish between these two kinds of observation, since there very definitely exists in certain cases a form of what is called *participation mystique* between men and animals, whereby they do indeed to some extent partake of one another's natures. Such a phenomenon exists in somewhat attenuated form among ourselves to-day in the relation between cats, or dogs, and their owners. People having close relation with cats are apt to develop somewhat feline characteristics, and even the cats themselves, those most independent of animals, develop a taste for human company. Much more so is this the case, of course, with dogs. We all know the doggy person with the brusque manner fostered by intimate company with this 'friend of man', and the community of fellowship existing between the real (not the superficial) rider to hounds and not only the hounds he leads but also the fox he hunts, together with the actual honour and admiration he accords to the objects of the chase. This is a fact, whatever we may think of the often artificial nature of fox-hunting to-day.

Nature of the connection between Hares and Witches

This kind of *participation mystique* might well account for the well-known relation existing between witches and cats—particularly black cats, which are, or are said to be, their frequent companions. It is doubtful, however, whether it can account for their association in the popular mind with hares, which appears to me to be due, not to the way in which witches regard themselves, but rather to the way in which *others* regard *them.*

This leads us to inquire just what a witch is. With regard to this question, there is little doubt that, in the first place, a witch is a woman with a highly developed intuitive faculty. There are, of course, white witches and black, that is to say, women who use their intuitive faculty or second-sight for good purposes or bad. In either case, intuition is to the onlooker always a surprising faculty, one that takes short cuts, leaps to conclusions (whether right or wrong), and generally behaves in what, to the less gifted in this way, appears to be an odd and somewhat mysterious manner. That is to say, that the intuitive faculty behaves not unlike a hare with regard to the hare's sudden appearances, its fleetness, its power of leaping so often met with in these pages, as well as its March madness when during the mating season it throws all other considerations to the winds in its pursuit of the desired object.

In the second place, witches, being introvert, usually compensate for their intense inner activity with an outwardly retiring nature giving the appearance of timidity or reserve, corresponding to the proverbial timidity of the hare, which gives rise to such expressions as 'he (or she) is timid as a hare' and to the refusal of certain peoples to eat the hare lest it would make the eater faint-hearted.

Coupled with these is the soft appearance of the hare, which (as in the case of the cat, another animal popularly associated with witches, especially when black) tends to make us think of it as a 'female' animal rather than as a male;[1] just as, in the opposite sense, dogs, whether in fact male or female, tend to be regarded as 'male'. Examples of the interchangeability of cats with hares in Europe are very frequent. Such are the contrasted statements that 'At Aurich, in East Friesland, the man who reaps the last corn "cuts the hare's tail off". In mowing down the last corner of a field French reapers sometimes call out, "We have the cat by the tail".'[2] And, with regard to witches, we have the numerous examples given by Frazer of the 'wounds inflicted on a witch-hare or witch-cat . . . seen on the witch herself'.[3]

Lastly, hares are hunted animals, and so, commonly, in Europe at least, was the witch.

[1] Hares are popularly referred to by huntsmen as 'puss', a term that appears to have originated in the seventeenth century, that is to say, in the age in which witch-hunting was so prevalent.

[2] J. G. Frazer, *The Golden Bough*, Part V, 'Spirits of the Corn and of the Wild', London, 1933, vol. i, p. 268.

[3] Frazer, *The Golden Bough*, Part VII, 'Balder the Beautiful', London, 1936, vol. i, pp. 316 sqq.

Witches transformed into Hares

Examples of witches being thought to turn themselves into hares are so numerous that only a few must be cited. Thus, Henderson tells us that 'The Hare is the most common disguise of the witch in all the northern countries of Europe'.[1] For example, 'Fishers of Fifeshire "look on all maukens (hares) to be devils and witches, and if they but see a sight of a dead mauken it sets them a trembling".'[2]

More familiar are such examples as those given by Frazer in his quotation of the sixteenth-century writer who states that the Irish 'account every woman who fetches fire on May-day a witch, nor will they give it to any but sick persons, and that with an imprecation, believing she will steal all the butter the next summer. On May-day they kill all the hares they find among their cattle, supposing them the old women who have designs on the butter. They imagine the butter so stolen may be recovered if they take some of the thatch hanging over the door and burn it.'[3]

Burning the Witch-Hare a purificatory measure

Not quite so familiar is the statement that in the Isle of Man, on May-day (Old Style) the break of day 'was the signal for setting the ling or gorse on fire, which was done for the sake of burning out the witches, who are wont to take the shape of hares'.[4]

This cannot fail to call to mind the catching alight of hares hiding in bracken cited near the beginning of this inquiry,[5] and its association with the spectacle of the self-sacrificing Buddha leaping into the flames in order to purify himself. The burning of witches, whether under the guise of hares or not, is also a purificatory sacrifice, but one of a very different kind,

[1] For this and other references see C. J. Billson, *Folk-lore*, vol. iii, p. 455. Witches also, apparently, had the power of changing men into hares, as was the case with the famous wizard, Sir Michael Scott, who was turned into a hare by the witch of Falsehope.

[2] W. G. Black, *The Folk-lore Journal*, vol. i, pp. 86–7.

[3] Frazer, *The Golden Bough*, Part I, 'The Magic Art and the Evolution of Kings', London, 1932, vol. ii, p. 53.

[4] ibid., p. 54. [5] See p. 106.

being indeed quite the other way round, since, instead of the corruptible body of the hare-Buddha sacrificing itself in order to transform itself for the good of the world into spirit, it is here the evil spirit of the witch which is supposedly destroyed in order to re-humanize the witch. Thus, in Frazer's view, which is most probably correct, 'the reason for burning a bewitched animal alive is a belief that the witch herself is in the animal, and that by burning it you either destroy the witch completely or at least unmask her and compel her to resume her proper human shape, in which she is naturally far less potent for mischief than when she is careering about the country in the likeness of a cat, a hare, a horse, or what not'.[1]

Nevertheless, it is more than possible that the belief concerning the self-sacrifice of Buddha and the practice of sacrificing the hare-witch, the first positive and the second negative, may have a common psychological origin, since Frazer regards the burning of witches and their supposed changelings as but a faint echo of the august rites of Beltane and Hallowe'en. Thus the burning of the hare-witch on the Isle of Man just cited occurred during the May Day rites attendant on what he refers to as '"the Druidical anniversary of Beil or Baal. . . . On the first of May, 1837, the Baal fires were, as usual on that day, so numerous as to give the island the appearance of a general conflagration." By May Day in Manx folk-lore is meant May Day, Old Style, or *Shenn Laa Boaldyn*, as it is called in Manx.'[2]

This burning he refers back to the practice, still mirrored in our present burning of Guy Fawkes on November 5th, of including the burnt sacrifice of men and animals at the ancient fire festivals of Beltane and Hallowe'en, and considers it to be due to a desire 'to break the power of witchcraft by burning or banning the witches and warlocks',[3] saying that 'the mode of

[1] Frazer, *The Golden Bough*, Part VII, 'Balder the Beautiful', London, 1936, vol. i, p. 321.

[2] ibid., p. 157.

[3] Frazer, *The Golden Bough*, Part VII, 'Balder the Beautiful', vol. ii, p. 41. He adds 'the victims most commonly burned in modern bonfires have been cats, and . . . cats are precisely the animals into which, with the possible exception of hares, witches were most usually supposed to transform themselves'.

execution by fire was chosen because . . . burning alive is deemed to be the surest mode of getting rid of these notorious and dangerous beings'. This seems to me to be a very negative way of looking at it (a view most certainly held by the actual burners of witches, and of the hares or other animals into which the witches may have been deemed to be transformed), but I submit that with regard to the human and animal sacrifices of the so-called Druids it would appear far more probable that this burnt-sacrifice was much more akin to the burnt-sacrifices of the Old Testament and many peoples in the pre-Christian era, and that these also were due to the same motive that inspired the Buddha when in the form of a hare he leapt into the flames in order to destroy his earthly body, not as a punishment but as a fulfilment whereby flesh was transformed into spirit for the benefit of all people.

The degradation of this positive sacrificial concept of purifying *oneself* into the negative one of getting rid of the evil in *others* is a typical misconception only too common in everyday life among all those who persist in seeing the 'mote' in their brother's eye but not the 'beam' in their own, and so project their own faults on others, as the good Christians of the witch-burning period projected their own negative psychological contents upon the unfortunate witches whom they thus destroyed instead of looking to the purging of their own sinful natures.

Degradation of a symbol. The Hare an 'uncanny animal'

With regard to this final stage of degradation in the mythological hare's progress throughout the centuries, all far-seeing writers on the subject agree that this is due to a total misconception of the unseen forces that rule human life—in fact to the intolerance of established and over-intellectualized dogmatists towards the older manifestations of spiritual activity that later forms have, for the time being at least, superseded. To quote from one only, W. G. Black, speaking of the lost 'high estate' of the hare, says, 'It did not at once acquire the repute of being either stupid or inspired by a witch. . . . The animal had been sacred, and the tradition perhaps shown in the use of the hare in augury perhaps [*sic*] was that the remembrance of this holiness long lingered. From primitive regard the descent is generally rapid, and we readily find an explanation for the hare's connection with witchcraft in the degradation of its character from the days of Buddha—a sacred animal becomes an uncanny animal, as heathen gods become devils when their worshippers change their faith. The process is a very common one.'[1]

Use of Silver Coins for shooting the Witch-Hare recalls Moon-symbolism

Nevertheless, even in the degraded era of witch-hunting, the connection between the moon and the hare still subsists, though under a disguised form. It is well known that, of the two precious metals known to the ancient world, gold represents the sun and the male element, and silver represents the moon and female. Thus we are all familiar with the superstition of turning over the silver in our pocket when seeing the new moon, in order to render the moon favourable to us, in the same way that we are all taught as children to utter the word 'hares' or 'rabbits' on the first day of each new month. It is, therefore, of interest to read Frazer's statement, supported by references to a very large number of authorities on folk-lore, that 'the only way to make sure of hitting a witch-animal is to put a silver sixpence or a silver button in your gun'.[2] Black also cites two cases of a similar nature.[3] It is sometimes stated that only a crooked sixpence will do. This is presumably an allusion to the 'crooked' nature of the witch's negative intuition, but the insistence on the round silver object representing the moon is quite clearly due to the kind of symbolism which speaks of 'paying a man out in his own coin', that is to say, that in order to counteract the intuitive moon-knowledge of the witch an equally powerful moon-symbol must be used. The value placed on this is indicated by the use else-

[1] W. G. Black, *The Folk-lore Journal,* vol. i, p. 89.

[2] Frazer, *The Golden Bough*, Part VII, 'Balder the Beautiful', vol. i, p. 316. Compare the account given on p. 173 of the game of thrusting a silver coin into the Easter egg.

[3] W. G. Black, *The Folk-lore Journal,* vol. i, p. 87.

where for the same purpose and in the same way of a consecrated wafer. Thus, 'Again, in the Vosges Mountains a great big hare used to come out every evening to take the air at the foot of the Mont des Fourches. All the sportsmen of the neighbourhood tried their hands on that hare for a month, but not one of them could hit it. At last one marksman, more knowing than the rest, loaded his gun with some pellets of a consecrated wafer in addition to the usual pellets of lead. That did the trick.'[1]

Degradation of attitude towards Witches and Ghosts

One of the most recent writers on the hare says, 'We are probably right in assuming that the lunar association of the hare made the shy animal "uncanny" in the eyes of primitive folk.'[2] This may be partly the case, but only, in my opinion, in so far as the feeling of awe is degraded through lack of real spiritual understanding into one of fright, as we now almost universally fear ghosts, whereas among truly primitive people ghosts are not considered as being hostile, but as being fundamentally friendly unless offended from one cause or another. Among most so-called (but not really) primitive peoples, love, reverence, and fear of ghosts alternate and intermingle according to circumstance, though among those Malekulans amongst whom I have lived the dominating feeling is one of love and reverence, unless the ghost has been injured in some way, either at the moment of death through being killed and so denied due burial, or else because after death it has not been duly honoured.[3] The problem with regard both to ghosts and to the hare, as to all other mythologically conceived phenomena, lies in the extent to which spiritual forces are honoured or not. It is a fact that if they are not honoured they become evil, and are responsible for the evil elements in the world, whereas if

[1] Frazer, *The Golden Bough*, Part VII, 'Balder the Beautiful', vol. i, p. 318. For further information on Hares and Witches, see article on the Hare in the *Handwörterbuch des deutschen Aberglaubens.*

[2] Alexandre H. Krappe, 'Old Celtic Taboos', *Folk-lore*, vol. liii, Dec. 1942, p. 201.

[3] See John Layard, *Stone Men of Malekula*, pp. 629 sqq.

they are honoured they become good, and yield up their power for the betterment of mankind, instead of this same power tending otherwise to its destruction. No primitive man, as no modern man who is not sunk in materialism, has any doubt that such powers exist, but if the heart that wields this power is evil, evil will ensue, and *vice versa*. But power it is, and cannot be destroyed, and if it is not allowed to work for good it will inevitably work for harm. As I envisage the problem, this has all along been the trouble with European witchcraft. For there have always and among all people been evil witches and good, that is to say, that there have always been women with strong intuitive powers, who have been forced to use these powers in an occult way, partly because society is in most places dominated by men, and partly because women are more closely in touch with earth-forces than men, who tend more towards social and less towards hidden modes of expressing their vital force.

This brings us back to the alleged 'fickleness' and 'unpredictable' nature of women (a reputation imposed on them naturally by men, because women's logic happens to be different from theirs) and to their consequent association with the vagaries of the moon, and, so far as the subject of this inquiry is concerned, with the elusive hare. There is little doubt that, logical thinking being predominantly a male function and intuition a female one, the persecution of witches in Europe was largely due to an over-systematized phase of man-dominated religion that led men to suspect all truly intuitive activities of women as bad and therefore as something to be eradicated at all cost—at the cost, as it has indeed turned out, of devitalizing men's own spiritual understanding, as is so evident to-day.

The uncanniness of the Hare as evidence of former sacredness

However this may be, the moon, having become the object of mere astronomical observation, has suffered a similar eclipse so complete that we use the word 'lunatic', derived from the Latin *luna*, the moon, exclusively as a synonym for 'insane'. The hare, too, once the symbol of radiant dawn and positive intuitive knowledge, has suffered a similar eclipse, and has come to be regarded, as Black puts it, as 'one of the most melancholy of animals in popular opinion'.[1] Thus, not unnaturally, 'Sir Thomas Browne tells us that in his time there were few above threescore years that were not perplexed when a hare crossed their path'.[2] He refers, of course, to a dying superstition, even in his day remembered only by the old. Even the hare itself seems to be conscious of its despised state, if we are to judge by the statement in Turberville's *Book on Hunting and Falconry* that 'the hare first taught us the use of the hearbe called Wyld Succory, which is very excellent for those who are disposed to be melancholicke: shee herselfe is one of the most melancholicke beasts that is, and to heale her own infirmitie she goeth commonly to sit under that hearbe'.[3]

Instances of the hare's uncanniness and of the consequent tendency to regard it as an unlucky omen could be multiplied, but space and patience will not allow, and I will content myself with one more quotation from Billson regarding his view of the reason. He says, 'The main evidence for the ancient sacredness of the hare rests upon its subsequent unpopularity, and the superstitions which cluster round it. It is of course a matter of common observation that the deities of one age become the devils of another; that, in the lapse of years, objects which were formerly worshipped and held in pious honour become, under a new dispensation, the most ill-omened and outcast. Thus we may often argue back from the present unpopularity of an animal to its former divinity.'[4]

With regard to those two factors most commonly associated with the hare, namely 'Moon' and 'Women', we have in a nutshell two of the most far-reaching transformations in history, from moon-worship to sun-worship, and from matriarchy to the almost exclusively patrilineal system that has ruled the

[1] W. G. Black, *The Folk-lore Journal*, vol. i, p. 85.

[2] ibid., p. 84.

[3] Quoted by W. G. Black, *The Folk-lore Journal*, vol. i, p. 85. Compare Prince Henry's question in Shakespeare's *King Henry IV*, Part I, Act 1, Scene 2, 'What sayest thou to a hare, or the melancholy of Moorditch?' to which Falstaff replies, 'Thou hast the most unsavoury similes.'

[4] C. J. Billson, *Folk-lore*, vol. iii, p. 453.

modern world and now only shows signs of being modified, or at least balanced by the rediscovery of the true role of women in our man-ridden world, a role that will not be one of rivalling men at men's jobs, but of reinstating the earth-value of the female element in life, to the neglect of which the instability of modern life is so largely due. Perhaps, when this is accomplished, we shall return to the view expressed in Russian and Chinese folk-tales, that the hare is associated with the Waters of Life,[1] or to the more moderate one expressed in many other tales of it as 'an exceptionally wise and crafty spirit, the guide of men, and the protector of other animals', as in China where the hare appears as 'the guardian of the wild beasts, and defends the lamb from the wolf',[2] though it is true that yet other folk-tales represent him as 'the crafty guardian and shifty schemer'.[3]

The Hare as symbol of the Repentant Sinner

I may perhaps quote here a phrase pregnant with meaning which I happen to have run across almost by chance in a Dictionary of Art to the effect that the hare is 'a symbol of the repentant sinner returning to God, as for example, in a representation carved in marble in the Catacombs of a hare running towards a dove which has an olive branch in its beak'. The entry closes, 'The hare later becomes a symbol of fear'.[4]

What better epitaph could there be on the death of spiritual love, and its substitution by all that is most negative under a superimposed feeling of the wrong kind of guilt?

HARE TOTEMS AND TABOOS

Many authors, including Andrew Lang, Black, Billson, and others, have discussed the claims of the hare to be a totem animal. There is no doubt that a number of non-European cases of hare-totemism occur. The definitions of totemism are

[1] C. J. Billson, *Folk-lore*, vol. iii, p. 461.
[2] ibid., p. 461, quoting De Gubernatis, ii, 79.
[3] ibid., quoting de Gubernalis, ii, 76–7.
[4] *Kunstlelexikon*, by Wilhelm Spemann, Berlin and Stuttgart, 1905, under the heading *Hase*.

so various, however, that I do not propose to go into this question here, but will simply refer to some of the supposed relics of hare-totemism in Europe.

The most frequently quoted of these is Julius Caesar's statement (*De Bello Gallico*, v, 12) regarding the Britons that 'they may not eat the hare, chicken, or goose, but kept these animals for pleasure'.[1] Krappe adds regarding the hare, 'There can be no doubt as to the correctness of Caesar's statement: as late as the nineteenth century the peasants of western Brittany could hardly endure to hear the name of the animal. In parts of Wales hares were not killed down to the reign of Queen Victoria; in the south-west parts of England the peasants, as late as the last century, would eat neither hare nor rabbit. The peasants of Kerry, Ireland, are even now said to abstain from hare, whatever the reason alleged.'[2] He further adds a long list of other countries or districts scattered throughout the world in which the hare is for religious reasons taboo.[3]

Taboo against pronouncing the names of the Hare or of Women at sea

There is also in the British Isles a widespread aversion to uttering the name of the hare, particularly at sea. Thus 'Mr. Gregor notes that to say to a fisherwoman of the north-east of Scotland that there is a hare's foot in her creel, or to say to a fisherman that there is a hare in his boat, arouses great ire, and calls forth strong words; the word "hare" is not pronounced at sea. In Cornwall a maiden who has been deceived and dies, haunts her deceiver in the guise of a white hare, sometimes saving his life, but in *the end* causing his death.'[4]

Billson also records that the prohibition against uttering the word 'hare' at sea is found amongst the fishermen of the west of Ireland.[5] The writer of this article is himself familiar with

[1] 'Leporem et gallinam et anserem gustare fas non putant; haec tamen alunt animi voluptatisque causa.'

[2] A. H. Krappe, *Folk-lore*, 1942, pp. 198–9.

[3] See also C. J. Billson, *Folk-lore*, vol. iii, p. 450, for an even longer list.

[4] W. C. Black, *The Folk-lore Journal*, vol. i, p. 87.

[5] C. J. Billson, *Folk-lore*, vol. iii, p. 452.

the fishermen of a Cornish village, among whom, even as late as twenty-five years ago when he himself went fishing with them, it was still absolutely forbidden to mention either a hare or women on board a fishing-boat. The taboo against mentioning women is commonly attributed to the fear of mutual jealousy among the crew, but no reason is given for not mentioning hares. The taboo against uttering the name of the hare may of course be a relic of totemism, itself a highly specialized and socialized form of the kind of *participation mystique* which I have spoken of above, but which, though it presumably had its origin in individuals, has in totemic societies been adopted and, so to speak, conventionalized by a whole community.

There is, indeed, with regard to the subject under discussion, at least one relevant attribute held in common between hares, women, and the sea which might give rise to the phenomenon known as 'linked totems', and this is the unpredictability to men of the way in which all three appear to behave. It will be remembered, however, that the sea is subject in the movement of tides to the moon, so that to this trio the moon must also be added, which seems to bring this superstition in line with the general configuration of hare associations now seen to be almost world-wide. Whether this be indeed a totemic configuration or not I am unable to say. The taboo against mentioning hares or women may, on the other hand, be a quite simple case of it being considered unwise to mention lightly, while under her sway, the goddess that rules the waves. Or, alternatively, it may be that formerly the hare-moon-goddess was necessarily invoked during sea voyages, and that this pre-Christian custom brought down on it the anathema of the Church according to the law by which many heathen customs become prohibited on the introduction of a new religion, but nevertheless live on under a negative guise.

THE HARE IN CLASSICAL ANTIQUITY

The connection of the hare with Easter, and through this with the Anglo-Saxon goddess Eostre, and in later times in Europe with witches, leads on to the last lap in this summary of the hare's mythical attributes, namely, to the beliefs held concerning this animal and to its symbolic use in classical times in Greece and Rome.[1]

THE HARE AS AN OMEN. AESCHYLUS'S ACCOUNT OF THE TWO EAGLES DEVOURING A PREGNANT HARE

A few references have already been made in passing to the use made by the Romans of the hare as an omen and in various other symbolic ways.[2]

Perhaps the best-known reference to the hare in classical Greek writing is, however, the famous passage in Aeschylus's *Agamemnon* (lines 104–39) in which the chorus reports an omen that appeared outside the palace as the army assembled under the leadership of Agamemnon and Menelaus before setting out for the siege of Troy. The chorus tells how two eagles, one black and one white, were seen feeding on a hare 'richly pregnant with young which had missed the last laps of its race' (see Fig. 15). Calchas interpreted the two eagles as representing the two princes Agamemnon and Menelaus, and declared

[1] It is worth mentioning that, though in late classical times the ancients sometimes confused the hare with the rabbit and the Greeks called the rabbit by a variety of names formed from diminutives of the word λαγῶς meaning a hare, such as 'half-hare', 'little hare', etc., no such confusion can have occurred earlier than the first century B.C. before which rabbits were unknown in classical lands, having been introduced, probably from Spain, for the first time about this date. As all the most important references cited in this section date from before the time when the rabbit was introduced, there is no doubt whatever that the animal referred to in them is definitely a hare.

[2] See pp. 189, 190, 205.

FIGURE 15. Two Eagles feeding upon a Hare

(see Aeschylus's *Agamemnon*, lines 104-39) Silver tetradrachm of Akragas, in the British Museum. About 413-6 B.C. After Hill, *Select Greek Coins*, Pl. 58, 2

that the omen signified that the army would capture and pillage Troy. The passage ends with the assertion that Artemis, who was antagonistic to the expedition, was angry with the two eagles for eating and killing the hare.

In view of what the hare symbolizes in other parts of the world, it is clear that we have here a symbolic representation of these two princes imbibing intuitive knowledge of what would be necessary to the success of their quest. In terms of what they set out to achieve, the hare which they devoured presumably represented Troy, that city of so great mythological import symbolizing the womb pregnant with the stolen graces of Helen, who was herself a pre-Christian symbol of the Holy Grail abounding with all those spiritual gifts symbolized by physical beauty that men desire and for which the Greeks were willing to sacrifice so much life, treasure, and time.[1] On yet another level of interpretation, it is clear that the hare having 'missed the last laps of its race' indicated the sacrifices that yet had to be made, or possibly the time that must elapse, before the end was achieved and the full pregnancy of satisfaction could be attained. It will be remembered that the moment of victory came when the Greeks sprang fully armed from out the belly of the horse (Aeschylus elsewhere refers to them as the horse's nestlings—in Norse mythology the horse gave birth to all the world), and it would be quite typical of the dream mind from which mythology is made to use this as a symbol for the birth of the hare's young representing the spiritual power that had been incubating inside the bodies of the Greek leaders until the final release of these powers resulting in the capture of Troy and the redemption of the lost treasure in the form of Helen.

The obvious connection, in this account, of the hare with

[1] Compare Oliver St. J. Gogarty in *Others to Adorn*, London, 1938, pp. 39 and 82, on the cock about to mount the hen, 'your body all a Troy to house desire', and 'I give more praise to Troy's redoubt, For love kept in, than was kept out'. For these and some other references in this section I am indebted to my friend Mr. W. F. Jackson Knight, who has a very great perception for the symbolism underlying much classical literature.

love and pregnancy, leads on to an examination of two aspects of Greek culture with regard to this animal that are so different from anything hitherto mentioned as to be almost in a category by themselves. The first has to do with beliefs about the actual animal's own supposed peculiar reproductive ability, and the other with what is clearly connected with this, namely, the symbolic use to which this reproductive ability is put in the employment of the hare in Greek art and literature as a love-symbol and aphrodisiac.

BIOLOGICAL BELIEFS REGARDING THE HARE'S FERTILITY

For Greek beliefs regarding the abnormal fertility and peculiar reproductive ability of the hare I am indebted to the account given in Pauly-Wissowa's great Classical Encyclopaedia,[1] from which the following quotation taken from the article on the Hare, and translated into English, is made. The part of the article cited itself consists entirely of summaries of and quotations from classical authors. It says:

'Hares mate at very frequent intervals, that is to say, every month during the whole summer, and females conceive even while still pregnant. They produce milk even before the young are born. Nor do they bring forth their young all at one time, but at irregular intervals whenever they wish, and the young are born blind.[2] It is said further that during pregnancy the uterus contains nipples within itself (for the unborn young to suck from).[3] Herodotus certainly exaggerates when he asserts that, while the female is still carrying her young, some of whom are already befurred, while others are not, and a third part are only beginning to take shape, she conceives yet again. It is, however, pertinent to note that the Father of History [Herodotus] remarks that God bestowed particular fertility on

[1] Pauly's *Real-Encyclopädie der Classischen Altertumswissenschaft*, neue Bearbeitung von Georg Wissowa, Stuttgart, 1894.

[2] Aristotle, *Historia Animalium*, vi, 33, p. 579b, 30.

[3] ibid., iii, 1, p. 511a, 29.

all creatures that are at the same time timid and edible.[1] Aelian[2] relates a remarkable tale which I will here give in his own words: "A huntsman of my acquaintance, an honest fellow incapable of lying, told me this queer story. He affirmed that male hares not only beget, but bear young and suffer the pains of labour, and rear as many as two or three. This seemed to me at first to be quite unbelievable, but the following incident confirmed it. He assured me that he had himself found a male hare half-dead, whose belly was swollen. He cut it open, and in fact found within it a uterus containing three young. When he took them out, they lay as still as a lump of meat; but as soon as the sun warmed them they came to life. One of them stirred, then opened its eyes, put out its tongue, and opened its mouth for hunger. He naturally gave the little ones milk to drink and successfully reared them, which seems to me proof of their miraculous birth. I cannot bring myself to doubt this story, since, as I have said already, the man was neither a liar nor a boaster." Female hares are said also to bear young without having a male to impregnate them.[3] According to Aristotle, the great fertility of the hare is caused by the possession of a womb divided into several parts,[4] shown outwardly by the unusual thickness of the fur.[5] All animals have an evil smell during their mating season,[6] so that the hare has it almost the whole year[7] though it is true that young hares have it also.'[8]

Apart from noting that the ancients had, of course, many erroneous notions regarding natural history, it is not necessary

[1] Aristotle, *Historia Animalium*, iii, 108; cf. Pliny, *Historia Naturalis*, viii, 219, x, 179, 182; Xenophon, *Cynegeticus*, v, 12; Aristotle, *Historia Animalium*, v, 9, p. 542, 6, 31; *Physics*, ed. Ideler, i, 178; Plutarch, *Moralia*, 829b.

[2] Aelian, *Historia Animalium*, xiii, 12. (It should be noted that Aelian is a humorous Roman writer who wrote in Greek but is said never to have been in Greece.)

[3] Archelaus, quoted by Pliny, *Historia Naturalis*, viii, 218.

[4] Aristotle, *Problemata*, x, 14, p. 892b, 1.

[5] ibid., *de Generatione Animalium*, iv, 5, p. 774a, 31.

[6] Theophrastus, *de Odoribus*, 61.

[7] ibid., *Historia Plantarum*, vi, 20, 4.

[8] Xenophon, *Cynegeticus*, v, 13.

to comment on these very interesting beliefs except to point out the obvious connection between the attribution of miraculous fertility, here attached to the hare as an actual animal, and the attribution of divine reproductive power akin to 'grace' attached by other peoples to the hare as a symbol. It may well be asked which of the two attributions, the symbolic or the material, came first. Folk-lorists of the materialistic school will doubtless favour the latter, but I incline to think that while the hare may indeed be prolific (and it must not be forgotten that hares and rabbits were in late classical times often confused) this would not by itself be enough to account for the above reports, and that the widespread ideas about the supernatural attributes of the hare may also have played their part in producing these 'miraculous' stories.

THE HARE AS A LOVE-SYMBOL

Very different from the crude biological beliefs cited above are the conceits mentioned in Greek literature and above all depicted in Greek works of art regarding the hare as a love-gage, and in particular its close association with Aphrodite and Cupids and the Bacchic mythical and ritual cycle.

When the Greek gods were gathered together by man's ingenuity upon Olympus and had become the objects of speculation and the pegs on which the mingled intellectual and artistically imaginative fantasies of this gifted people could be hung, among other things the hare had its place in this cosmogony. How far the love-gage was conceived as actual—for it is depicted also as taking place between mortals—and how far it symbolized a more spiritual union I leave the reader to judge from the evidence cited below, culled mainly from an article on vase-paintings published as long ago as 1862 in the *Compte-rendu* of the Russian Imperial Archaeological Commission,[1] relevant passages from which I here render in English.

[1] Ludolf Stephani, *Erklärung einiger Vasengemälde der Kaiserlichen Ermitage, Compte-Rendu de la Commission Impériale Archéologique pour l'année* 1862, St. Petersburg, 1863. The pages quoted are pp. 62 to 73. I am indebted to Dr. H. Meinhard for calling my attention to this work. I here give only some of the numerous refer-

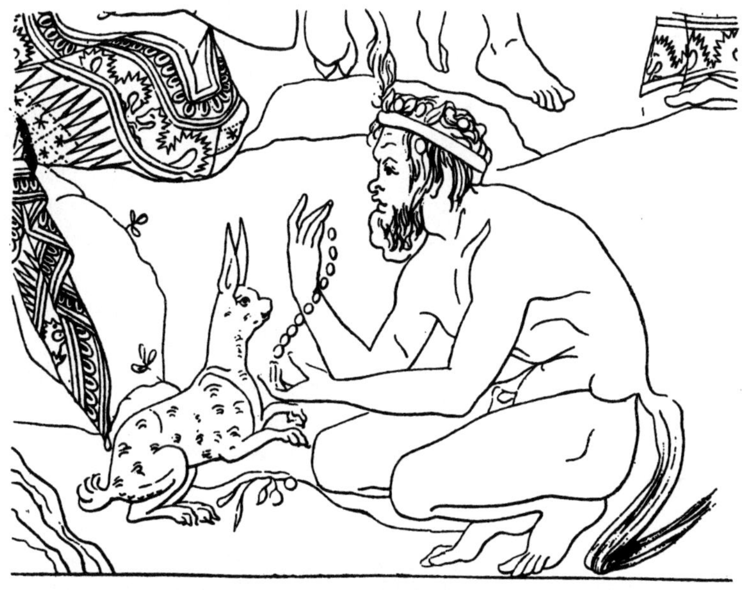

Fig. 16. A Satyr playing with a Hare

From a clay calyx-krater in the Jatta collection at Ruvo. Attic work of the early fourth century B.C. After *Monumenti dell' Instituto*, 2 Pl. 59.

Satyrs, Maenads and the Bacchic ritual cycle

The author begins with a catalogue of the various appearances of the hare in connection with Satyrs without any too obvious mythological or symbolic import. On the first vase he mentions, a Satyr wearing a white band in his hair is seen trying to catch a hare which in its turn tries to escape. He goes on, 'Similarly on a coin of Messana, Pan is about to seize a hare,

ences to the Greek and Latin authors cited. Those interested in further study are referred for more detailed references to the work in question.

The subject is very briefly handled in the article 'Hase' in Otto Keller's *Die Antike Tierwelt*, Leipzig, 1909, p. 216, containing a few further items of information, as for instance that wedding-rings were often decorated with the image of a hare.

and on an incised gem the same god is seen in the act of disembowelling a game animal, apparently a hare, hung on a tree'.

'In a famous representation of the myth of Io, a Satyr[1] is seen playing with the same animal, holding out to it a string of beads (see Fig. 16). On a marble relief a Satyr is seen teasing a panther by dangling a hare before it, while another Satyr in the form of a Herm[2] offers the same animal to the young Dionysus himself to play with. A vase painting by Amasis shows two Maenads presenting a hare to the bearded Dionysus, and in another beautiful vase-painting a Maenad named Tragoedia does the same.[3] On an incised gem the cult image of Dionysus himself appears to be holding a hare in his hand.'

'One vase-painter portrays six Satyrs armed with clubs chasing a hare. On the base of a candelabrum in the Imperial Hermitage is depicted a Satyr bringing a captured hare for sacrifice, and on each of two incised gems is seen a Satyr triumphantly holding up his prey.'

'Another vase-painting shows a hare in a cave attending a meeting between Dionysus, a Maenad, and a Satyr, while in a third Dionysus joins the Satyrs and the Maenads in greeting Apollo who is seen approaching upon a swan (see Fig. 17). On a fourth vase-painting two Satyrs watch a pair of hares playing together, and on a Roman marble relief a hare puts in an appearance at a Bacchic sacrifice.'

'Lastly, with regard to a relief in the Villa Albani, the meaning of which is difficult to grasp, the presence of the *thyrsos*[4] and the mask can hardly leave any doubt of the fact

[1] The Satyrs and Cupids that figure so largely in the following account both have the common characteristic that they playfully do everything and anything they like, a fitting symbol of that carefree attitude to life that also informs the Graeco-Roman symbolic attitude towards the hare.

[2] A herm is a small pillar surmounted by a human head, with the human genitals carved on the pillar. It has been supposed that all Greek gods were originally represented in this way, but by the fourth century B.C. in Athens they were all held to represent Hermes, whence the word 'herm.'

[3] The Maenad in this painting holds the hare behind Dionysus's back.

[4] A sacred wand.

FIGURE 17. Apollo riding upon a swan, with Hare beneath

The other figures are of two women (Muses?) and a Satyr. Clay bell-krater in the British Museum. Attic work of the early fourth century B.C.

FIGURE 18. Luxuria, accompanied by a Hare
Drawing by Pisanello now in the Albertina in Vienna

J. Mathey, *Portraits and Studies of Women*, says (p. vii) that Luxuria is a symbol of sensual delight and carnal pleasures, and that the hare is assigned to her as the symbol of fertility that here, too, the hare is present by virtue of his connection with the Bacchic mythical and ritual cycle. The same motive obviously lies at the root of Aeschylus's well-known phrase: "Bromios [Dionysus] haunts the place, I know it well, since the time when the god took command of the Maenads and contrived death for Pentheus like a hare."'[1]

Aphrodite, Eros and the Cupids

'It was quite natural for the ancients to place the hare in this context on account of the marked analogy between the nature of the hare's being and of the ideas centring round the Bacchic myth and ritual. Such qualities possessed by the hare are swift-footedness, curiosity, fearfulness, and aphrodisian lasciviousness, qualities which are as conspicuous in the character of the Satyrs as in the hare. That it was particularly the last-mentioned of the hare's supposed characteristics on which the ancients laid most stress is clear from the fact that they connected the hare also so closely with Aphrodite and Eros.'

'The passage in Philostratus in which he gives the clearest indication of it is well known. It is the one in which he speaks of "the most acceptable sacrifice to Aphrodite: you know of course the legend of the hare, that it possesses the gift of Aphrodite [i.e. fertility] to a superlative degree".'[2]

'We thus find the hare regarded as an emblem (or attribute) of Aphrodite in two indisputable representations of her and may therefore, with more or less probability, be justified in thinking of her in connection with other female figures [painted on vases] accompanied by a similar emblem.'

'With regard also to the close relation existing between the hare and Eros we may recall to mind above all the information given us on this subject by Philostratus when he describes a painting that is said to have represented Cupids hunting hares, in which he says, "and let not yonder hare escape us, but let us

[1] Aeschylus, *Eumenides*, 24; referring to the fact that Pentheus had tried to suppress the worship of Dionysus.

[2] Philostratus, *Imagines*, i, 6. Compare Eustathius, *Commentaries on the Iliad*, A, p. 87, 37. The hare is an offering to Cupids. It should be noted that Philostratus wrote as late as the third century A.D.

join the Cupids in their hunting". This creature sits under the apple-trees and feeds on the fallen apples, but leaves many half-eaten. The Cupids hunt him up and down and rout him out, one with clapping of hands, another with a cry, a third waving his cloak. Some fly over him with shouts, others follow his trail on foot, and one starts him up as if he were going to hurl himself on him and the hare goes off on another course. Another schemes to catch the hare by the leg, but the hare slips away just when he thought he'd caught him. So they laugh and fall over, one on his side, the other on his face, and others on their backs, in every attitude of disappointment. Nevertheless, none of them shoots an arrow, but they try to catch him alive [as Aphrodite's favourite offering].'[1]

'In agreement with this we see on a vase, in a wall-painting and on a glass vessel representations of Cupids, with or without dogs, running in pursuit of a hare. Elsewhere they fly in pursuit. Thus, on one, a relief, are represented two Cupids, one of them armed with a club, trying to catch a hare in a trap; and on a cornelian, a Cupid rushing upon a hare emerging from a snail-shell.

'Other classical artists depict Cupids who have already caught their prey and are hurrying away with it either by flying or running, or resting with it when caught. In yet other ancient works of art we find, for example, Cupids watching two hares playing together or themselves playing with the beloved animal, kissing it or driving a chariot drawn by hares.[2] In yet other representations a hare may be seen quietly sitting at the foot of a Cupid-herm or near a Cupid completely formed.'

'Lastly, in a well-known marble relief representing a sumptuous banquet in a world populated only by Cupids and Psyches, one Cupid brings in a hare, while another plays with a second hare on the ground.'

The Hare as love-charm and customary love-gift

'It was on account of this emphasis by the ancients laid on

[1] Philostratus, *Imagines*, i, 6.

[2] It should be noted, however, that the hare is not the only animal that is depicted as being harnessed to the Cupids' chariot.

FIGURE 19. Eros with Hare

From a clay amphora of Panathenaic shape in Naples. Attic work of about 490-480 B.C. After Beazley *Der Berliner Maler*, Pl. 10.

Eros carries in his right hand a flute-case, to which is attached a box containing the mouth-piece. In his left hand he carries a lyre with its tortoise-shell sounding-box. Beneath crouches a hare

the hare's aphrodisian nature that they endowed it with the power of a love-charm,[1] so that it is not surprising to find, on a beautiful necklace recovered from a Crimean tomb, among other amulets one representing a hare, and also to meet with a representation of the same animal on a magic nail.'

'This fact explains also a great number of other works of art which otherwise would be unintelligible, in which hares are found closely associated with youths, men, and women, and obviously have the meaning of love-gages.'

'So we meet with youths in the act of presenting a hare, or having just given one, to a beautiful woman to win her love.'

'We see men handing the same animal as a gift to youths, or *vice versa*; youths having just received one from men who in the picture appear to be occupying themselves with the gift; or paintings in which hares are hung up between men and youths, thus clearly indicating the nature of their relationship.'

'Also in cases where individual men, or individual youths or boys, are in various ways brought together by means of a hare, or where hares are being exchanged as gifts between youths, there can no longer be any doubt that these gifts have the same meaning.'

'If, therefore, a hare is depicted in connection with the meeting of Poseidon and Amymone, or with the attack of Nessos on Deianeira;[2] if it is associated with Herakles reposing from his

[1] Thus, Philostratus, *Imagines*, i, 6: 'But perverted lovers recognize in the hare a certain power to produce love, and try to secure the objects of their affection by the compulsion of magic art'. It is to be noted that Philostratus wrote in the third century A.D. when magic had acquired a much greater importance in the classical world than hitherto.

So also Pliny, *Historia Naturalis*, xxviii, 79: 'The people think that if you eat a hare your body acquires sexual attractiveness for nine days, a vulgar superstition, which, however, must have some truth in it since the belief in it is so widespread.' [Pliny probably refers to Italian rather than Greek folk-lore.]

So also Martial in one of his tart epigrams (Martial, v, 29): 'Whenever you send me a hare, Gellia, you say to me, "You will be beautiful for seven days". If you are not making fun of me, my love, if you mean what you say, you, Gellia, have never had a hare to eat.'

[2] Poseidon and Amymone were lovers, and Nessos's attack on Deianeira was a sexual assault.

labours, who, as is well known is at such a juncture wont to apply himself to every kind of material pleasure with no less energy than ordinarily to heroic deeds; if a hare peeps at the

Fig. 20. MAN OFFERING A HARE TO A YOUTH

From a clay calyx in Boston. Attic work of about 500 B.C. After Hartwig, *Meisterschalen*, Pl. 26. The symbolism of this love-scene is an interesting study in the psychology of complementary opposites. The man pursues the youth, but inwardly he is pursued by his desire. Therefore the sought-after youth brings the dog (the hunter), and the man brings the hare (the hunted).

orgiastic dances indulged in by girls and youths, or if it is present during the quiet conversation between a man and a woman, no-one who has read the evidence given above, can remain ignorant as to the meaning the artists intended to convey.'[1]

[1] The author says in a note:

'It is as a symbol of aphrodisian delight and not as material food that, on a Roman sarcophagus (Garrucci, *Mus. Lateran. Tav*, 30), the hare is represented as being brought to a festive meal. For the hare is depicted as being alive, and is not brought like the foodstuffs upon a

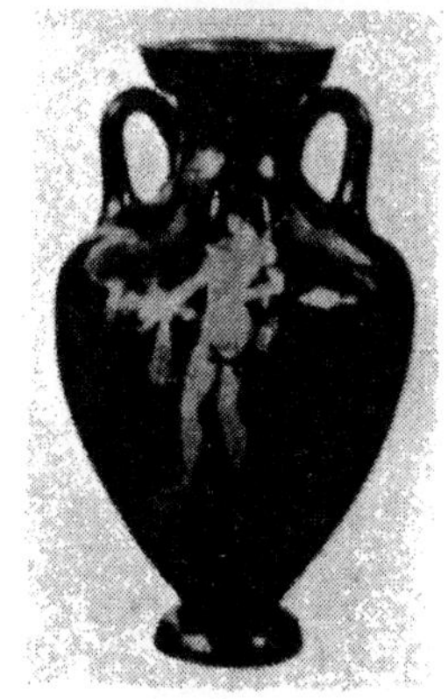

FIGURE 21. The Victorious Athlete receives tribute, including a dead Hare, from an admiring friend

Clay amphora of Panathenaic shape in Boston. Attic work of about 490 B.C. After Caskey and Beazley, *Attic Vase Paintings in the Museum of Fine Arts, Boston*, Pl. 5

The author then goes on to say that not all representations of the hare in Greek art are symbolically significant, since the hare is often used, as are so many other animals, with purely decorative intent or to fill in unwanted gaps in the design, such as the space between a horse's legs. He goes on, however, to say that 'if this happens in the Bacchic *thiasos*,[1] if the rider is a Satyr and the animal on which he rides is a panther, it cannot be doubted that the artist, in depicting a hare of all animals between the panther's feet, was led to choose this animal by virtue of its close connection with Bacchic concepts.

'If we notice the same animal beneath the horse of Oenomaus or that of Tertus, this probably hints at a love relation.[2]

'The hare is, however, depicted elsewhere in a similar position without our being able to presume any other reason for it than that which would apply to any other hunted animal.

'The hare as a quite ordinary object of the chase is in this way closely connected with gods and heroes, not only in legend but also in works of art.

dish. The same is true with regard to the African tombstone of a Roman soldier, on which his small son is represented as bringing a hare, while his daughter holds in her hands a dove and a bunch of grapes (*Revue archéol.*, 1863, pl. 8).' It appears doubtful, however, to the present writer whether this offering of a hare by a boy to his dead father is capable of an aphrodisian interpretation, unless it were an indication of carnal pleasure in the hereafter. Could not an alternative explanation be that it was an expression of filial love, as appear to be the dove and grapes brought by the daughter?

Elsewhere (on p. 64, note 5), however, the authors calls attention to the large number of hares represented on Roman tombs, where they are depicted usually as eating grapes.

I here put forward the suggestion that if, as in other parts of the world as we have seen, the hare is a symbol for intuition, this may possibly represent a union between divine intuition and the red blood of earth.

[1] *Thiasos* is a body of worshippers, here referring to the famous 'Bacchus and his rout'.

[2] It has been rightly pointed out that as the horse's chief attribute in this connection is fleetness, so also is the hare's. I suggest, however, that, if the horse symbolizes physical fleetness, the hare symbolizes a fleetness of spirit that is akin to the intuitive faculty that we have seen associated with it elsewhere.

'In the first place, Artemis herself is called λαγωβόλος[1] [shooter[2] of hares]; in a remarkable bronze object she is depicted as holding two hares in her hands, and is elsewhere often seen closely associated with them. In such scenes she is often accompanied by her brother Apollo, and by her companion Aura.

'Next to the fox, the hare is the game most frequently hunted by the Centaurs, such as Chiron, Pholos, and others.

'Adonis also, and Perseus and Orion hunt hares, and in a famous vase-painting Theseus, Actaeon, Tydeus, and Castor are seen hunting together.

'Elsewhere mortals, unidentifiable men and youths, are seen bent on the same form of amusement, or dogs without huntsmen alone chasing and catching hares. Zeus's eagle also pursues the sport, and the hare is also depicted in kitchen scenes.

'The hare thus also becomes, in later times, a regular attribute of the seasons, whether these latter appear in the form of women or of boys or Cupids.'

As a seasonal emblem[3] the hare in the late Graeco-Roman world appears to fall into line with its use as a zodiacal sign in China and among the Aztecs, but in all other respects the Greek view of the hare, both in its supposed biologically miraculous fertility and in its use as a love-gage, is unique. It seems to me to mirror not only the extraordinary ingenuity of the Greek mind but also what might be called its whimsically agnostic and materialistic outlook, an outlook that placed it for a few centuries in the very forefront of the world's cultural development but lacked that second sight or sense of complementary opposites without which stability and durability cannot exist.

As I have said above, just how far the aphrodisian attribute

[1] Thus Nonnus, *Dionysiaca*, xxxiii, p. 126, depicts Eros as saying, 'But if the Archeress [Artemis], the huntress of hares, moves her [Aphrodite] to anger, I will draw the fiery Olympian sword of Orion to harry Artemis, and I shall drive her out of heaven'.

[2] i.e. with bow and arrow.

[3] It seems to have represented winter, possibly on account of the alpine hare's coat turning white in winter in order to approximate its colour to the snow.

of the hare was materially conceived and how far it may have been thought of also as symbolic of spiritual truth I cannot say, and can only leave it to the reader to decide.[1] It does seem at first sight, however, as if we are here dealing with the degradation of a symbol. If we may judge from all that has been said about hare symbolism in other parts of the world it would appear that the hare was venerated in the first place on grounds quite other than purely sexual ones as symbolizing the transformation of instinct into spirit, and that its use for symbolizing simple untransformed sex is purely secondary.

The Hare sleeps with its eyes open

Finally, there is the widespread belief already mentioned,[2] which is of no little interest, that the hare sleeps with its eyes open. Thus, Xenophon[3] says, 'When he is awake he shuts his eyes, but when he sleeps his eyelids remain open though his eyes do not move'. Various attempts have been made to explain this curious statement on physiological lines, but to the psychologist it is clear that this is a symbolic way of saying that the hare 'sees with the inward or spiritual eye', which has been misconstrued by the material-minded in classical times to refer to physical fact.

Later on in the same work this author remarks, 'When going quietly it springs; no-one ever saw or will ever see a hare walking',[4] which brings to mind the symbolism of the hare as a 'leaper' so often met with in these pages and giving rise to its use as a symbol of dawn and of the faculty of intuition.

[1] Those interested in following the trail of the hare as a love-symbol in modern European folk-lore will find much material to hand in the article on the hare in the *Handwörterbuch des deutschen Aberglaubens*.

[2] See pp. 128 and 190.

[3] Xenophon, *Cynegeticus*, v, 11, quoted by Otto Keller, *Die antike Tierwelt*, Leipzig, 1909, p. 217.

[4] Xenophon, *Cynegeticus*, v, 31.

CONCLUSION

This survey, which makes no claim to completeness (since literature is inexhaustible, and in any case this is no academic treatise), has at least touched, however briefly, on most recorded aspects of the subject of which I am aware, and, for lack of both time and space, I propose now to draw it to a close in the hope that it may nevertheless have added something to our knowledge of a small corner of archetypal research.

We have ranged over a fair area of the world's surface, as well as a stretch of some six thousand years of time, and have witnessed on the one hand a remarkable uniformity in the fundamental symbolic notions connected with the hare by mankind throughout the ages, and on the other hand a great variety of detail.

Let us now turn back and gather the threads, so far as is possible, of the various mythological concepts we have met with.

The Hare as (often a Willing) Sacrifice

Beginning with the central motive of Mrs. Wright's dream, which is that of sacrifice, we have seen this in highly developed form in the case of the Buddha as a hare sacrificing himself by leaping into the fire and so transmuting his fleshly instinct into spirit and its immediate connection with the moon, that 'light in the darkness' which illuminates the inner life of man.

The motive of sacrifice we have seen reflected in the Déné Hareskin legend about throwing the head of a white hare into the fire whereon it immediately became dawn, and more faintly in Europe in Dr. White Kenneth's quaint report about the hare that 'kills itself', in the 'black broth' of Sparta made of the blood and bowels of a hare, in the feeding of the Kings of Tara upon 'the hares of Naas', in the widespread harvest custom of 'killing the hare' and drinking of the 'hare's blood', in the Pomeranian custom of eating the Easter Hare, in the English custom of killing a hare on Good Friday, in the

Leicestershire rite of 'Hunting the Hare' on Easter Monday, and the subsequent eating of 'hare-pies'.

Hare Deities

Various taboos on eating the hare at ordinary seasons and on mentioning its name probably indicate its sacred nature. As god of the nether world the hare is found associated with Osiris as moon-god of the dead, and with the goddess Unnu-t. Among the Algonkin of North America the Great Hare is the creator, and in Europe we find the hare-headed goddess, tutelary deity of the Moon-day we now call Monday probably associated with the Anglo-Saxon Eostre, whose name is equivalent to our Easter. The Teutonic goddess Frejya is also said to have been attended by hares.

Association with the Moon

The association of the hare with the moon is almost world-wide, being found in India, China, North America, Ancient Egypt, among the Hottentots, and, by virtue of the connection of the hare in Europe with Easter, among ourselves also, since Easter is the great moon-festival which also ushers in the spring.

Symbol of Dawn, Easter and the 'east'

This festival follows, and is entirely dependent on, being the result of, the supreme sacrifice of Good Friday, which is the darkness which ushers in the dawn. It is therefore significant to what an extent the hare itself figures as a dawn-symbol. It does so, in fact, almost universally. We may begin with Ancient Egypt, where, in Le Page Renouf's view, the very word for hare means 'leaper' and is connected with such concepts as 'uprising', 'opening', 'becoming' (hence the use of the hare hieroglyph for 'to be', and also 'to be created'), so that the word *Unnu* itself becomes 'an appropriate appellative of the rising sun, who springs forth in glory and triumph'.

The sun rises in the east, so also the Indian god Sakka who translated the image of the hare into the moon has his place in the east, and the Algonkin medicine-lodge has its door opening to the east and summons the east in the name of the Great Hare, the creator-deity. In Europe the hare is also connected with Easter, the name of which feast has been shown to be derived from Sanskrit roots meaning 'the east' and 'dawn', from which also are derived through different channels the Greek ἕως and the Latin *Aurora*. Mention has also been made of the Easter Egg, laid by the Easter Hare, and of the eastern European custom of making sugar images of it with little windows looking into them, through which are seen pictures of religious subjects such as Christ rising from the tomb.

Association with Whiteness and Snow

Closely connected with the east is the colour white (if that which has no colour, or includes all colours, may be so called). Mythological allusions to the hare and its accompanying phenomena are throughout the world extraordinarily insistent on white and whiteness, which is itself equated with the brightest possible light. Beginning with Mrs. Wright's dream, it will be remembered that, though her hare was brown (fawn-coloured), outside the house the ground was covered with a miraculous snow on which no footprints were left, and inside the kitchen in which the sacrifice took place 'there was a great light and everything was as white as it was outside'. Also the bowl in which the hare sat was white. If we now turn to the mythology of the hare throughout the world, we notice, first, that the stone seat on which the god Sakka sat, and which through the power of the Hare-Buddha's renunciation became so warm, was covered with a white woollen blanket. Then, when the hare leapt into the fire but was unharmed, it is said that it was as if he had leapt into snow. This might at first sight be taken to be a simple figure of speech to express its coldness, but it means also the pure light of intuition as opposed to the earthly light of the fire.[1] It is therefore interesting in this connection to

[1] Compare the descriptions of Our Lord at His transfiguration, when He first spoke of His coming sacrifice, that 'His face did shine as the sun and His raiment was white as the light' (Matt. xvii, 2). Mark (ix. 29) says of His raiment that it was 'white as snow', and Luke (ix, 29) that it was 'white and glistering'. The same language is used of the appearance of the angel who rolled back the stone from the tomb, whose raiment was 'white as snow' (Matt. xxviii, 3; see also Mark xvi, 5).

note the reference among the Algonkin to the Great Hare's 'brother, the snow'. Brinton points out also that the syllable *wab* occurring in the Great Hare's name also means 'white'. In China also, though red and black hares are mentioned, the most prominent hare in mythology is the white hare, which lives a thousand years and becomes white when half that period is completed. There is here doubtless a reference to the arctic hare, which in fact turns white in winter, but what is significant is the choice of this white hare as the chief mythological symbol. It is said also in China that the white hare is the Moon Queen's servant. It will be remembered also that it was the head of a white hare that in the Déné Hareskin story was thrown into the fire and produced the dawn. Whiteness—usually described as 'silveriness'—is also commonly connected with the moon. For this reason we turn the silver in our pockets on sight of the New Moon, and it will be remembered that in the Austrian game of piercing the Easter-egg laid by the hare the object that pierces it must be a silver coin. Silver is also useful in the hunting of the witch-hare in Europe. Thus, as has been stated, 'the only way to make sure of hitting a witch-animal is to put a silver sixpence or a silver button in your gun'. Sometimes it must be a 'crooked sixpence', but a still more efficacious method is to use for the same purpose a consecrated wafer—also a round white object—mixed with the shot.

Symbol of Intuition

Mention of the moon and silver, both symbols of intuition, brings us once more to the subject of the hare as representing pre-eminently this psychological function. Too much has been said about this throughout this survey to need stressing it any further, so that all I will do now is to bring together a few of the possibly subtler forms of expressing it. Intuition is a peculiar function—possibly the most fundamental—which enables a man to receive instantaneous perceptions about things, which are correct though not based on logical deduction but rather on direct subliminal knowledge. Children have it, of course, and animals, but we are apt to lose it as we grow up. Spiritual understanding of the 'other side' of things depends on its recovery, that is to say on its 'redemption' or 'salvation' from the dark recesses of the soul into which it has been thrust as into a kind of cold-storage. This is particularly the case to-day when purely intellectual processes are so overestimated that we are apt to distrust and so be afraid of our 'intuitions', which, since we do not honour them, are indeed apt to revenge themselves on us by coming up in a negative or unreliable form. This, however, is only the case in so far as we dishonour them by not joining them to our other, more generally considered to be 'respectable', functions of thinking, feeling, and sensation, because they need precisely the check which these other functions can provide. Coming, as they do, directly and without any apparent intermediary into consciousness, they do in fact bear messages from the 'other' world of non-conscious values. Therefore, it is not surprising to find the hare (itself a fleet-footed animal appearing in surprising places) saying, in the Indian story, 'I am the ambassador of the moon, and this is what the gods say to you by my mouth'; or, in the Hottentot story, being charged by the moon to bring a message to man to tell man of his immortality (though it is true he forgot the message by the way); or that the hare-moon in Egypt should be equated with Thoth, himself equated with the Greek Hermes and the Roman Mercury, who are themselves messengers of the gods as shown by the wings they bear on head and feet.

The Hare as Omen

Different from these but possibly to be classed under this heading is the use of the hare as an omen according to the direction in which it runs, as described by Pausanias, and in the case of Boadicea, and of the running of a hare portending fire.

Association with Picture-writing

It is a characteristic of intuitive knowledge that it often makes itself felt in the form of pictures, seen in dreams or visions which present themselves in pictorial form. It is therefore not surprising that the Great Hare of the Algonkin should be accredited with the invention of picture-writing, and Thoth with the invention of hieroglyphs, of which the hare-sign itself is one.

The Hare makes the Elixir of Life

Another magical attribute of the hare is the widespread view of it as the maker and purveyor of the elixir of life. This is the case in China, where the hare mixes the Herb of Immortality on the moon; in North America where the Great Hare is the founder of the medicine hunt and in whose house at the place of sun-rising the souls of good Indians feed on delicious fruits; in its connection through association with Thoth and Hermes who, as Hermes Trismegistos, became later the patron of alchemy; and in a degraded literal sense in medieval Europe where parts of the hare's body were said to have many healing properties. All but the last of these are connected, of course, with the gift of, or search for, immortality, with which the hare-amulets of Ancient Egypt, China, and Greece are also doubtless connected. It is with a message of immortality that the moon sends the hare to mankind among the Hottentots, and in the South African myth the moon sends the hare with the message, 'Like as I die and rise to life again, so you shall die and rise to life again'. Doctrines of immortality are, of course, implicit also in the worship of the Great Hare of the Algonkin, as in our own Easter festival and in the Easter eggs laid by the hare at this season, and if a hare lays eggs she must be previously pregnant, as is the Anglo-Saxon hare-goddess who clasps the moon to her belly. Artemis also sees eagles feasting on a pregnant hare, and the hare-moon, Lucina, assists at parturition. In Ancient Greece this motive is translated into pure superstition regarding the biological productivity of hares, and the hare becomes, as we have seen, a symbol of love.

The Hare as Witch-animal

Finally, in a totally negative way, hares, from being goddesses, are in medieval and modern Europe reduced to the status of witch-animals, using their intuitive-productive capacity for negative purposes.

Influence of the Hare Dream on Mrs. Wright

In Mrs. Wright's own dream-history the sacrifice of the hare in Dream 9, surrounded by bright light and with its snow-white setting, did indeed bring about a transformation of instinct, and thereby of her whole personality, in the direction of intuitive knowledge and of a spiritual pregnancy benefiting not only herself but her daughter Margaret to an extreme degree. It will be remembered that her next dream (Dream 10) contained the direct message that 'Margaret and her mother may sleep together', meaning that the mother-love that had been cloyed was now purged of inhibiting misconceptions and could now flow directly into her daughter. This was followed by Dream 11 confirming the last by emphasizing Mrs. Wright's release from the authoritarian influence of a falsely intellectual external world. Then, when the analysis had made her conscious (which she had not been before) of the full meaning of these dreams, came Dream 12 marking the descent of spirit from on high (symbolized by the supposed air-raid), together with the prayer before the fowl-house containing the unseen Easter eggs, symbols of new life, followed by the Good Friday scene of parting from her school friend for three days. Then came Dream 13 referring to the Last Supper and the adumbrated recovery of Bertha, and after that Dream 14 introducing the motive of human flesh seen in the flesh-pink material, leading up to the sacrifice (dreamt of as an 'operation') of the young well-set-up Jewish butcher symbolizing Christ. This in turn was followed by Dream 16 introducing the dark aspect of God in the form of the black pony, and Dream 17 referring to sanctification and 'marriage to God'. And so the analysis proceeded.

She was, of course, as totally ignorant as I was of the world-wide mythology of the hare that has just been summarized. Nevertheless, some of the chief motives in it, namely, the sacrifice, the whiteness symbolized by the snow, the bright light symbolizing the dawn and direct intuition (a light which occurred again with much more defined meaning later in her career, as will be described in a subsequent volume), the association with Good Friday and Easter and Easter eggs, and the realization of divine love, all came into her dream-series, showing the deep connection existing in the inner world of the psyche of individual modern men and women with the whole mythological history of mankind. The fact that the dream of sacrificing the hare had no effect on her till enough of its meaning was explained, and that it then produced this great effect, demonstrates clearly—and it is only one of innumerable examples—not only the power of the archetype but also the part it plays in the redemptive process that lies latent within us all, though it remains comparatively inoperative till joined to consciousness, but becomes so potent a force for good when activated by being recognized and honoured.

Part Three

MORE DREAMS ABOUT HARES AND RABBITS

SHOWING THE MYTHOLOGICAL MOTIVES ON WHICH THEY ARE BASED AND THEIR RELATION TO EVERYDAY LIFE

Since making the foregoing investigation into the Mythology of the Hare, I have taken particular note of the occurrence of dreams about hares and rabbits in the analysis of other patients, both past and present, and have been so impressed by the references they all contain to different aspects of the mythological hare cycle that I have thought them of sufficient interest to include some of them here. I take this opportunity of thanking the respective dreamers for kindly allowing me to do so.

It is the nature of archetypes, as they appear in dreams, that, while preserving their archetypal characteristics, the details and context of their appearances have always a special bearing on the dreamer's own problem. Just as different localities emphasize different aspects of any one myth, thereby presumably indicating the state of inner development of the particular communities in which they are found, so in the case of individuals a similar selective process is seen to be at work. Thus in dreams, which deal fundamentally with universal problems, we get an infinite number of variations, all of which nevertheless centre round one feature or other of the archetypal pattern.

As will be seen from the dreams about to be cited, just as no one mythological cycle includes all the mythological attributes associated with the hare, so also no single dream embraces them all, but each dream includes a definite reference to one or other of them, elaborated in terms of the dreamer's own personal problem. It would make an interesting theoretical study to determine what characteristic of a particular dreamer causes the correspondence with a given variation of the mythological pattern associated with a particular locality or perhaps era in the world's history. But such speculation is outside the scope of this book, and would demand a far greater body of evidence than I am here able to present. I will therefore content myself merely with citing such dreams as have recently come to my notice, and it is important to note that in all these cases the dreamer had no conscious knowledge whatever, any more than had Mrs. Wright, that the hare was of any importance as a mythological figure, and much less of any of the beliefs held concerning it that have been described in this book, except possibly a vague memory of the connection of the hare with witches in Europe, a motive that incidentally does not enter into a single one of these dreams.

Association of Hares with Rabbits

It may surprise some readers that, among hare dreams, I include also dreams about rabbits. Though rabbits differ from hares in many essential ways, notably in their methods of self-defence, which for the hare is running and for the rabbit burrowing, and in the loneliness of the hare as opposed to the gregarious habits of the rabbit, they belong to the same genus and have so much in common that town-dwellers to-day often fail to distinguish between the two. As pointed out on p. 208, note 1, they were sometimes confused also by the ancients, the Greeks calling the rabbit by diminutives of the common word for the hare, such as 'half-hare', 'little hare', etc. It is also to be noted that before the first century B.C. there were no rabbits in classical lands, rabbits having been introduced thither from Spain for the first time about this date. Spain is also said to be the land whence they were introduced into Britain, having originally been brought to Europe from North Africa, as they were later introduced with disastrous consequences from Europe into Australia. Hares and rabbits are also so closely allied that instances (though rare ones) are on record of their interbreeding, and the grey rabbit of North America is a kind of intermediate species which normally does not burrow, though when hard pressed it may escape into any accessible hole.

H. Kunike goes so far as to write a whole article on 'The Rabbit in the Moon'. He speaks of the Great Rabbit of the Prairie Indians in the same way as we speak of the Great Hare of the Algonkin, and adds that they sometimes refer to the moon as 'Rabbit's Eye'. He also perceived the truth which I have emphasized in this book regarding the archetypal nature of this mythological cycle, which he associates with the rabbit and which others associate with the hare. Thus Siecke in reviewing his article says: 'The remarkable agreement [regarding this cycle] found in the beliefs of different peoples of the earth who otherwise have no connection with one another forces us, as Dr. Kunike rightly shows, to the conclusion "that they must be due to some common underlying natural cause".'[1]

We have only to think of the White Rabbit in *Alice in Wonderland* to realize the obvious connection between this visionary character in the Lewis Carroll mythological cycle and the association both of hares with whiteness, and of the hare as the 'opener of the way' or 'of the womb'[2] (which is what the White Rabbit is in the Alice saga, by showing her the way into the rabbit hole which is the gateway into the inner world), to realize the universality of the symbolic imagery connected with both hares and rabbits in the collective psyche. The child-mind is well aware of it, as seen in the nursery custom of say-

[1] H. Kunike, 'Das Kaninchen im Monde, insbesondere in der Mythologie der Nordamerikanischen Indianer', in the journal *Die Sterne*, Potsdam, 1925, pp. 267–75. Dr. H. Meinhard kindly called my attention to this after my Part II on *The Mythology of the Hare* was already in print. I have been unable to find a copy of the original article, and the above quotation is from a review of it by E. Siecke, in the *Ethnologischer Anzeiger*, Stuttgart, vol. i, 1928, Abteilung B, p. 31.

H. Kunike has also written another article on the Toad in the Moon ('Die Kröte im Monde') among the American Indians in *Die Sterne*, 1924, pp. 79–83, to which also I have been unable to gain access, but which should prove of interest in connection with the Frog accompanying the Hare in the Moon in the Chinese T'ang mirror illustrated in Fig. 9.

[2] See pp. 151–2, 155, 223.

ing 'hares' last thing at night on the last day of the old month and 'rabbits' (sometimes 'white rabbits') first thing on the first morning of the new, a quite obvious symbol of 'dawn' and 'new life' fittingly connected with the moon despite the calendrical convention that the month no longer coincides with the moon's phases though it originally did. This is supposed to be a 'lucky' act just as the white hare was regarded as an auspicious omen in China (see p. 128). Sometimes in nursery custom the roles of hare and rabbit are reversed, and 'rabbits' is said at the end of the old month and 'hares' at the beginning of the new. But the association between the two animals and their symbolic meaning is clear.

If any doubt is still entertained as to the propriety of associating hare-dreams with rabbit-dreams I think the way in which the dreams dealing with rabbits fit in with the archetypal pattern of the hare will prove sufficient answer.

Dream of a doe-rabbit having to transfer her habitation underground or else be burnt.

The first dream I propose to cite, though it is about rabbits, recalls so definitely the self-sacrifice of the Hare-Buddha by leaping into the fire that I have no hesitation in including it. In case the similarity of this dream-motive to the mythological material might be ascribed by the critical reader to some kind of unconscious suggestion or telepathic influence passing from analyst to patient, I should like to point out that, like Mrs. Wright's dream, this one occurred and was recorded more than a year *before* the analyst himself had any knowledge that such world-wide mythology existed.

The dreamer was a married woman of highly over-extraverted nature, who dreamt that she saw two conical earth-mounds. The right-hand mound was intact, but the left-hand mound was partly demolished, showing it to be the hutlike dwelling-place of a doe-rabbit who was sitting inside, and that its earth-covering had an internal lining of straw. A buck-rabbit was standing outside, between the two mounds, and was engaged in setting fire to the doe-rabbit's hut with a lighted stick. The doe-rabbit inside the hut complained to the buck, 'Please, *Monsieur Lapin*, do not set fire to the thatch of my house!' The buck-rabbit, with which the dreamer identified herself, replied, 'If you are idiotic enough to build such an erection on the surface of the ground instead of burrowing deeply where you belong, I must'. The dream was very vivid and had all the impact of a vision.

Fig. 22

The buck rabbit burns down the doe-rabbit's hut to 'send her underground.'

This dream is a very deep one. The maleness of the buck-rabbit is emphasized by the phallic emblem he wields in the shape of the lighted stick representing the external or male fire, and the doe-rabbit's female nature is emphasized by the fact that, with her, the fire is an internal one represented by the lighted thatch *inside* the roof of her hut. In Freudian terms the action of the dream would represent an attempted sexual union refused by the woman. But the union desired by the male and refused by the female is not one of sex but of the spirit, and the buck-rabbit states quite clearly what is the obstruction, namely, in terms of the dream, that the female has made her dwelling above ground and not below 'where she belongs'. That is to say that the female has rivalled the male instead of supporting him from below by developing the truly female and earthy part of her own nature. Though not stated in so many words in the dream, it is clear that the right-hand mound is also a hut and belongs to the male who represents not only the husband but also, if the dream is taken on the purely subjective level, the dreamer's own properly extraverted side. But a balanced psyche needs equal weight on both sides of the dividing line, namely a strong inner life to balance the outer. The dreamer in fact lived so much on the surface (as shown by both huts being above ground) that at the time this dream was dreamt she could achieve real creative union neither with her husband nor with her own internal *animus*.

Since, like the hare, the rabbit stands for intuition, the two rabbits together with their two huts may be interpreted as representing the two aspects of intuition, the male on the right hand representing extraverted intuition and the female on the left hand the complementary function of introverted intuition. It is an axiom of psychology that no element of the psyche is in itself wrong, but that any wrongness there is arises from the misplacement of any given element, whereon what would be positive when in the right place becomes negative when in the wrong. The two conical huts may be likened to the two triangles in the Shield of David mentioned on p. 168, of which the triangle pointing upward represents external reality and the triangle pointing downward represents internal reality. In that symbol the two are creatively united, each being the mirror opposite of the other. But in this dream they are not so united, and the female triangle corresponding to the doe-rabbit's hut is in its wrong place, that is to say above ground and pointing upward, causing the dreamer at that time in actual life to project her own unrecognized internal contents externally on to others in a negative way, giving rise to difficulties in her relationship with just those who possessed the feminine qualities which she lacked through not recognizing them in herself, difficulties which she was either unable to account for or else found rationalized excuses to explain.

With regard to external and material things the dreamer was thoroughly well equipped, having her feet well on the ground, so that in the dream the right-hand (extravert) hut is solid and in its right place and is in no need of being changed. But she could not make proper contact either with her husband or with society as a whole (except with people very similar to herself) because she was always invading their spheres and trying to dominate them. It is to remedy this state of affairs that the buck-rabbit in the dream proposes the burning, that is to say the transformation, of the left-hand hut which should have been the positively introverted one but was, instead, negatively extraverted with the above-mentioned results. Two sames cannot unite, and so, in order to bring about their creative union, the left-hand dwelling had to be transferred underground, involving the dreamer's withdrawal of negative projections and their transformation into positive self-knowledge of her own inner nature.

The transforming medium is the fire, wielded objectively by her husband and subjectively by her own *animus*. But here again the same conflict is seen, since she identifies herself with the *animus* as represented by the buck-rabbit and not with the female rabbit, which means that intellectually she has the desire but emotionally she still rebels. Still, the desire is there, and when the feminine side of herself agrees the transformation will doubtless take place, and it is a fact that the dream occurred at a moment when she was beginning to realize the need for some such fundamental revision of habitual attitude. At the same time, the use of the French language by the doe-rabbit when she addressed the buck-rabbit as '*Monsieur Lapin*' showed how very much of a foreign language to her the world of the spirit still was.

The existence of two fires, the external fire of the buck-rabbit and the internal fire of the doe, is a particularly interesting feature. This juxtaposition refers to a symbolic truth that I have observed in dreams, namely that whereas the Pentecostal fire descends upon men from above, as on the Apostles' heads, for women it arises out of the earth, as seen in women's dreams in which their shoes catch fire (as this woman actually dreamt some time later) or the floor or wainscoting of a room (as opposed to the roof) gets set alight. This represents the internal fire which the buck-rabbit was driving the doe to accept through sacrifice of her negative externalization (in other words, unconscious pride) as symbolized by the burning of the externally usurping hut and the transferring of the doe-rabbit's dwelling to below the ground. This corresponds to the self-sacrifice of the Hare-Buddha in the fire and the transference of his image into the moon which is the 'light in the darkness' that rules the night, symbolizing the inner world. Everyone is, like this doe, afraid of sacrifice, but it should be noted that, just as the Hare-Buddha, because a willing sacrifice, did not himself get burnt, for 'the fire was powerless to heat so much as the pores of a hair on his body . . . it was as if he had leapt into snow' (p. 110), so also the doe-rabbit will not get burnt if she obeys, but will if she does not. This means that the woman *will* get psychologically and spiritually burnt up if she continues her double externalization (symbolized by *both* huts being above ground), but will find self-realization both within herself and in relation to her husband and to society as a whole if she becomes humbly receptive enough to the command of her *animus* to internalize that half of her nature which belongs inside, that is to say, become really acquainted with herself.

Dream of cooking the white meat of a Rabbit which turns into a child

Another rabbit dream is that of a young woman who dreamt: 'I am in a kitchen cooking, standing over a stove, and with a spoon in my hand am stirring some white meat in a saucepan. The meat is the size and shape of a rabbit. As I turn it over it becomes whiter till it seems almost luminous, and a girl friend standing beside me shows me that what I am cooking is no longer a rabbit but is a child. In the dream this mysterious business seemed quite natural, but when I woke up I felt utterly horrified at what I had done.'

This dreamer had been forced through highly unsatisfactory home conditions into living an unnaturally extravert life, underneath which was a nameless cavern of unoccupied because unrecognized spiritual power, of which she felt terrified as of a vortex into which she might some day be suddenly dragged, and of which for this reason she had become mortally afraid. She was, at the time of dreaming, on the point of opening up the deeper levels of her psyche, but the life she found there was all so strange to her that its various manifestations often appeared both frightening and, to her, quite incomprehensible.

This dream has in it the luminous whiteness so frequently associated with the hare (see pp. 224–5), which in the deep psyche represents direct intuitive knowledge and at this level always carries with it a mysterious and ghostly feeling somewhat akin to awe. Only when, as in this case, the inner meaning is not recognized does this feeling of awe turn into dismay or horror, which it will be noted did not occur within the dream itself since to the dream mind the process that was taking place was a perfectly natural one, but which was felt acutely on waking.

The dream actually represented a very positive advance. As in real life cooking means the transformation of raw food into something that can be more easily digested, so cooking in dreams also means transformation but in a spiritual sense, that is to say the making of some difficult truth digestible in order that it may be swallowed and, as in the previous dream, internalized. Ezekiel swallowing the roll of the Law (in order to 'inwardly digest' it) is a case in point. Such food might to the conscious mind not seem very appetizing, yet when he had eaten it he found it 'as honey for sweetness'.[1] What actually happened in this dream was that by means of a spoon, which is a receptive instrument symbolizing female or introvertly intuitive thinking, the dreamer was 'turning over' her problem, that is to say, was seeking what lay beneath the external appearance, and so was confronted with the 'illumination', which she herself took simply to be the white meat of a rabbit. It needed the greater knowledge possessed by her girl friend, a real person who had herself been successfully analysed and thus

[1] Ezekiel ii, 8 to iii, 4.

represented the dreamer's own 'positive shadow', to show her what was indeed the fact, namely that her hitherto unrecognized intuitive knowledge as represented by the rabbit was capable of being made conscious, as symbolized by its transformation into a human child. This was, of course, the 'holy child' trailing with it the 'clouds of glory' of which Wordsworth speaks, that is to say, her own divinely childlike nature, that had been so damagingly obscured by fear and by a superimposed religious education that had proved worse than useless by turning her against religious symbolism in all its forms and thus yet further divorcing her from the reality of her own inner life. This mysterious dream was then, when understood, far from being a horrid act, but, on the contrary, was pregnant with all the possibilities of new life. It is, incidentally, of interest to note that the cooking took place in a saucepan, which is a round vessel corresponding in this respect to the round white bowl in which Mrs. Wright sacrificed her hare, and to the round full moon in which the transformed image of the Hare-Buddha was displayed. This brief dream thus includes four motives of the Buddha story: the sacrifice, that is to say the transformation, represented by the cooking, the luminous whiteness, the round container, and the rebirth.

The analytical process was proving that the apparently frightening symbols were in fact pregnant with healing virtue, and that the mystery, far from being an insult to the dreamer's intelligence (which so many at first take anything mysterious to be), was on the contrary the revelation of a profundity in her own psyche before which her conscious ego could only prostrate itself in grateful acceptance and do its best to understand. This dream was one of many, all dealing on different levels with the acceptance of the childlike intuitive faculty in herself, whereby the power of emotion within herself could be transformed, from being a merely negative force inevitably dragging her down into an abyss of nameless fears, into a positive guide illuminating the deep recesses of her soul and so leading to creative life.

Dream of sacrificing a Rabbit by hitting the right side of its head with a white stone

Another rabbit dream also represents the rabbit as a sacrificial animal—as, in fact, all hare and rabbit dreams that have come to my notice do. This dreamer was a woman in middle life, who dreamt:

'I am standing at a desk in a square room (the desk resembles partly my own and partly the analyst's), trying to kill a small animal with a lovely brown fur coat. I am trying to do this by grasping its body in my left hand and rapping the left side of its head on the desk, and have been trying to do so for twenty-four hours.

'While I am absorbed in this job of killing, an unknown man who clearly has every right to be there comes in through the door behind me and to the left, and crosses over to the window on my right and stands with his back to it, watching what I am doing. I say to him, "I have been trying to kill it this twenty-four hours", as if I am acting on some preconceived and unconsidered notion that I must kill, but do not question why, or whether I want to or not. But it won't die, but on the contrary looks uncomplainingly at me with its bright eyes set in a remarkably broad face. It makes no attempt to defend itself or to escape, nor does it display any kind of animosity, but playfully bites me with mouse-like teeth. I wonder whether I shall be infected by the bite, but do not feel pain or fear, in fact have no feeling sensation or emotion at all.

'Up till now I have been trying to kill it by grasping its body in my left hand and striking the left side of its head against the desk. But now, still keeping it in my left hand, I try to kill it by hitting the right side of its head with some object which I had in my right hand and which I think was a white stone.

'At last I think that I have killed it, and see the result, which is the *left half* of a bleached rabbit's skull such as one may find anywhere on the downs. The right half of the skull was not there, but what was particularly remarkable was that the left half which I now saw had, to my surprise, the dead white brain still in it. It did not seem possible that this was the animal that I had just killed, but there it was.'

Though the dreamer had no knowledge whatever of the mythology described in this book, the dream nevertheless includes four of the hare's most widely attested attributes: (*a*) its sacrificial nature, (*b*) that it is a willing sacrifice, (*c*) its bright eyes (also attested by Mrs. Wright), and (*d*) the whiteness so often associated with the hare, represented (though the animal itself was brown) by the bleached skull, the white brain within the skull, and the white stone with which it was killed.

It would take a long time to analyse the dream fully, and there is space here to refer only to certain salient points.

In the first place the room is square, a shape so often symbolizing the inner psyche, witness the square house in which Mrs. Wright sacrificed her hare (see p. 48), and the desk quite clearly represents the sacrificial altar, as did the operating table in Mrs. Wright's Dream 15.

'This twenty-four hours' meant to the dreamer at first simply 'all night and all day', but later she thought that it referred to that period twenty-four years ago when she was battling with certain peculiarly severe problems of adolescence. Later still, following the suggestion that it might also mean 'all my life', it dawned on her that twenty-four signified her own age reversed, which was forty-two, so that on this level the number symbolized a return to the beginning, in other words rebirth.

The animal's bright eyes set in a broad face reminded her of a mentally deficient girl she had once dealt with, and indicate, in my opinion, the intuitive knowledge[1] of all mental defectives that lies deep hidden behind an appearance of inability, the unexpressed wisdom of the newly born child as yet uncontaminated by the illusions of a materially minded and disbelieving world, a deep wisdom of which the so-called mental defective is the unconscious carrier precisely because the conscious does not supervene, and from whom this pearl of great

[1] Compare the Prairie Indians' reference to the Moon as 'Rabbit's Eye' (see p. 232).

price can be dug out through right handling based on an unreserved belief in human instinctive knowledge as mirroring the divine will. There is no space here to expand this thesis, which will form one of the main themes of a future volume. All I wish to point out here is that the 'bright eyes' thus also indicate a rebirth motive, that of regaining the inborn wisdom of the child.

This also explains why the effort to kill the rabbit by crushing the *left* side of its head was not allowed by the dream-mind, but on the contrary the successful sacrifice consisted in striking it on the *right* side of its head with the white stone held in the right hand, thus, as it turned out, demolishing the right side altogether but leaving the left side of the ancient bleached skull intact. This is because 'left' represents instinctive (and therefore potentially spiritual) life symbolizing the wisdom of the ages, while 'right' signifies external control. Thus we speak of the 'right arm of the law' (meaning man-made law), and not the left. It was the wrong kind of control over the instinctive-spiritual process exercised by the 'right' or conscious side due to fear and disbelief that had to be sacrificed, and not, as she had been doing all her life (symbolized by 'these twenty-four hours') the 'left' or unconscious side from which these processes spring.

As seen throughout *The Mythology of the Hare* and summarized on pp. 224–5, luminous whiteness represents direct intuitive knowledge corresponding to Wordsworth's 'clouds of glory' trailed by the child at birth, and this accounts in the dream for the bleached appearance of the ancient skull representing the wisdom of the past containing the apparently dead white brain, which, however, cannot really have been dead, else it would have long since disappeared. The whiteness of the skull and of the brain, which impressed itself particularly on her mind, as well as the whiteness of the stone with which the sacrifice was eventually performed, corresponds very closely with the luminous whiteness of the rabbit's flesh that was being cooked in the previous dream and that in fact turned into a child. The bleached ancient and now apparently lifeless skull corresponds to the lack of emotion and feeling sensation in the dream, and might superficially seem negative, but becomes positive if taken as representing deep buried and ancient wisdom which may be difficult to get at, but is, when found, more positive than anything the merely rationalizing ego can ever know.

Important was the feeling that the dreamer was acting on some preconceived and unconsidered notion unknown to herself. This is exactly what Mrs. Wright did on sacrificing her hare, and is also seen in the apparent meaninglessness (until interpreted) of the action of the two other dreams that I have just cited. It is characteristic of the internal redemptive process that it acts *for* and *in spite of* one's conscious self in accordance with laws which the conscious ego has so largely forgotten but which have to be obeyed and, in so far as possible, understood. The internal redemptive process is, however, inoperative unless it has conscious support, and the change-over from the mistaken attempt to destroy the left side of the skull representing instinct to the successful sacrifice of the right side representing her former mistaken conscious attitudes, and the use for this purpose of the white stone in the right hand representing the dreamer's newly recovered belief in the correctness of her intuitive faculty, indicates that she is on the point of realizing this and of taking action accordingly.

The question once more is: What did the rabbit which she was sacrificing represent? That it wanted to be sacrificed is clear from its lack of any kind of resistance, from the trusting look in its bright eyes, and from its playful biting of her with its needle-like teeth. Biting in dreams (even when it looks like attack, and may look very frightening) is always a love-act symbolized by the merging or entry of each protagonist into the other, the teeth of the 'attacker' (the male, active, intrusive element or 'lover') entering into the 'attacked', and the flesh (the female, passive element) of the 'attacked' one simultaneously entering into the mouth of the so-called 'attacker'. It is only the one-track thinker who ignores this symbolic meaning of 'attack' by failing to understand the mirror-opposite nature of the deeper levels in the unconscious, and that love is only mistaken for assault when it is refused. This is the meaning of the dreamer's fear of 'infection'. Infection in dreams means 'impregnation', and, the dream always being an effort at integration, infection here means impregnation by the primaeval instinct which is at one with spirit and signifies the acquirement of spiritual power.

On a more personal level the rabbit represents (with its bright childlike eyes and mouselike teeth) the 'mousily' diffident and unassuming side of the dreamer's nature that has to be transformed by more self-assertive action.[1] Indeed, her perfectly natural instincts had, both forty-two years ago when she was born and again twenty-four years ago at adolescence, all seemed to her to have been 'knocked on the head' (as in the dream she first knocked the left side of the rabbit's head), and it was now time that she put things right again by knocking on the head, in other words sacrificing, the right-hand side representing the consciously resulting 'mousy' feeling that the unmerited rebuffs of her childhood had caused in her and that had proved only a false refuge, and that she now took matters into her own hands by recovering her belief in her own instinctive reactions. The unknown man (her positive *animus*) silently watching her quite clearly approved of what she was doing, and himself represented what, if she succeeded, would be her reward through union with him, internally in the form of instinctive-spiritual power, and externally, if matters took that course, in the form of union with a real man.

It is of interest that, after realizing the various implications of this rabbit-dream, she recalled another dream that she had had a little earlier of all the animals in the Zoo coming out of their cage. Like the three objects in her rabbit-dream, all the animals were white, representing externally things unaccustomed to the light, such as her wrongly repressed instincts, but internally the white light of self-knowledge. Her immediate reaction on having this dream had been 'The lion shall lie down with the lamb', meaning that now the union of opposites was at hand, and that, after all, instinct was right

[1] It is worth noting that the dreamer is not, as are so many women, in real life afraid of mice, but likes them, and thinks of them kindly as 'wee timorous beasties'.

and could go hand-in-hand with spirit and with right social behaviour, since, however opposed they might appear to be, they were ultimately one.

Dream of shooting a Hare which flies up into the sky and then returns

The last dream I propose to cite is a real hare-dream, dreamt by a young priest well versed in psychological thinking, but, like the other dreamers, having no knowledge of the mythology of the Hare and being quite astonished when he heard of it and of how his dream fitted into the archetypal pattern.

'I am out shooting (formerly a favourite occupation of mine) in a very green countryside, with long grass and luxuriant hedges. I put up a hare from close by my feet. My gun is at the ready, and I put it to my shoulder and snap the left-hand barrel at the hare, which is just entering the hedge. I know that I have hit the hare, but fear it will escape. It goes through a hole in the hedge, beside which, on my side of the hedge and to the right, is standing an unknown older man with longish white hair and wearing a white shirt and dark trousers. Scared apparently by him, the hare when it reaches the field on the other side of the hedge turns to the left. It runs some distance, and then flies up into the air, turns on its back and dies as it turns over, and falls to earth dead. I set out to retrieve the hare. It is of the golden-brown, tawny colour I associate in particular with the hares found in my home county.'

By Freud the gun would be regarded as a phallic emblem, as indeed it is if it is realized that a phallic emblem is not a sexual organ, but, on the contrary, a symbol representing the transformation of sex into spiritual power. Shooting with the left-hand barrel means conscious use of the internal intuitive faculty always associated with the 'left', indicating that the dream has to do with spiritual values as opposed to direct sexual ones, which would have required the right-hand barrel. This much would have been deducible from the bare symbolism of the dream without the aid of any personal associations. It turned out to be indeed the case, since it later transpired that the dream was the culminating one of a series dealing with what the dreamer had thereby discovered to be a totally unresolved attitude towards celibacy, which was the goal that he had set himself.

The dreamer was practised in that particular form of self-analysis which consists in holding written conversations with his own *anima*, who had by now become his constant inner guide. As an example of such conversations, I here give, with his consent, that part of the subsequent day's discussion with her that touched on this dream:

'*She:* Hence you can sacrifice the hare; and you know all about hares!

'*He:* Do they fly through the air? I must ask my psychologist.

'*She:* Never mind about him for the moment. This one did. What's flying?

'*He:* Taking wings? Becoming spiritualized?

'*She:* Yes. Compare the wind in yesterday's dream. In the air the hare dies. It can then return to earth, the sacrifice accomplished. The blood of the sacrifice is always poured on the ground, or on some sacred object.

'*He:* And the unknown man?

'*She:* He is the old, pre-sacrifice man who didn't accept the female. The hare goes past, that is beyond him; breaking through the hedge, which is the restraining limit set by the man, into the *open* ("he brought me forth . . . into a large place", Psalm xviii, 19), where it can fly up, and die.'

The female referred to here as being something that the pre-sacrifice man did not accept is, of course, on the one hand the *anima* herself who represents the contrasexual or spiritual aspect of the man, but is, in a more general sense, also the whole 'other side' of life represented by the other side of the hedge, in other words the world either of sex (if untransformed) or, if transformed, of spirit. The death or 'sacrifice' of the hare symbolizes precisely this transformation. Though the psychologist himself could have said all this (in fact had said it before he heard the *anima's* comment), she quite rightly overrides him, and thereby proves the efficacy of the analytical treatment, since for a man the main goal of such treatment is the establishment of effective contact with the *anima* and so freeing the patient from the analyst, just as for a woman the chief aim is the re-establishment of contact with her *animus*, as was the case with Mrs. Wright.

The whiteness so frequently associated with the hare is seen in this dream in the unknown older man's white hair and shirt, though in this case it takes on a special meaning owing to its association with the darkness of his trousers. The upper parts of the body as contrasted with the lower are symbolically in the same relation to one another as is the conscious in its relation to the unconscious, or as the mind in its relation both to sex and to spirit (which is transformed sex). In his case the illumination does not extend below the belt, meaning that his sex has not been transformed, and it is for this reason that the *anima* refers to him as the 'pre-sacrifice man', in other words the Old Adam representing the dreamer's unresolved 'shadow'. The same dichotomy that is seen in the upper and lower parts of the man is seen also in the two sides of the hedge. The dreamer, being illuminated in his mind, consciously shoots the hare on the near (conscious) side, but the transformation takes place on the other side, that is to say, that the illumination has to become more internalized. The hare, representing the sex desirous of being transformed,[1] is naturally averse to the unresolved 'shadow', and so runs to the left in order to avoid it, and thereby leads the dreamer's attention still more deeply into the spiritual world. It is in this doubly deep level (represented both by the 'other side' and by the 'left') that it flies up into the air, as the image of the Hare-Buddha was elevated into the moon, both being resurrection symbols. Then it turns on its back, again symbolizing the turning or transformation of sex or extraverted intuition into spirit or introverted intuition. As it does this, it dies, indicating a certain finality in the process, or, as the *anima* says, that 'the sacrifice is accomplished'.

The *anima* does not, however, say just what sacrifice, or rather what extent of sacrifice. If the dreamer had been the

[1] See pp. 112, 185.

consummated Buddha, the hare doubtless would not have returned to earth at all, but would have soared ever upward. But even the Buddha had to undergo successive rebirths before attaining full Buddhahood. And so the hare still has to return to earth, that is to say, in one sense to be reincarnated, or in a more everyday sense to bring the dreamer to earth to attend to his still unsolved problems.

With this, I will take leave of the reader, with the promise that in the not far distant future the story of Mrs. Wright's development and that of her daughter Margaret will be resumed, not in the simple narrative form adopted in Part I of this book, but in the form of a somewhat deeper analysis of Mrs. Wright's dream process as it continued later quite independently of the analyst, and of the role her daughter played in it.

INDEX

In the absence so far of any adequate Dictionary of Symbols (supposing such a complex undertaking to be possible) this Index has been made with a view to furnishing future compilers of such a work, as well as the reader, with some sort of a key to the meaning of the dream symbolism and its associated mythology that have been outlined in this book.

For expert assistance in this attempt I have to thank Mrs. Alice Meinhard, who also compiled the index to the ritual and mythological material in my *Stone Men of Malekula*.

INDEX

INDEX

INDEX

INDEX

INDEX

INDEX

INDEX

INDEX

INDEX

INDEX

INDEX

INDEX

INDEX